BORN LUCKY

It was fun writing about these things, 60 years after they happened.

Fun yes, but not nearly as exciting.

Harry

VANWELL
VOICES
of WAR

Craig B. Cameron (signature)

CRAIG B. CAMERON

BORN LUCKY

RSM HARRY FOX, MBE
ONE D-DAY DODGER'S STORY

Harry Fox (signature)

Vanwell Publishing Limited
St. Catharines, Ontario

Vanwell Publishing acknowledges the financial support of the Government of Canada through the Book Publishing Industry Development Program for our publishing activities.

Vanwell Publishing acknowledges the Government of Ontario through the Ontario Media Development Corporation's Book Initiative.

Design: Linda Moroz-Irvine
Front cover: Portrait photo of Harry Fox, newly promoted to Warrant Officer Class 1, and newly appointed Regimental Sergeant Major of The Queen's Own Rifles of Canada, May 1942; QOR 75th Birthday Guard at University Armoury, Toronto, Ontario, October, 1935. Cpl Harry Fox, back file furthest from camera.
Back cover: Cap badge of the Hastings and Prince Edward Regiment.

Vanwell Publishing Limited
1 Northrup Crescent
P.O. Box 2131
St. Catharines, Ontario L2R 7S2
sales@vanwell.com
1-800-661-6136

For sales in the United States, please contact Casemate Publishing at 610-853-9131 or
    casemate@casematepublishing.com.
For sales in Great Britain, please contact Helion & Co. at 0121 705 3393 or
    books@helion.co.uk.

Printed in Canada

Library and Archives Canada Cataloguing in Publication

Cameron, Craig B., 1953-
    Born lucky : RSM Harry Fox, MBE : one D-Day dodger's story / Craig B. Cameron.

(Vanwell voices of war)
Memoirs of Harry Fox, rewritten by the author.
ISBN 1-55125-102-7

1. Fox, Harry, 1914-. 2. World War, 1939-1945--Campaigns--Italy.
3. Canada. Canadian Army. Queen's Own Rifles--Biography.
4. Soldiers--Canada--Biography. I. Fox, Harry, 1914- II. Title. III. Series.

D811.C248 2005   C813'.6 940.54'215'092   C2005-906535-4

CONTENTS

The Fox family in England, 1917. Harry stands next to his mother.

PROLOGUE

Regimental Sergeant Major Fox's military memoirs were originally created to honour the seventieth anniversary of his enlistment in the militia. They have been rewritten and are now presented to the general reading public. Harry Fox's service to Canada in the military has been significant. As a friend and serving member in the Canadian Forces, I wish to honour him by passing his story on to subsequent generations. It is my hope that others will be similarly motivated and encouraged to serve our country as Harry Fox has done.

Harry Fox was born in England and emigrated with his family to Ontario, Canada, in 1920 at the age of six.[1] The Foxes moved to Toronto in 1929, and Harry left school that same year to work for the T. Eaton Company. Continuing a family tradition of military service, Harry chose to enlist in one of the country's oldest military units, The Queen's Own Rifles of Canada (QOR) in 1932. He participated in the regiment's seventy-fifth birthday trip to England three years later. Harry Fox was a sergeant when the Second World War began in 1939. When the 1st Battalion, QOR, was mobilized for overseas service in June 1940, Harry enlisted and was promoted to Warrant Officer Class Two. He was subsequently appointed Company Sergeant Major for Charlie Company. Harry Fox served in this capacity at Borden, Newfoundland, New Brunswick and in England until May 1942. Company Sergeant Major Fox was selected to be Regimental Sergeant Major (RSM) of the battalion at that time. He served in that capacity until October 1943, when he was sent to Italy with other senior soldiers to gain combat experience.

In January 1944, Harry joined the Hastings and Prince Edward Regiment (Hast & PER) and became a permanent replacement for their famous Regimental Sergeant Major, Angus Duffy. Serving with the Hast & PER throughout 1944 and early 1945, Harry ended up in Holland in the spring of 1945. He returned with his adopted regiment to Ontario in October 1945. He promptly moved back to Toronto, and rejoined Eaton's department store. Harry returned to The Queen's Own Rifles for a second term as Regimental Sergeant Major in 1947, serving for a year before retiring permanently from military service. Harry Fox is unique in this respect, as he has served as Regimental Sergeant Major of two different regiments on *three* occasions, both in wartime and in peace.

Along with a number of other veterans, Harry participated in a tour of Normandy, France, in June 1994 for the Fiftieth Anniversary of D-Day. It was his first visit to Normandy, and he was quite moved by the ceremonies, especially visiting the cemeteries where some of his old friends are buried. Harry was also privileged to make a "pilgrimage" with the Hastings & Prince Edward Regimental Association to Italy in 1998. A third trip of a commemorative nature followed in May 2000, when he went to Holland for the Fifty-fifth Anniversary of VE Day with various members of The Queen's Own Rifles Association. His fourth and most recent trip was in 2004 with the QOR Association for the Sixtieth Anniversary of D-Day celebrations.

The title of the book is taken from an old proverbial expression used by Harry to describe many of his wartime experiences; it is better to be *born lucky than rich*. Indeed, some historians claim that Napoleon Bonaparte is purported to have asked about each candidate for general rank, "Yes, I know he is able, but is he lucky?" Harry feels he was saved from death at least ten times in Italy and twice in Holland. While I would ascribe his deliverance to divine providence, the phrase nonetheless captures his notion of being fortunate in combat. The sub-title "D-Day Dodger" is taken from a term coined in England to describe those soldiers fighting in Italy who would miss D-Day, the beginning of the long awaited "second front." A song was composed and set to the tune of the well-known wartime song, "Lille Marlene," and entitled, "We are the D-Day Dodgers." Because of his transfer to the Italian front in late 1943, Harry Fox did indeed dodge D-Day (6 June 1944) with the QOR.

Note: All photographs are from Harry Fox's collection unless otherwise noted.

ACKNOWLEDGEMENTS

G rateful acknowledgement is extended to many people for their assistance and cooperation. The Queen's Own Rifles of Canada and the Hastings and Prince Edward Regiment supplied photos as well as articles from their respective regimental magazines, *The Rifleman* and *The Plough Jockey*. Harry Fox wrote an account of his involvement at San Maria di Scacciano that was printed in *The Regiment*, by Farley Mowat, in 1955. I am grateful to Dr. Myles Leitch, an academic friend, who read the first manuscript, and made many helpful suggestions regarding the structure of the memoirs. The Honorable Barnett J. Danson, PC, OC, and Lieutenant Colonel Steven D. Brand, CD, also read and made helpful comments on the text. I also appreciate the fine maps drawn by Hannah Torrens. My wife, Donna, provided encouragement and a critique of the text as a non-military reader.

I offer special thanks to Vanwell Publishing and especially, Angela Dobler, editor, for believing in this book and agreeing to publish *Born Lucky* in the "Voices of War" series.

Finally, I am especially grateful to Harry Fox himself, for his willingness to talk about his war experiences and his patience in explaining many aspects of combat experience to a peacetime reserve Army chaplain. Through the fall and winter of 2001–2002, he and I had lengthy conversations about different aspects of his war service. Indeed, after the first version was produced in April 2002, Harry began to provide me with additional recollections until just a few months before publication. Any inaccuracies in the text are attributable to my work as writer. Although Harry was a key member of The Queen's Own Rifles of Canada and the Hastings & Prince Edward Regiment, these memoirs do not claim to be *official* histories of either regiment in the Second World War. I have endeavoured to express accurately Harry's military experience, and memories, as well as his viewpoint on many related and controversial issues.

Craig B. Cameron
August 2005
Toronto, Ontario

On Parade

QUEEN'S OWN RIFLES OF CANADA,
TORONTO

A souvenir postcard of The Queen's Own Rifles of Canada, Toronto, "On Parade."

CHAPTER ONE

The Home Front

Beginnings

I was born in West Hartlepool, County Durham, England, on 28 April 1914, the year World War One began. I come from a family with a history of military service. Ernie Fox, my father, served with the British Army in Burma and India. He developed malaria in Burma in 1896 and eventually left the service in 1902. Upon the outbreak of war in 1914, he volunteered to fight as part of "Kitchener's Army," and eventually served in Palestine in the artillery. Tom Sargentson, one of my uncles, was a sailor on the first British aircraft carrier, and died of stomach trouble in 1923. One of my grandfathers was a Royal Marine in the Crimean War.

One of my earliest memories occurred during the First World War. I recall seeing an object in the sky, which looked like a lit cigar. My mother rushed me inside when she realized that it was a German Zeppelin that had bombed our town, West Hartlepool, located on the North Sea coast.

Our family moved to Canada right after the First World War. My father and older brother came first and settled in Timmins, Ontario; my mother, sister and I came in 1920. My father worked in the mines there but he soon decided he didn't want his sons to be miners, so he moved the family to Toronto in April 1929. I had had enough of school by that time and got a full-time job at Eaton's department store in May 1929, just six months before the stock market crash. I lied about my age to get the job, as sixteen was the minimum age for employment there. Eaton's accepted me because I was tall and looked older. I recall that my first pay was nine dollars a week. My father got a job at Simpson's department store but he was soon laid off in the early thirties. This brought considerable hardship to the family, like many others in those Depression years. For a short time I was the sole breadwinner in the family. Fortunately, I didn't get laid off and was, in fact, earning more than some married men.

I joined the QOR in April 1932, at the height of the Great Depression, when I turned eighteen. The country was so poor that militiamen received almost no pay and what little pay we received had to be signed back over to the regiment. If we were desperate (broke), we would be given a streetcar ticket and a hot dog. There was almost no equipment, the rifles were Lee-Enfields from World War One, and there were no machine-guns or virtually any other weapons in the militia. The uniform was the Great War issue with puttees.

What are puttees you ask? A puttee was a strip of green cloth about four inches wide and eight feet in length that was wrapped around the top of one's boots and bottom of one's pant legs. They kept the dust out and as the British discovered coincidentally, they could also help minimize the effect of snakebite. In India and Burma, there were many poisonous snakes, including the very deadly pongyi snake, a striped krait. The thick puttee absorbed some of the venom and saved a few soldiers' lives.

Training on Wednesday nights in the regiment consisted largely of drill and basic weapons handling. I was in Baker Company of the 2nd Battalion QOR at the time; we lost the battalion in 1936 due to Army restructuring.[2] Summer camp was reduced to a weekend during most of the thirties. The deployment to Niagara-on-the-Lake for a seven-day musketry camp in 1937 and 1938 was the exception.

In the years before World War Two, I was on the regimental rifle team. We competed in shooting competitions at places like Long Branch (now in Etobicoke). One rifleman I remember well from the rifle team was Ernie Stock; he was always shaking before he shot but when he got behind the rifle's sights, he was a fine shot. He was a Company Quartermaster Sergeant at the beginning of the Second World War, but was boarded out as unfit in England.

My shooting ability was one of the reasons that I was chosen for the 1935 trip to England. I was one of only two riflemen below the rank of sergeant who participated in the seventy-fifth birthday trip of the QOR. I was a corporal, as was Bill Lennox.

As a sergeant in 1939, I was a designated alternate (sub) for the regiment's rifle team that went to Connaught Ranges, outside of Ottawa. We were given a single round at a time to fire at targets up to nine hundred yards away. In the City of Ottawa Match, we fired ten rounds and I scored forty-nine out of fifty. It was the best shooting I ever did!

The militia was full of unusual and eccentric characters. Our medical sergeant was a short man from Belfast named George O'Driscoll. He had grown up in the Falls Road area of Belfast, which was a rough Catholic area of the city, and, as you can imagine, he was tough and scrappy. "Geordie" as we knew him, went with the regiment to Newfoundland and Sussex, but was boarded out after we got to England.

Another unusual soldier I remember was Rifleman Cuthbertson. He was known as the longest serving QOR rifleman with over 40 years of service. He was obviously over-age and hence did not go with us to Newfoundland. While we were in Sussex we learned that he had dropped dead in a drug-store on Sherbourne Street in Toronto. It was only through reading his obituary in the paper that we learned that Cuthbertson had been incarcerated for murder and had joined the regiment after his time in prison.

Seventy-Fifth Birthday Trip to England, 1935

One highlight of my service during the lean thirties was being selected to be part of the QOR Guard that went to England in 1935 for the seventy-fifth birthday of the regiment. Three officers and twelve enlisted personnel were chosen to represent The Queen's Own. Captain John Strathy, Sr., was the officer in charge, along with two lieutenants. The two company sergeant majors were Joe Adams and Bert Couchman, and they were the most senior non-commissioned members in the Guard. I was a young corporal and one of the junior members of the group. It was an exciting prospect to go to England, which was my parents' native land. While there, I managed to get away from the group for a few days and visit my relatives, including my uncle in Durham. It was a real thrill to meet them for the first time.

The QOR Regimental History states that Regimental Sergeant Major Jim Kennedy was part of this guard; he did *not* participate in the trip, however, as drill was not his strength. We anticipated being in a formal parade while visiting the Buffs, The Royal East Kent Regiment, one of our allied regiments and so a Regular Force corporal was brought in to drill us. After the parade with the Buffs at Canterbury, Kent, our English comrades took us over to Belgium and France where we visited various Canadian memorials and battle sites of the First World War. One highlight was going to Ypres, "Wipers," as old soldiers call it. The Menin Gate at Ypres, now known as Ieper, has all the names of the Commonwealth soldiers with no known grave who died in Belgium. Since 1922, a wreath-laying ceremony with buglers playing the Last Post has taken place every day at 8:00 P.M. It was personal for me as there are five Foxes' names on the Gate; they were all cousins of my father, and he remembered each one of them. They were serving in the Durham Light Infantry in the Great War when the Germans exploded a mine under them. Nearly the whole battalion was wiped out, five hundred men in one blow! The Pozières Memorial also has a listing for the men of that regiment.

Another highlight was visiting Vimy Ridge, the site of the Canadian Corps' successful battle on Easter Monday, 9 April 1917. The Canadian World War One monument was under construction when we were there. King Edward VIII dedicated it during the opening in 1936. While he was king, this was his only official duty. Our group also visited Passchendaele in Belgium where the Canadians fought a successful battle at the end of October and November 1917, under horrendous conditions.

Mobilization for War

A number of riflemen came to the regiment after the Second World War was declared in September 1939 but before the QOR was mobilized for overseas service. A young fellow named David Kingston was one of those riflemen. I was a sergeant, which is the equivalent of a warrant officer today. After Wednesday parade nights the question was asked in the Sergeants' Mess, "Who are your best men?" The answer was always the same: "Kingston, Stanton and Forbes." Dave Kingston eventually became Platoon Sergeant of 14 Platoon in Charlie Company. He commissioned at the end of the war with the Guards at Royal Military College, Sandhurst, England. Bill Stanton eventually became Provost Sergeant and Jack Forbes achieved the rank of Warrant Officer Class Two. Forbes became Company Sergeant Major of "D" Company and was killed at Le Mesnil Patry in Normandy on 11 June 1944.[3]

When the QOR was mobilized for overseas service, most of the militiamen like myself automatically enlisted. Anyone physically intact in the militia was taken on when the regiment was mobilized in June 1940. Some who were not as fit or too old were sent to the 2nd Reserve Battalion. For example, Gordy Fox, our Regimental Quartermaster Sergeant, in the militia, had very poor eyesight. His glasses were like the Coke bottles we had in those days, about half an inch thick. No one in the infantry was supposed to have glasses, as 20/20 vision was the standard. There are many reasons for this requirement. The first is shooting, of course, which is the heart of the infantryman's job. Glasses can be a real hindrance in combat; they get dirty, fogged, lost and broken. Most infantry patrolling is at night, and a near-sighted man would be a real handicap to his patrol. The scenes from Hollywood movies, such as in *The Longest Day* when actor Roddy McDowall pauses on Omaha Beach on D-Day to clean his glasses, are just nonsense.

The Canadian government reluctantly accepted the reality that the war was going to be a long one and that more than two divisions would be needed in the Army. The Queen's Own was placed in the Third Infantry Division and was authorized to mobilize an overseas battalion on 5 June 1940, almost exactly four years to the day of D-Day. This was just after the fall of France, and the evacuation from Dunkirk. The 1st Battalion was mobilized at the University Avenue Armoury, in Toronto, where the QOR had paraded on Wednesday nights since 1893. My enrollment date in the 1st Battalion (Active) was 12 June 1940 and I was given regimental No. B 63612. I was promoted to Warrant Officer Second Class the next day, and soon became Company Sergeant Major of Charlie Company.

The letter "B" was the designation for units in south-central Ontario, Military District No. 2, with headquarters in Toronto. Units in southwestern Ontario used an "A" for Military District No.1 and those in eastern Ontario (that is, the Hastings & Prince Edward Regiment), got a "C" for Military District No. 3 based in Kingston. Those who volunteered for overseas service in infantry units like the QOR received a five-digit number. Our original allotment of numbers was B 63500 to B 64449 with provision being made for two QOR reserve battalions to be given numbers B 64500-66499. My predecessor as Regimental Sergeant Major, Gordon R. Alexander, received the first number of our allotment, B 63500.[4]

Some of our militia non-commissioned officers were seconded to Military District No. 2 for recruit training soon after the war began in 1939. The Horse Palace at the Canadian National Exhibition grounds was taken over for this purpose. Our QOR quota consisted of Sergeants Fred "Lucky" Rowell, Eddie Fox, Jack Bray, Ernie Stock, Harry Kippax and Stan Love as well as Corporal Glen Love. Nearly all of these men rejoined the regiment but almost none saw combat with the QOR. Later on in my story, you will hear more of Eddie Fox, Ernie Stock and Glen Love.

Peacetime service in the Non Permanent Active Militia (NPAM) stood us in good stead for the basics of Army service: how to teach drill, saluting, rifle handling, and so on. Those riflemen who joined during the war and who became non-commissioned officers, lacked the formal training in how to teach soldiers. For instance, at the end of the Second World War, when the Hastings & Prince Edward Regiment was in Holland, I was sent on leave right about VE Day. Company Sergeant Major George Ponsford, MBE, MM, was acting Regimental Sergeant Major in my stead. The Commanding Officer told him to teach the junior officers how to salute properly, as he felt they were sloppy. George Ponsford had never been in the peacetime Army and therefore had not been formally taught how to instruct. He had to look up saluting in an Army manual and then try to teach it.

"Potato Sackers"

Those who enlisted in June 1940 became known as "potato sackers" as the Army did not have enough duffle bags for all of us and we were issued fifty-pound burlap potato sacks with a piece of rope to tie the top. After being issued uniforms, we largely did drill because most of the men were new recruits. Rifle drill and rifle regiment distinctives had to be instilled into them. In our new battle dress, we went on a route march up University Avenue behind the band, and we all felt pride in being in the regiment.

We left Toronto for Camp Borden in late June and settled into tents, as there was insufficient hard accommodation for us. Huts were in the process of being built, and as soon as they were finished, men moved in. This was a relief because the warmth of July coupled with the ever-present sand, produced breathing problems for some of the lads.

Training in Borden consisted of drill and learning the rifle. Unfortunately, not all the men got to fire the basic machine-gun, known as the Bren gun. Only a few select riflemen were sent on a small-arms course to Connaught Ranges outside Ottawa. Equipment was issued and then exchanged, and then more and better equipment was issued. The battalion had nearly a thousand men at that point and was organized into four rifle companies as well as a headquarters company. All the men who had a driver's licence, and not many had in the thirties, automatically became drivers. Prior to the war, each company had four platoons of forty-five men. The companies were reduced to three platoons with the surplus men being transferred to support tasks in Headquarters Company. This was especially true of older riflemen who it was thought might not stand the stress of front-line action as well as the younger men might. Eventually a separate Support Company was created, with platoons for mortars, anti-tank, carriers, and pioneers.

Some of the officers and non-commissioned officers went on courses while in Borden, and there were personnel changes. Some men were declared medically unfit for military service and were sent back to the depot in Toronto. Others came up to take their places. The order came to move to Newfoundland and by early August we were ready to go. The train left Toronto on 6 August and pulled into Montreal the following day where we boarded, I think about nine hundred strong, the ship, the *Duchess of Richmond*.

The *Duchess* was a cruise ship that would eventually be converted into a troopship. However, for this trip, riflemen travelled in second class and officers were in first class. For three days we experienced a level of luxury we would never see again while in uniform. Whiskey was three half pennies, (British currency was in use), and Wild Woodbine cigarettes, the poorest cigarettes made in Britain, were tax free. The *Duchess of Richmond* was the largest ship to navigate the narrows leading into Botwood, which was a base for seaplanes. The small town of Botwood, where we would be stationed, was located on the Bay of Exploits on the northern shore of Newfoundland, northwest of Gander Airport. British Imperial Airways and Pan American Airways used the facilities there; the British seaplanes came from Ireland.

Newfoundland

In 1940 Newfoundland was not yet a province of Canada and was under direct control of Britain by a Commission Government. The island colony had had serious financial trouble during the Depression years, forcing Britain to intervene. Newfoundland was vital to the defence of Canada and indeed, North America, and hence Canadian infantry units were stationed there for defence against possible German attacks. You have to remember that this was the era of the mighty German battleship *Bismarck.*

Able and Baker Companies and part of Headquarters Company remained in Botwood on the Bay of Exploits after our arrival in early August. Charlie and Don Companies, with the Commanding Officer and the rest of Headquarters Company, headed east by train to Gander Airport. Gander became one of the main refuelling stops for bombers being flown from the

United States to Britain and our prime job there was to guard the bombers and other planes against saboteurs.

We replaced the Black Watch (of the Second Infantry Division) who had been there since June, and they were only too happy to go: conditions were primitive, to say the least. They at least had had decent weather. It was close to the end of summer and Newfoundland is never as warm as southern Ontario. The two men who were inadvertently left behind by the Black Watch, mentioned in the Regimental History, were placed in our company. They were Riflemen John Fells and John Showers. Showers would be one of the sixty-one fatalities suffered by the QOR on D-Day.

Charlie Company was organized on the following basis: 13 Platoon was comprised of men who had previous militia experience or Regular Force military service; 14 Platoon was generally made up of older men who were in their late twenties and thirties such as Dick Ayton and Len Craig; 15 Platoon was largely made up of the younger fellows, eighteen to twenty-two years of age with no military training.

Charlie Company exchanged with Able Company in early September and took up the Botwood duties. One of the responsibilities while Charlie Company was stationed at Botwood was sending a four-man detachment to the outpost at Lewisporte, a hamlet on the eastern side of the Bay of Exploits. While the weather was still good in September, I went out with a relief of riflemen to spell off my friend, Sergeant Dave Hazzard, who had been at Lewisporte for about a week.[5] We had to take a small boat to get to the outpost at Lewisporte. We tried not to keep them out there long as it was fairly tedious watching the sea for German ships or submarines and there were very few distractions.

Even though life was a struggle in Newfoundland, there was the occasional humorous moment. For instance, one day I had Charlie Company formed up perfectly and the fall sunlight reflected off the soldiers' polished equipment. I gave the "stand at ease" command and started to address the troops. "Now listen to this," I said to them, trying to get their full attention. I heard a noise in the distance where sheep were grazing on the hillside. "Now, listen up" I continued, allowing for a small pause. It was at this very moment that a sheep said, "Baaa." The men collapsed with laughter.[6] These kinds of experiences reminded me *not* to take myself too seriously, a good lesson for an Army sergeant major.

It was while we were at Botwood that the first serious winter storm of the year developed. Two feet of snow fell and the temperature dropped to minus twenty degrees Celsius. The storm began on 18 October and lasted for nine days.

The Queen's Own Rifles was stationed in Newfoundland in 1940 because of the Battle of the Atlantic, which had already begun. Britain was dependant on Canada for many of its necessities as well as weapons of war and the Germans sent several battle cruisers into the Atlantic in 1940 to try to cut off Britain's lifeline from North America. The first two cruisers that went up and down the Atlantic raising havoc with the convoys were the *Gneisenau* and the *Scharnhorst* and they sank the British carrier *Glorious* off Norway in May 1940. This was before U-boats were available in large numbers. We had one advantage over the Germans in that we got meteorological reports from Northern Ireland and Iceland. There had been a rumour that the Germans had established a weather station on Greenland, but that was never proven to the best of my knowledge. This was before the *Bismarck* and the *Prince Eugen* were able to break out from the Baltic into the Atlantic in May 1941. By that time the other two battle cruisers were in port at Brest, on the Brittany coast of France. As quoted in Whitsed, *Canadians*:

> There was a major kerfuffle one day in the fall while we were at Botwood. We were told to expect a visit from the *Admiral Scheer*, a German pocket battleship. We made ready to move out. The Commanding Officer, LCol MacKendrick, met with the mayor of Botwood and then announced that we were about to blow up the railway. All military personnel were to withdraw to Grand Falls. He declared that the best way to protect the town would be to declare it an open city.[7] The poor mayor was stunned. When he got his breath back, he reminded the Colonel that the QOR were supposed to be there protecting Botwood, not deserting it. The plight of the Botwood man became worse when LCol MacKendrick asked him if he had any idea of the destruction an eleven-inch shell could cause? Six and the whole town would be in flames. This "near-tragedy" vanished when the Germans stayed at sea.[8]

On their off hours, the men would often go fishing for trout in a local stream with swords (bayonets to other soldiers), if you can believe it. The water was only six inches deep and the trout were plentiful. Another favourite pastime was drinking, naturally enough. The men's canteen was reached by walking along the narrow gauge railway track. As the train schedules were quite erratic, it was necessary to check the line to ensure that no rifleman was passed out on it. The men developed quite a taste for Newfie Screech, the local rum. By the end of four months on the "Rock," many of our lads were seasoned drinkers and figured they could drink with the best of them.

Transportation is always a concern in the Army and we used whatever we could find to get around. Our dispatch riders used big Norton motorcycles and so I thought I would give it a try. As quoted in Whitsed, *Canadians*:

> We were going down a street in a group. The rider ahead put on some speed. I did the same. Ahead was a barracks block with a flight of wooden steps in front. As the bike drew near, for some unknown reason it wheeled left, pranged the steps and hurled me into a mess of what had become brand new kindling. The street instantly filled with men in loud voices asking what had happened and equally loud voices explaining what had happened. They picked me out of the mess, strapped me onto a stretcher and I was taken to the aid post. There was nothing wrong, not a scratch, as it turned out. In the Army this was my first escape from injury or worse. There were many more, for the next five years, in England, in the Italian fighting [where] I missed shaking hands with a mortar bomb. I was a lucky man.[9]

I have always had a high regard for military chaplains and the important work they do for our soldiers. The QOR did have a chaplain assigned to us while we were in Newfoundland. The only story I know about him concerns a visit he made one day to an isolated outpost on a hill. The men had done some "scrounging" and come up with fresh eggs to eat. While there, the chaplain ate with them, consuming all the eggs. The men were not impressed! He did hold Sunday church services in town, but we hardly ever saw him. We did much better with Cecil Stuart in Sussex and then Jack Clough, whom everyone in the regiment admired and remembers fondly.

Towards the end of November we knew we were moving when an advance party from the Royal Rifles (a sister rifle regiment from Quebec) appeared in Botwood. Their regiment was not placed in one of the first five divisions for overseas service as it was deemed by the higher-ups to be not up to combat standard. Yet despite this perception, the Liberal government of MacKenzie King still allowed the Royal Rifles, along with the Winnipeg

Grenadiers, to go to Hong Kong in 1941 as a token defence garrison. We were in Aldershot, England, when we heard that they had been sent to Hong Kong and for a short time, we were quite envious. This was before Pearl Harbor, and no one really imagined them fighting against a battle-hardened force like the Japanese Army. Incidentally, one of our original "potato sackers" named Barnett, B 64068, took sick while we were in Sussex and didn't sail with the regiment to England. Somehow he found his way to the Royal Rifles, went with them to Hong Kong and was killed in action there. Barnett was the only QOR rifleman killed in the Asian theatre of war.

Charlie Company was in the first "flight" to depart Botwood on the ship SS *New Northlands* on 30 November for Halifax. This was the only ship available and it held just a couple of hundred soldiers. It was winter and bitterly cold on board; we wore all our winter kit and balaclavas. The sea was rough, and many of the men were seasick. We took several days to reach safe harbour in Nova Scotia. From there we took a train to Sussex, New Brunswick, to join the rest of the newly created Eighth Brigade of the Third Infantry Division.

In reflecting on what the time in Newfoundland meant for the regiment, the late Company Sergeant Major Charlie Martin commented that, "The Queen's Own Rifles were firmly welded into a family unit."[10] The main benefits for the regiment were primarily in the area of physical toughening and adapting to adverse circumstances. I think we got shortchanged, however, on the normal procedure of training for an infantry battalion. For example, we should have spent the first two months doing nothing but parade square bashing, kit inspections, building up our physical fitness and then moving on to master our weapons, the rifle, the Bren gun, the mortars and so on. We hadn't had enough time in the period before Newfoundland to do these things. We did finally get rifles and spent some time on improvised ranges as well as in map and compass work (navigation). Still, we were far from a well-trained outfit at that point.

Sussex, New Brunswick

It was in Sussex that we started to get into more formal training for combat. We did more rifle shooting, rucksack marches, unarmed combat and some communications work. A school for non-commissioned officers was established and various courses were given to our corporals and sergeants.

How Cold Can It Get in Canada?

When I was about thirteen, our family lived in Timmins, in northern Ontario, and I had to walk about one and a half miles to school. One winter's day, I didn't just walk, I shivered all the way there. It was a nice, bright, clear day, the coldest type of day, as those who come from the North or the Prairies can testify. I noticed that the wood smoke from the houses was going straight up, slowly spiralling its way up to about four hundred feet where it spread into a thin grey cloud. When I got home after school, I was told that the mercury had plummeted to minus fifty-one degrees Fahrenheit. Now that is cold!

While we were at Sussex, there was a memorable experience of Canadian cold. Charlie Company was on the Sussex rifle range, and the "Quarterbloke," Ernie Stock, had a fire going so that we would have hot water to clean our rifles.[11] I noticed something odd: the steam from the fire was not rising into the air but blowing in a straight line about eight feet off the ground. Another peculiar thing was that the men were not gathered around the fire as was normal on a cold day, but were standing in smoke and sparks.

Lance Sergeant Clay Bell came to me with a very unusual expression on his face. He had fired one round from his rifle and when he pulled the bolt back to reload, the bolt handle broke off in his hand. So I took the broken piece, and went to the major suggesting that if it was this cold, perhaps we should go back to the barracks. He barked at me, "You are a Canadian and so should be used to the cold. Now get back to your post and issue ammunition for the next relay," which I did. However, when I gave my instructions to the non-commissioned officers, I told them to tell the men to forget aiming; just fire the rounds off and then get back to the camp and get warm again. After all the ammunition was expended, we made the quickest route march I can remember back to the warmth of our barracks. It didn't hurt that we had a wind blowing from behind us about fifty-five miles per hour. I don't know the actual temperature, but it was brutally cold.

Transport

We also received a supply of new vehicles in Sussex, and we needed to learn how to operate them. There were occasions when we marched out to the ranges but more often than not we got rides on Army trucks. The British had laid it down as a law of the Medes and Persians, that is, unchangeable, that vehicles in convoys would travel at a speed of twelve miles per hour, and no faster. We had to keep exactly seventy-five yards between each vehicle. One day I had the company ready to get in the backs of the open trucks. The Transport Corporal came along and asked me just how far seventy-five yards was. I looked around and judged the distance to be about three telephone poles apart, and I told him so. The corporal looked skeptical so I told him that the exact distance didn't matter as long as he kept each of the trucks three poles away from the vehicle ahead. I looked over to the major and he was visibly angry. He snarled at me, "Get back to your truck." As was so often the case in the Army, it didn't pay to use too much common sense.

There was an exercise laid on by Eighth Brigade to try to get this aspect of transport to work properly. The other two units had tried and failed. So then it was the turn of The Queen's Own. With the entire brigade staff and even a divisional representative present, we launched into the exercise. We measured the distance out in the camp precisely and then had a motorcycle go along until seventy-five yards had passed. He would turn off, and a truck would come out from behind the barracks onto the road. At precisely 0900 hours the first truck moved out and the convoy began. The staff then retired to a spot on a hill outside the camp where they could observe. Our drivers kept up a precise speed of twelve miles per hour and three poles apart. Everyone was delighted and said the QOR was tops in transport work.[12]

Anyone who has served in the Army knows that what goes around comes around. On another field exercise with the artillery, someone in Four Platoon, the Carrier Platoon, suggested that they practise convoy work on the way to and from the local beach and then do tactical exercises on the sand itself. This was surprisingly approved by the higher-ups and off they went. It was probably a handy cover for a picnic or something, I suspect. During the tactical training on the beach, one carrier threw a track and everyone pitched in to fix it. However, someone forget to check the state of the tide, and water was soon lapping up around their feet. This was the Bay of Fundy with the highest tides in the world; the carrier was soon under water and had to be abandoned. I imagine the Platoon Commander must have received quite a reprimand from the Commanding Officer as one of his brand-new vehicles was gathering barnacles in the Bay of Fundy.

In typical Army fashion, a paper trail is always needed, so a Vehicle Casualty Report was filed and sent on up the chain. Both brigade and division were incensed and declared this to be the worst foul-up in Canadian military history. One week we were transport kings and the next, a bunch of transport incompetents. The Carrier Platoon truly earned the nickname "Mad Four" Platoon through repeated fiascos and outlandish ideas over the next three years.

One of the activities that we used to build up our fitness was cross-country skiing. Rumours were floating about at Sussex that some Canadians, including several of our riflemen, had volunteered during the previous winter to fight for the Finns against the Soviets. These volunteers had to be excellent cross-country skiers, but in the end they were never sent. I know we did have some men that were fine skiers like Corporal (later Lieutenant) Ken MacLeod, a section commander in Baker Company. I am told that MacLeod was clocked at an amazing thirty-seven miles per hour on the flat; someone drove a truck on a nearby road to check his speed. This is about the speed that the current Olympic cross-country skiers clock in the sprint events.[13] There were other fine athletes in the regiment such as Lieutenant (later Captain) Pat Green and Lieutenant (later Major) Sid Heyes who taught many of the men to ski, although we had only enough skis for one company. We also had six very good boxers who won the Third Division championship while we were at Sussex.

One of the best-known athletes in the regiment was Corporal (later Flying Officer) W. E. "Ed" Hinchcliffe. He had been the North American double-sculls champion with Mark Thompson and had also played football for Ottawa. Hinchcliffe transferred to the Royal Canadian Air Force while we were at Sussex, and qualified as a pilot; he was killed over Berlin, Germany, in September 1943.

We lost some good men to a strict medical board before going overseas. On a positive note, we gained many fine men who made excellent contributions to the regiment, including Lieutenant W. D. "Bill" Stewart and Honorary Captain Jack Clough as our chaplain.

There was an Eighth Brigade route march in the spring of 1941, and I was concerned about what blisters would do to the men's feet. I had this brown powder called potassium permanganate that I mixed with warm water and had each man in the company use on his feet. I had them soak their feet for about five minutes in this purple Kool Aid-looking water. Many complained that it discoloured their feet, but it nevertheless had the desired effect of hardening their feet and helped prevent blisters.

The brigadier later complimented me because Charlie Company of the QOR was the only company in the brigade not to have a man fall out. I appreciated the compliment but never did tell him about my "secret" foot powder.

Inoculations

One of the unpleasant aspects of life in the wartime Army was inoculations. Prior to embarkation for England, everyone was to receive shots. On the designated day I marched Charlie Company from Highland Park Camp to the Regimental Aid Post, near Follies Point. When we arrived, I told them to lay their rifles, webbing and battle dress blouses down on the ground. They were going to get a shot, and after they were done, they could come out and have a smoke if they wanted. They were to wait for the whole company to assemble before marching back to our barracks.

Sergeant George O'Driscoll, the medical sergeant, came out on the veranda, called me over and told me that I would have to give some new orders to the troops. This inoculation against cholera was one that produced considerable side effects; there would be no marching after this shot, he said! I changed my orders accordingly.

I took out my nominal roll and called the names out alphabetically for each man to go inside. As they started coming back out, I could see that O'Driscoll had not been exaggerating in the least. Some of the men looked pale and were rubbing their arms and nearly all looked sick. One rifleman even fainted. As they walked slowly up the road, as individuals, not in platoon or company formation, they looked like the tail end of Coxey's Army.[14]

I was the last one in and signed an affidavit saying that all the men of Charlie Company had been through. Then I got my own shot. By golly, did it hurt! It felt like a thousand red-hot worms crawling inside my left arm and shoulder. I got dressed and then started back to camp. There was only one man visible in front of me, and he appeared to be in rough shape. He held his rifle by the sling in one hand and his webbing in his other, dragging both as he stumbled along. Normally, if a rifleman is in trouble, his buddies help him out. I caught up to him, slung his rifle as well as his webbing over my shoulder, and then put my arm around him to help him along. I had a difficult time getting him moving and to make matters worse, the "red hot worms" in my arm had now turned to ice. At the top of a gentle rise as we neared our barracks, I noticed three officers standing under a tree. They all had red bands around their hats, so they were generals. I thought, "Oh, no, what a time to have an inspection!" However, I took no notice of them and trundled on by with my burden. I finally got the man into his bunk, and was heading for mine when something else came up. I never did get to "press the blankets" that day.

The soldier who fainted was not popular in his platoon and this was why no one helped him on the march back. His fellow riflemen had given him a leather medal, which aroused his ire. I found him to be a rather sarcastic man with a chip on his shoulder. But just to show that people can change, when we arrived in England and got better training, especially as D-Day approached, he earned his stripes as a lance sergeant. Unfortunately, he was one of the sixty-one QOR riflemen who died on D-Day on Juno Beach, in the water in front of Bernières-sur-Mer.

Norm Varley and Harry Fox (foreground) at the Long Branch rifle range, 1935.

George O'Driscoll, left, and Harry Fox, "coat exchange" at Niagara camp, 1938.

QOR Guard, England trip 1935 at University Avenue Armoury, Toronto.
Capt. Strathy, CSM. Joe Adams, Sgt. Reg Wallace, Cpl. Harrison, CSM. Ber Couchman, Cpl. Lennox, Sgt. Ted Harshman, Sgt. Les Smith, Ship's Doctor, Cpl. H. Fox, Sgt. Bryant, Sgt. Mark Thompson, CQMS Walter Goldner, Lt. J. Cream.

Rfn Cuthbertson in Niagara, 1938. He served with the QOR for over 40 years.

The *Duchess of Richmond*'s Montreal to Newfoundland trip, 1940.

Harry Fox and J. Haynes on the way to Lewisporte, September 1940.

L/Sgt Clay Bell, QOR, during the unit's move from Newfoundland to Halifax on the SS *New Northlands*, December 1940.

Rfn J. Showers, left, Rfn J. Fell, and Rfn St. John at Botwood, Newfoundland, September 1940. Showers was killed in action on D-Day.

CSM Harry Fox posing for the camera at guardpost in Lewisporte, Newfoundland, September 1940.

Cpl Wallis in front of the accommodations at Botwood, Newfoundland, fall 1940.

Sgt Dave Hazzard, Newfoundland, 1940. He was later killed in action with Baker Company, QOR in Normandy on July 5 1944.

Sgt Bill Simmons, 1st Hussars, Christmas 1940. He was captured and murdered by the 12 SS Panzer soldiers in Normandy in June 1944.

CSM Harry Fox, Camp Borden, 1940.

Charlie Company portrait photo. England, October 1941. CSM Harry Fox, front row, seventh from left.

Newfoundland: CSM Harry Fox and Company NCOs after inoculation.

CSM Harry Fox with 4 C Coy Rfn Moore "Moose" Jackson in Sussex, NB, January 1941.

Harry Fox, left, and Ernie Stock in Sussex, NB, 1941.

L/Sgt Clay Bell, left, and Rfn Sully Rosenthal, Sussex, NB, 1941.

Cpl William E. "Bill" Hinchcliffe in Sussex, NB. He was later killed in action while serving with the RCAF, over Berlin in September 1943.

Sgt O'Driscoll, QOR, was the Medical Sergeant at the Regimental Aid Post in Sussex, NB, 1941

Charlie Coy on the march to rifle ranges in Sussex, NB, January 1941.

L/Sgt Clay Bell, left, and Sgt Ed Fox (no relation) at Sussex, NB, 1941.

CHAPTER 2

England: Getting Ready for Combat?

A Memorable Night

We set sail for England from Halifax on the HMS *Strathmore* on 21 July 1941. Also on board ship with our nine hundred QOR riflemen went le Régiment du Chaudière of our Eighth Brigade and the Highland Light Infantry of the Ninth Brigade. The entire Third Division sailed in this convoy and it was correspondingly well guarded by corvettes, destroyers and even a few cruisers. Although there were a few interesting moments, on the whole the journey was uneventful. The *Strathmore* docked at Gouroch, Scotland, on 29 July and by next day, the regiment was at Mandora Barracks, in Aldershot, England.

Soon after we had got settled into our new quarters at Mandora Barracks, the whole battalion was given leave. We marched down to the train station in groups depending on our destination. I chose to go north to visit my relatives in County Durham. My train seemed to stop at every town between Aldershot and West Hartlepool, and it was dark by the time I arrived.

West Hartlepool is a small town with a notable history. The Romans had built a fort there, anchoring the east end of Hadrian's Wall. The Angles came in the fifth century and pushed the older Celtic inhabitants out. In the Middle Ages, it was the English residence of a branch of the de Brus family, descendants of one of William the Conqueror's Norman knights. In the seventeenth century, West Hartlepool became known as "Monkey Town" after an incident where a judge ordered the hanging of a man whose pet monkey had stolen a loaf of bread!

During the First World War, the German Navy shelled the town and my house lost some of its slate roof from the shrapnel. Later in that war Zeppelins regularly bombed the city and in 1917, our anti-aircraft gunners managed to shoot one of them down.

I got off the train and headed out to my uncle's place. Everything had changed since my last visit in 1935. All along the streets were sandbags in front of the shops, and nothing seemed familiar. Finally, after falling down a curb and jarring my whole body, I decided to head back to the station to get a room for the night.

At the hotel an elderly gentleman showed me the bathroom and then my room, saying, "If you don't mind, sir, please leave the door ajar. You see if a bomb falls nearby, the whole building shakes, and a closed door could jam, and we would have a difficult time getting you out." Strange advice, I thought to myself but then I had just arrived in wartime Britain. What did I know about such things?

I was just about asleep when a person entered the room. I sat up and found myself staring into the muzzle of a pistol! There was enough light for me to recognize it as a German Luger, and I froze. Out of the darkness, a voice snarled, "So you call yourself Harry Fox, and you claim to be from Toronto? That's a likely tale, and I'm going to investigate." The light came on and I recognized a British police officer. He put the pistol away and laughed, "Eee, that frightened you, didn't it?" I confessed that it had. The bobby introduced himself as Assistant Inspector so-and-so; his job was to check all arrivals on the trains. He had noticed from the guest book that I was from Toronto, and as he had lived there for a period of time, he thought he'd come up to introduce himself. What a way to introduce yourself!

I told him to pull up a chair. My green field service cap was on the chair, and he picked it up, saying, "Hey, it's the old cap badge, I haven't seen one in years." It seems that he had gone to Canada as a young man, landed a job in Toronto and then joined the QOR. He served with the 3rd Toronto Regiment in World War One and then took his discharge in England after the war.

The inspector asked whom I was visiting, and I told him the name. He was certain he had done an investigation regarding someone by the same name. I said "No way. They are strict Baptists and would never be involved in any crime." He was determined to make the connection, and then asked if there had been any other notable incident involving someone in the family. I recalled that my uncle's father-in-law had been killed in a motorbike accident. Yes, he knew the name and it was a colour. I replied, "Whyte." The investigation determined that the vehicle that killed the man on the bike was an Army vehicle. The Army's reply was to the effect that there were no vehicles out on that night, in that location, et cetera. When it comes to civilians, especially in wartime, the Army does look after its own. We shook hands, he said "Best of luck, Canada" and left. I have never forgotten the sight of that Luger just three inches from my nose.

Back in Aldershot, I learned that Queen Mary, who was our Colonel-in-Chief, had graciously consented to visit the regiment. We held a parade in her honour on 10 September. It was a little hard for her to inspect the troops however, as we did a double past, the prerogative of a Rifle regiment on parade. It was one of the last occasions that our regimental band and buglers led us on parade in the Second World War. Shortly thereafter it was broken up and the musicians distributed to different organizations. Many of the buglers, like Ted O'Halloran, became stretcher-bearers and did very commendable work under fire as non-combatants. Those who were willing to become combatants, changed to the role of anti-tank gunners.

Drivers and Dances: Lost in England

We had been in England a few weeks when a message came through that a dance was being laid on in the town of Reading, several miles from Aldershot. The Telephone Service girls were hosting the dance and had specifically asked for Canadians as partners. The message went on to say that on previous occasions some Canadian troops had acted in an uncivilized manner and the British now regarded us as "wild colonials." Third Canadian Division was going to alter that perception. In order to realize this goal, restrictions were placed on who could go to the dance. If anyone got out of line or was cause for complaint, it would be instant court-martial and heavy punishment. It was decided that twelve sergeants would go as the battalion's contribution, and they had a first class time.

We decided to return the favour and invite some of the girls back to our Mess for a party. However, we needed to go and get them, so a truck and driver were requisitioned for the job. As the truck was about to leave, Regimental Sergeant Major Alexander came to me and said, "You are the senior man; if anything goes wrong, you'll find out what big trouble is all about. It's your neck, so watch your p's and q's."

We drove to Reading and picked up the girls at their individual homes. As each one got into the back of the truck, I gave her a pack of Sweet Caporal cigarettes. It was a happy truckload, with laughing, giggling and talking until the truck suddenly stopped. The assistant driver came to tell me that the driver wanted to talk to me. So I went up to the front, and the driver told me bluntly that he was lost and didn't have a clue where we were.

To say that this news shook me is an understatement; I was horrified. Here I was, lost in the south of England with a truckload of soldiers and local civilian women at night. I could see a trial and seven years in the "glass house" staring me in the face. Needing time to think, I walked into the middle of the intersection and looked around. It was a T-intersection on a main four-lane road. I could see the cat's-eyes blinking in the centre but there were no signposts of any kind as they had been removed because of the fear of invasion. When in doubt about navigation at night, always look up. I saw the Big Dipper and the North Star and figured that this road ran east to west and that we should likely go east.

I told the driver to turn left and go on for fifteen minutes or until he hit another main road. I crawled into my spot in the back, and they asked why we had stopped. I told them, and there was an instant change in the atmosphere. You could feel the women's fear, and I can't say that I blamed them. One fellow asked what I had done, and I told him the instructions I had given the driver. His rather caustic reply was that if we were lost before, we were even worse off with me giving directions! This put the girls into a real tizzy, and I had quite a time trying to calm them down.

The truck stopped again and I saw on one side of the road a pub sign with a rooster painted on it and the words underneath, "The Home of Alton Courage Ales." Now I had drunk my share of Courage ales and I knew that the town of Alton was south of Aldershot. I gave the driver the same directions, and much to my surprise, lo and behold, the next stop was right in front of the Sergeants' Mess at Mandora Barracks.

At 2330 hours, the party broke up and we drove the girls home, dropping each one at her own residence. This meant we were quite late getting back to barracks and did not have much sleep that night, but lack of sleep is just a part of Army life you learn to accept. As Shakespeare put it, "All's well that ends well." But that wasn't quite the end of the story. The driver told a rather exaggerated tale to the other drivers about how I had given him such perfect directions even though we were "lost." The upshot of this was that my reputation with the Transport Platoon was so strong that I had total co-operation whenever I wanted a vehicle. They had complete confidence in me. Later when I was Regimental Sergeant Major, I even had the use of the Commanding Officer's personal station wagon on several occasions. The strange thing about that night is that I was just guessing and was as lost as the driver!

Route Marches

An essential part of our training was route marches: we started slow and built up to marches of eight hours' duration. The normal routine was fifty minutes of marching and ten minutes of resting every hour. As Company Sergeant Major, I usually marched at the head of the company with the Officer Commanding, who was responsible for all the details of the march. Occasionally I was able to drop back to join one of the platoons. Sometimes we sang, and as I knew more songs than most of the men, I often led. I was also the source of fun. For instance, when we passed a cemetery, someone would ask why there was a fence around it; to keep people in or the rest of us out? No matter what my reply was, I was wrong and this helped keep them in good humour.

As a rule, though, the men simply plodded along like mules with their heads down. Their legs were getting stronger but that was about the only benefit. To make things more interesting I decreed that all the corporals and sergeants would draw a sketch of the day's march including any interesting features. I took the best sketch and put it on the company notice board along with a trace of the actual map itself. Of course, there was the usual complaining: "why do we have to do this, the other companies don't," et cetera. Eventually the idea caught on, and the riflemen in the sections began to help their corporals with the sketches. I recall that one sketch had a drawing of a hedgehog in a bush. All the men knew what this meant and where the bush was located. The sketches helped the troops and helped me as well. For example, I learned that men at certain locations wore red caps (military police were called "meatheads" because of their red caps) and the lesser types wore blue.

I recall one particular route march in England when Company Sergeant Major Charlie Martin had a Tommy gun and his finger was on the trigger. He was constantly looking around at the trees and hedgerows, always anticipating trouble, like the Boy Scouts' motto, "Be Prepared." This alertness stood Charlie and his men in good stead on many occasions in combat.

The reason I knew what Charlie was doing in Able Company was that I had to fall back during route marches to catch my breath. I have had a weak heart all my life; it's a valve problem, and I'm not able to exert myself beyond a fast walk. With a heavy rucksack, it was worse. This condition was not picked up by the various medicals I had, and I did not tell them about it. If they had known, I would have been boarded out as unfit for combat. I only found out the reason for this physical limitation during the process of being demobilized after the war. At that time, physical training was confined to marches and calisthenics, and we did very little running.

Someone told me a story about Honorary Captain Jack Clough, our chaplain, who participated in all these marches. At a rest point he sat down on his haunches with his small pack on. Some joker came up behind him and pushed him and he fell over. He got up, and looked at the fellow and said, "If I had been standing, you would never have been able to do that," and the man knew it. Clough had been a wrestler while a student at Trinity College, University of Toronto. The troops liked Clough as he was a man's man. He was the regiment's chief swimming instructor in the period leading up to D-Day.

On our route marches we usually carried fighting order only. Very seldom did we march with full packs as they normally went by truck. We didn't carry picks and shovels, as the Company Quartermaster Sergeant and his staff would bring them up to the company. Interestingly, the Second Division did carry shovels on marches. We couldn't really understand why when you have to travel light and fast for combat. I guess it was things like that that gave rise to the reputation of the Second as "nutty as a fruitcake." From what I could gather, their Commanding Officer, Major-General Odlum, was a little bit of a nut. The CBC movie *Dieppe* (1993) certainly portrays him in an unfavourable light. He was relieved prior to Dieppe by Major-General Hamilton Roberts. The Second Division was well trained because they went through their assault training twice in the lead up to the Dieppe raid. The CBC movie suggests that Lord Mountbatten launched the Dieppe raid without the approval or knowledge of General Brooks, the British Army Chief of Staff. This is not really believable.

Here is one reason I don't believe it. We were at the coast and moved from Eastbourne to Hassocks in August 1942, just before the raid was launched. When we got there, we saw on a siding a train with Red Cross emblems on the cars. We just assumed they had always been there. But later we found out that Dieppe was on the next week. They knew there would be casualties, and they brought these cars down to the coast. So someone at the top knew, because even a division commander couldn't order ambulance trains without approval from the very top. The Dieppe raid needed all elements of the military for the operation: as well as the soldiers, the Navy's ships to transport the troops, and the Air Force to provide covering support.

Lost in England, Again!

The regiment was going on a training exercise down near the Kent-Sussex border, and we were to make a night move by truck. By this time we had been in England long enough that all officers and senior non-commissioned officers had been given maps, and navigation was one purpose of the exercise. As the drivers were from the Royal Canadian Army Service Corps, our infantry people were to give them directions. This meant that we had to use the flashlights in the trucks to see the maps. Unfortunately, this created a problem as the drivers complained that it ruined their night vision and might cause accidents. They were right, of course, so after I had crawled into the cab of my truck, I asked the driver if he had been on one of these exercises before. When he said, "Yes," I was relieved that I would not have to use my flashlight and wouldn't give him any trouble. I proceeded to get comfortable and drifted off to sleep. Sometime later I was awakened as the truck came to a stop. The driver politely informed me that he was lost. This news certainly woke me up completely. I told the driver that there were three things we could do: one, keep on driving and get more lost; two, stay where we were until someone came along to help us out; or three, we could backtrack. The driver thought the third option best, and we proceeded back to the last roundabout.[15] The driver was able to tell where the other vehicles had gone, and drove along until we found the drop-off point. The troops got out and we marched along for about a mile. I noticed Major "Long John" Pangman (one of several pairs of brothers in the regiment) who was in charge of Able Company; he grinned at me, pointing in the direction of Charlie Company. We finally arrived and I reported to Major Gianelli, the Officer Commanding. He was not too pleased and said, "Where in the blazes have you been?" I told him that our truck's engine had conked out, and it was only after daylight that the recovery team came along to fix it. That wasn't true but he couldn't disprove it, and so I got away with a white lie.

The battalion spent the next thirty-six hours tramping around Ashdown Forest in East Sussex and then returned to our camp. Much to our surprise, we relocated shortly after that exercise to Pippingford Park in the same Ashdown Forest.

Pippingford Park: Our First Casualties

We were stationed at Pippingford Park in East Sussex County through the winter of 1941-1942. One task that we had to perform while stationed there, was taking trucks to London and then returning with loads of rubble from bombed-out buildings. We would use the brick to construct parking lots and to build up the small muddy lanes in Sussex that we used as access routes to the bivouac areas. On one such trip in late February 1942, a truck went too fast around an icy curve and rolled. Several riflemen were crushed and one died of his injuries.

Some people think that the combat zone is the only place casualties occur or that it is somehow more "acceptable" to die in battle than in a rear area. A soldier's death is tragic no matter where it occurs! Seven QOR riflemen died from the time we arrived in England in July 1941 until D-Day. For instance, one rifleman's girl wrote him a "Dear John" letter during our first year in England, and he was frantic with grief and jealousy. He had been a good solid soldier in 14 Platoon but he changed overnight. He jumped out of a second-floor window at Mandora Barracks in Aldershot and landed on his shoulder. So we had Sergeant Ted Hartnell, (in Baker Company at the time), escort him handcuffed to the mental hospital at Basingstoke. Some time later, this soldier managed to get hold of a rifle and ammunition and shot himself. This was very sad!

Military vehicles travelled under blackout conditions in England with no lights. The result was that there were many road accidents, some of which took the lives of our men during those years. In one particular mishap, a civilian driver killed one rifleman just outside one of our camps as he was walking along the side of the road with Sergeant Fred Harris (killed on D-Day) and another rifleman. Another victim of a road accident was Captain Hugh S. McRae, from Winnipeg, whom I knew and respected, a likeable man and a good officer, killed on 30 April 1943.

Many other riflemen were injured in actual training. A rifleman in our company named Leonard Laird, a 1940 "potato sacker," had his leg crushed while jumping from the dock to the deck of the ship that was to take us to amphibious training at Inverary, Scotland.

From time to time, various unit personnel were sent back to the Canadian Infantry Reinforcement Unit or "Holding Unit," as we called it, at Crookham Crossroads near Aldershot. These men were deemed to be unfit for combat for a variety of reasons. While we were at Pippingford, Sergeant George O'Driscoll, previously mentioned, Sergeant Ed Fox, Company Quartermaster Sergeant Ernie Stock, Major Gianelli and others left the regiment for the Holding Unit. It was also the clearinghouse for reinforcements coming from Canada, for example, from the 2nd Battalion in Toronto, before being posted to the various regiments. After the war, I met Eddie Fox at a Mess function and he was a sergeant in The Royal Regiment of Canada. Major Gianelli eventually served in staff jobs in the Eighth Army in Italy. He had been our Officer Commanding of Charlie Company in Newfoundland and Sussex, New Brunswick.

The focus of our training in England from 1941 until the spring of 1943 was to repel seaborne invasion and airborne landings. There was no special plan or training given, though, on how to attack paratroopers on a Drop Zone (DZ). One exercise, called Exercise Fox, held from 19-21 June 1942 with the Home Guard, was geared specifically at repelling a seaborne invasion. Hitler's Wehrmacht had invaded Russia in June 1941 and was fighting a campaign there with several armies. German troops had occupied most of Europe from Greece to Norway. Field Marshal Rommel was leading the *Africa Korps* in the North African desert. I wondered, who is left to invade Britain in 1942?

Singed Boots and a Brush Fire

Another memorable incident occurred while we were stationed at Pippingford Park. Ashdown Forest had been logged off in the sixteenth century and all that was left when we were there was mostly low scrub, gorse and whin bushes. It was known locally as the Isle of Thorns.

Even though it was December and the middle of winter, we were still able to train due to the mild climate of southern England. The Army brought out a new battle drill that was intended to cut down on casualties and to save time. At the platoon level it consisted of the platoon commander waving his arms and saying, "There is our objective. We will do a left flanking. Move. Go." This tactic may have been better than a frontal bayonet charge against an entrenched position but I never observed it in use in Italy. There were many things like that about the Army. The battle drill for house clearing, as an example, proved totally ineffective. Instead, at Ortona several Canadian infantry units developed a more effective tactic called "mouse-holing" which involved blowing holes in the walls of adjacent buildings from the inside. The major advantage was that fewer casualties resulted due to less time spent in the streets.

In any event, during battle drill in Pippingford Park one day, we spent several hours galloping here and there until we were huffing and puffing like bull elephants. We eventually stopped for a rest, and I joined Sergeant Jack Forbes, the Second-in-Command of 15 Platoon. We took a break in a little hollow. In the south of England, there is an old adage, "Shine before seven, rain before eleven." On this particular winter day it held true and the rain came pouring down. Soon the little hollow where we sat had three or four inches of water in it. We were completely soaked but neither Jack or I complained. The rain felt so good on our hot, sweaty bodies!

During this exercise, the Mortar Platoon created some trouble for us. Several of their bombs had set fire to the peat moss. The fire spread quickly and the Commanding Officer had to call out the whole battalion to fight it. We soon found out that the eighteen picks and twenty-four shovels issued to each company weren't much use in fighting fires. Believe it or not, the most effective treatment was to stamp on the brush with our feet. We stomped and tromped the ground in the Ashdown Forest for the better part of two days!

One negative side effect however, was that it played havoc with the men's boots. Many were singed and cracked as a result of the heat. One of our Charlie Company riflemen had size fourteen feet. Back in Canada, this size wasn't a problem as the supply system simply had larger boots ordered for him. In England, it wasn't so simple. The Quartermaster declared that no one in the Army should have such large feet; what this meant was that supply did not have them, and was not going to bear the extra cost of getting them made. As a result of this deficiency, the rifleman was removed from the company and sent to Headquarters Company as a cook's helper. About a month later he was posted to the Holding Unit and I never saw him again. We were on six hours' notice to move at this time, as the higher-ups still believed that a German invasion was possible. This soldier was deemed to be a hindrance as he had no boots. So simply because this man had feet larger than the Army could provide boots for, he was removed from the regiment.[16]

Did Someone Mention Climate Change?

Earlier I mentioned an incident in Canada when we were desperately cold on the rifle range in Sussex. The coldest I have ever been during my Army experience however, was in *England* in January of 1942. The battalion was on six hours' notice to move to repel a notional German airborne landing. We were driven in Troop Carrying Vehicles (TCVs) for about twenty miles; then we unloaded, made a very quick march of about a mile, turned left and began to ascend the South Downs. The Downs are on a sixty-degree slope and are nearly four hundred feet high and at that time of year, are covered in ice and snow. The Major and I were leading the company, and it was one tough climb. Within a couple of minutes we were wallowing in sweat. About halfway to the top I heard some noises from below and I turned to look; one of the riflemen had slipped and fallen, knocking down four others who were all cursing the one who had fallen. I decided not to intervene, and let the platoon sergeant sort the mess out.

Upon reaching the top, I looked over a large flat area that resembled a skating rink with sprouted tussocks of grass, all nicely iced. The gale that struck us out on the top of the Downs was something you had to experience to believe. I looked at the Major's face: the beads of sweat were turning into icicles. I knew my face must look just the same. I could feel the sweat start to freeze all over my body, and my clothing was stiffening like a board. As I looked down the hill, I could see Lieutenant Ed Dunlop waving his arms and yelling but because of the wind, could not hear what he was saying. The straggling column of men began to turn around and go back down. The descent was much worse than the ascent! Once I slipped and sat down heavily, sliding about twenty feet. Apparently, the Commanding Officer, Lieutenant Colonel Hank MacKendrick, had come along and sized up the situation, and on his own initiative cancelled our participation in the exercise.

I got the company into a column of route and we marched for about a mile, where we turned into a field and met the Company Quartermaster truck. Al Newlands, our Quarterbloke, had a hot meal of baked beans ready for us. As usual, I was the last one to eat and found out that he had a whole gallon container of beans left over. When I asked what he was going to do with them, he said, "Throw them out." I replied "No way," and proceeded to eat the whole gallon. It was the best meal I ever had in the Army. I paid for it, though: as we boarded the trucks to return to Pippingford Park, I discovered that I could not buckle up my waist belt!

I hear some scientists are claiming that the world is warming up a degree or two, to which I respond, "I'm a Canadian, I have proven that I can take the cold, so go ahead, bring on the heat."

I Become Regimental Sergeant Major

The regiment moved from its well-established and reasonably comfortable bivouac at Pippingford Park to nearby Pulborough in late April 1942. Pulborough proved to be a short-lived location and for that we were all thankful, as our accommodations were in tents. The QOR moved just a few days later to Eastbourne in early May of 1942. Just prior to this move there came a big change for me.

Regimental Sergeant Major Gord Alexander, who was fifty at the time, had to leave the regiment on account of age (he later died of sickness in September 1943). There was some uncertainty as to which of the six sergeant majors would take over. Bill "Daddy" Hughes was senior and had British Army experience behind him. I didn't feel I had all the adequate preparation to be a Regimental Sergeant Major and was surprised when Jock Spragge, our Colonel, informed me that I had been selected. So I bade Charlie Company a sad farewell and took on a new and challenging job.

During these years, the QOR and the Third Division never actually worked with the other Canadian divisions. We worked on similar training schemes but were usually behind the Second Division in the training cycle. One of these schemes was based on the actual scenario that the Second would encounter at Dieppe. We were all divided into syndicates of several officers and non-commissioned officers. In my group there was a major, Company Sergeant Major Charlie Martin of Able Company, several others and myself. At one point, the major declared that he would send one section from our company to take the casino on the beach. Charlie spoke right up, "Oh no, sir, it's much too big for a section to handle alone." Charlie was like that. He was not afraid to speak his mind to anyone regardless of rank or position.[17] He felt that this was a poor leadership call, and he said so. In action, this kind of non-commissioned officer usually turned out to be a fine leader, even though he sometimes "reinterpreted" his orders.

I feel that many of these exercises in 1942 and 1943 were a virtual waste of time from a strictly training standpoint. All we did was march about, miss regular meals, and then just sit around. The troops didn't learn much about their trade as infantry soldiers on these exercises, which were primarily designed for higher staff. There was no emphasis on infantry tactics at a platoon, company or battalion level, as had been done in New Brunswick. In effect, many of these exercises were tactical exercises without troops but with live troops in attendance.

Breakfast is Served

It was one of those quiet English summer mornings with not a breath of wind, and soft rain was coming straight down. We were on a big training exercise, involving the whole Third Division, called Exercise Spartan, and we had been marching since dawn. It was fully light now, so we pulled off the road into a field, and the cooks had breakfast all ready for us. Normally the battalion was fed by company, with the one hundred thirty riflemen formed in a long queue. As the feeding process could be quite slow, I laid it down that corporals could either shepherd their section through as a group or lead them personally. The platoon sergeants had to wait, however, until all the men in the platoons had eaten. The Company Sergeant Majors would eat last, and accordingly, I was almost the last man to eat in the battalion and sometimes that meant a skimpy meal for me.[18]

There are good points to this system; perhaps the most important is the message conveyed that the riflemen come first in a Rifle regiment. Another is a practical one: the soldiers would keep an eye on me to see when I packed up my Mess tin. When I did this, it indicated to the troops "prepare to move," and so they would snuff their cigarettes out and get their webbing on. The Commanding Officer would then blow his whistle, and we had one minute's notice to move out. The troops would move out quietly without much noise or chatter. We call this "noise discipline."

On big schemes like this one, we had officers from other regiments with us as umpires. We thought of them more as "spies" because they would take note of everything that we did wrong and report it up the chain of command. One umpire complimented The Queen's Own Rifles about the way we did our feeding. In other regiments that I won't name, there was a mad rush for the chow line, every man for himself, with many of the sergeants getting in line ahead of the men.

The cooks had prepared porridge this morning, and few of the men liked it, taking as little as possible. As far as I was concerned, porridge to a Canadian soldier is a staple, as rice is to Asians and potatoes are to the Irish. In England, porridge is known as "bergoo." I had my Mess tin filled to the brim and was happily eating away. A few minutes later I noticed that my tin wasn't getting empty! This was rather odd, and I looked around to find an explanation. I noticed that the rain was dripping from my steel helmet into the Mess tin. I was eating rainwater and enjoying it!

This incident reminds me of another eating experience when I was on a course at the Advanced Infantry School in February 1942 in the West Highlands of Scotland. Have you ever been to Scotland? There it either rains or snows, with very little sun. We were out in the wilds near Loch Ailort, close to where the ferry goes to the Isle of Skye and when the skies cleared briefly, we could see the isles of Rum, Eigg and Muck in the Hebrides. We were on a three-day scheme called "Map Orientation" or something to that effect. In any event, we had been tramping around the soggy countryside doing navigation, and it came time to have our tea on the last afternoon. We were given tea mugs with some flour in them and told to go into the nearby field, cut as much grass as we wanted, and mix it with the flour. This was easily done, but as far as finding dry wood to make a fire, this was impossible in the middle of winter in the Highlands. On the good side, we didn't need to worry about cooking this meal; on the bad side, there were three hundred hungry men with mugs full of this dirty-looking mush, an inedible concoction that might have been good for hanging wallpaper but nothing else.

At this time in the war, things were not going well for the Allies. No one knew where and under what conditions our Army might have to fight, so they wanted to give us some exposure to adapting to different environments. Our troops were in Spitzbergen and Alaska, and we needed preparation for surviving in northern climates. Later that same day, one of the staff shot a stag, and we were given a lesson in how to dress and cook a wild animal. Very few of the men on this exercise had ever seen a dead animal of this size, and none knew how to prepare it for eating. It was a more complicated procedure than opening a can of Fray Bentos bully beef!

I have thought a lot about the food we received while serving in the Canadian Army in the Second World War. I have a funny feeling that if the Canadian government knew it could feed the soldiers on grass and rainwater, it would do so at once. Of course, the concoction would be called a fancy name, like "Aqua Pura de la Tranchees," but you would have to use your imagination to find a word to describe adequately what it tastes like. We had some dandy names for our rations. As for me, I'll settle for a good hot pot of bergoo any day. *Bon appétit!*

You Can't Keep A Good Man Down

About 1933, a new Second Lieutenant named Edward A. Dunlop was posted to my company (Baker Company of QOR Second Battalion). Dunlop had been in the Cadet Corps while at Upper Canada College, and he knew what he was talking about. He was an easy man to talk to and, more important, he listened to his non-commissioned officers.

Ed Dunlop was as keen as mustard (to use an old expression) on marksmanship and got a group of us together to shoot in a match at the Connaught Ranges in 1938. We did so well that we each won a Freysen shield for our efforts. I have it still; it's on my living room wall.

Like most of us, Ed Dunlop joined up in June 1940 when a battalion was mobilized for overseas service. After we were in England for while, he went off on an advanced infantry course in the Scottish Highlands. He came back very gung-ho and was soon sent off to join the British Army in North Africa to gain combat experience. After returning to the QOR from that theatre of operations, he was promoted to major and given command of "D" Company. Shortly thereafter, the company was soon reduced to nil strength during a reorganization of the battalion into three rifle companies during early 1943. The men were subsequently scattered among the other companies. The fourth rifle company was brought back some months later, however, on Field Marshal Montgomery's order and Major Ed Dunlop was given charge once again of a rejuvenated "D" Company.[19] Many of his riflemen were brand-new soldiers, mostly eighteen or nineteen years of age. Dunlop had a challenging job to try to get his new company up to speed with the other three companies.

By the summer of 1943 the training focus had finally shifted to preparing for an amphibious landing on the coast of France. In September the battalion deployed to the West Highlands of Scotland, near Inverary, for assault-craft landing practice. Near the beach that we used was a hill with an old stone watchtower on the top. One favourite drill was to land a company of men on the beach and then see how long it would taken them with full pack to climb to the top of that hill. No matter how soon they made it, though, it was never fast enough for the higher-ups. I don't believe many senior officers made that climb but I know Ed Dunlop went up with his men.

One day the whole unit was doing grenade training, and I decided to take the headquarters staff out to do the same. I demonstrated the correct technique: pull the pin, stand, throw and then duck behind a boulder to dodge the splinters. Sergeant Watson, the Orderly Room Sergeant (now called Chief Clerk), threw his grenade but just couldn't resist seeing it explode. As a result he caught a fragment in his chest. I told the rest of the group to stay put, and I escorted him to the Regimental Aid Post. After a couple of hundred yards he said he was all right and didn't need me.

So I turned back, and on the way I noticed a group of men who were hurrying along and they were carrying something. I could have interfered but decided that they had things under control, and I'd just mind my own business. Later that day I found out that it was Major Ed Dunlop they were carrying and that he had been badly wounded by a grenade. One of his men had dropped a grenade and Dunlop had scooped it up and thrown it, but it had exploded just as he released it. He lost two fingers and the sight in both his eyes.

An old adage has it that you can't keep a good man down. In Ed Dunlop's case, that was certainly the truth. After the war, he was active in the Regimental Association. He was also elected a Member of the Provincial Parliament for Ontario and I understand, was a very good one. Ed Dunlop also got involved in the organization of the *Toronto Sun* following the demise of the *Evening Telegram.* The paper prospered, and though it has changed considerably over the years, it is still in circulation. On the twenty-fifth anniversary of the paper's establishment, no one mentioned Ed Dunlop's name. This is a shame, as I knew him to be a fine officer and a responsible politician. He was a far better man than ninety-seven percent of those who have been elected to public office in Ontario. I stand on this assertion. Ed Dunlop deserves to be remembered.

The Infantry and the Guns

There was an artillery battery from the 13th Field Regiment (one of the supporting units in our division) in the camp, and their men ate in our Mess. When we had Mess meetings, their sergeants were there too. There was a lot of friendly rivalry with "the guns." We would often make wisecracks to them as we marched along the roads of England. However, once we had been in combat for a short time, we came to appreciate the gunners of the Royal Canadian Artillery whose role was essential in winning the war. George Blackburn, an officer with the 4th Field Regiment, relates an incident in August 1944 during the Falaise fighting. One day as the 4th Field's trucks drove by, infantrymen spontaneously rose to their feet and applauded the gunners.[20] It can be fairly stated that the artillery played a crucial role in defeating the German Army in combat. I think the highest compliment to our gunners was given by the enemy themselves. In Normandy, some German prisoners asked to see the Canadian "super 25-pounder," as they were convinced that no gun crew could load and fire shells with such a rate of fire.[21] As Blackburn explains, the high volume of fire directed at specific German targets was due to detailed fire plans for all Canadian guns, from the field regiments right up to the "heavies" at division and corps levels.

Leave

Soldiers love to grumble and complain. One of our very legitimate beefs was about the Canadian Army's leave policy. In the summer of 1942 we were at Eastbourne in Sussex for coastal defence. We went there to replace a Second Division unit that had been pulled out for Dieppe preparation. There was always the chance of a commando raid in that area because of the presence of a big hydro-electric plant. Every night or two a detachment had to go down there and stay for the night. It usually wasn't necessary, but we still had to do it. We were one hundred men under strength yet we were still required to have seventy-five percent of a full battalion nominal roll on the ground at all times. Only so many men could be away on leave at any given time. Instead of getting fourteen days' leave every six months, as we were entitled to, it happened only once a year. A sick rifleman admitted to hospital was immediately "struck off strength" from the battalion.

The troops could always get weekend leave, and many would go to London. Even though a rifleman's pay was one dollar and fifty cents per day at this point in the war, he could still afford to go if he economized.[22] If he was single, half of his pay was stopped. This practice began in the First World War so that the soldier would have that money later rather than spend it all on a binge and then be broke for months. If he was married, and many of our men were, there was an allowance deducted for his wife. I used to send one hundred dollars a month home to my mother because she needed it and my expenses were modest. As Warrant Officer First Class and Regimental Sergeant Major, my pay was four dollars and twenty cents per day; it had been three dollars per day as Warrant Officer Class Two.[23]

Ironically, only one man got leave with regularity and that was the Commanding Officer's batman. On one occasion I told him that he couldn't go because others hadn't had theirs' yet. Lieutenant Colonel Spragge said to me quite emphatically his batman *was* going on leave. I insisted that it wasn't right for the rest of the troops not to get their leave. The troops didn't know why; they just knew they weren't getting it. At night they would be allowed to go to the local pubs, but that was about it.

When the men did get their fourteen days' leave for every six months of service, some went as far as Scotland and Northern Ireland. This was usually to see the land of their ancestors and sometimes to visit relatives. They would be issued free rail tickets for travel to their chosen destination.

Army Training Courses

In addition to the leave policy, Army training courses were another sore point. Often we could send only so many men off to a course although we needed many more to be qualified in that particular trade or skill. Does this sound familiar? Some things in the Army never change! For example, sergeants should all have been small-arms experts but only a select few got the really keen courses. Sergeant (later Warrant Officer Class Two) Jack Forbes was one of these select few. He was originally in Charlie Company prior to being moved to Don and he went off on one of these small-arms courses. He came back with a "D" award. The "D" was for "Distinction," which in the British Army world was high praise indeed, something like having two moons in the sky. The British were very stingy about awarding medals and distinctions of any kind.

I've mentioned that we trained on many occasions in these years with the Home Guard. Sergeant Forbes was given the job of teaching these old soldiers the new weapons. Many of the Home Guard had been officers in the First World War, some with ranks as exalted as full colonel, and here they were taking instruction from a Canadian sergeant. Jack had a great time as he was a born instructor, and the Home Guard men were keen learners. He took along a small group of the better corporals from the company, with the result that Charlie Company gained some very fine small-arms instructors.

Another non-commissioned officer who got the really important courses was Charlie Martin of Able Company. I remember that Charlie had just come off an explosives and demolitions course. He showed us how to take a No. 36 grenade (the pineapple) and increase its destructiveness by putting the explosive charge into a long narrow piece of pipe with a penny to stop one end. Charlie had been taught that such a grenade could be thrown further and has much greater destructive power. I recall this incident like it was yesterday. As he finished this briefing, he rubbed his hands with glee.

Amphibious Landing Training

By 1943, pressure was strong from "Papa" Joe Stalin for a "second front." He had been pressing the Allies about this since the German invasion in June 1941. Sometime in 1943, the Third Division was selected to be the front edge of the invasion of France, and we began training for amphibious landings. We had some preliminary assault-boat training on the south coast of England before going to Scotland. This was prior to my departure from the regiment in October.

Teddy Hartnell, who took over from me as Company Sergeant Major of Charlie, related a story about one winter evening in 1942–1943 when the company was working with the assault boats. As they came through Portsmouth harbor, they came across an anchored anti-aircraft ship in the harbor manned by Royal Marines. The Marines invited them to come aboard for a drink so they tied up their assault boat and went on board. The guns were all at a high angle to protect against planes. You have to remember that the Royal Marines used to have a Blue Division, which was artillery and a Red Division, which was light infantry. After the First World War, all Marines were cross-trained as infantrymen and gunners. One platoon of Charlie Company was with the Sergeant Major and they spent the whole night aboard ship while all the rest of the troops were jumping off into salt water. The other platoons were royally cheesed off when they heard of the platoon "swan" that night.

Incidentally, one of the lessons learned at Dieppe was that stronger assault boats were required for the D-Day landings. The Second Division had been given wooden boats, and when they came in to land, the German machine-gun fire went right through the hulls and killed men even before they reached the beach.

We were at Inverary, on the west coast of Scotland, in the fall of 1943, to do advanced amphibious-landing training for the upcoming invasion of France. One concern was how to keep the vehicles afloat once they hit the water. The answer was to make them waterproof, and a paste-like substance was invented for this purpose. The men in the Mad Four (Carrier) Platoon applied it to a jeep and once they had finished, it needed to be tested. Rifleman Harry Baxter volunteered for the trial and drove the jeep into the water. Marvel of marvels, it worked! But once again, inspiration went ahead of practicality in Mad Four: someone had forgotten to take the tide into consideration (they were definitely not Maritimers). It was going out, and Harry and the jeep were being taken out to sea. Fortunately there was a small Royal Navy vessel nearby, and some of the sailors spotted Harry in the water in his jeep. What a sight that must have been! The ship came over, hooked on and kindly towed him back to shore, to Baxter's great relief. For a short time, he had been panic-stricken and thought he was going to float all the way back to Newfie. The Platoon Commander too was mightily relieved, as he had not forgotten the Bay of Fundy episode two years earlier!

Company Sergeant Major Teddy Hartnell was a friendly fellow, much more outgoing than I, even though I know our men didn't like him at all. He had been a sergeant in Baker Company first before taking my place as Sergeant Major of Charlie Company. He eventually succeeded me as Regimental Sergeant Major in October 1943 when I was pulled out for service in Italy. Why didn't the Baker Company Sergeant Major become RSM? Sammy Score (anglicized form of "Scoresisio"), who was the first Sergeant Major of Baker Company, had gone for officers' training. Bill "Daddy" Hughes, who had seven years in the British Army, took his place. He was a little bit old but I nevertheless recommended Hughes for Regimental Sergeant Major as he knew all the drill and weapons. Another factor in my recommendation was that he wouldn't "crime you," that is, he wouldn't put various minor infractions on a soldier's conduct sheet.

Discipline

One of my main jobs as Regimental Sergeant Major was discipline. When the soldiers got into trouble with Army regulations, we had to take action. Charges were most often laid at the company level and they were recorded on a form called a conduct sheet known as MFN 6. After the first six months were up, a soldier's first MFN would be destroyed. However, any new charges that were placed on the next conduct sheet became permanent. Those soldiers being considered for promotion had to have a clean record. For instance, if a rifleman was AWL (Absent Without Leave, or as we called it, "Over the Hillo") and came before his company commander, he would be fined and then "confined to barracks." This would go on his conduct sheet. Most of the infractions (apart from leave) had to do with conduct in British towns and other minor things such as a dirty rifle or unpolished boots. In this respect, the Canadian Army was very good because they tore up the record of the charge after six months. But a second one stayed with you wherever you went.

In certain cases, however, charges were laid a little too readily. I recall one officer who was overly zealous in this regard. He had his Sergeant Major, Fred Rowell, put twenty-nine men on charges, mostly for minor barracks infractions. Rowell later told the officer when asked where the men where, that he had lost the paper with the names. He knew that charging so many men in one company could only have a negative impact on their morale.

This same officer, who was known as "Granny," objected to the men singing dirty songs while out on route marches. The word got back to the men pretty quickly, and then they took to singing "Onward, Christian Soldiers" in not exactly an attitude of reverence. As a serious churchman, the Major later admitted that it was preferable to have lewd songs sung than to have them make a sham out of a fine old hymn.

In early 1943 we were out on one of our many battalion route marches. The troops had been walking for hours and they were pretty tired. Toward the end of this particular march, we were told that we had to wade through a small pond that was almost five feet deep. For most of the men under six feet tall, the water was up to their mouths. Sergeant Rollie Guiton stood on one bank to help the non-swimmers, and Padre Jack Clough was stationed on the other side. Normally we didn't do this sort of thing, unlike the British Army who felt that such activities "toughen the men up." When I had learned about the water route planned for the conclusion of the march, I had advised the Commanding Officer that the troops should leave their weapons behind. My reason for this counsel was that the battalion had just been issued the No. 4 Lee-Enfield rifle. It was this weapon we would use throughout the Northwest Europe campaign. Mud in the barrel would have compromised its effectiveness before we got into combat.

Padre Jack Clough came alongside Rifleman Bill Lewin of Baker Company as he struggled along in the water, the mud sucking on his boots with each step. Clough told him to tilt his head back because the water was up to his nose. His group of riflemen staggered out of the pond totally soaked, water running off their clothes and their boots full of mud. As you can imagine, it was quite difficult to stay in any kind of formation after that "dip." These men of Baker Company were dragging themselves along in loose groups of four or five when, the officer in charge of the company, Major "Granny" Hudson, came along in a jeep. Compared to his soaking men, he was the picture of cleanliness, as he had not gone through the water with them. Hudson told

Sergeant Major Fred Rowell to charge this group of stragglers with conduct unbecoming and a group of riflemen was confined to barracks.

Normally as Regimental Sergeant Major I only got involved with charges when they went from the company to the battalion level. I happened to be walking by the Baker Company lines later that same day and I saw Rifleman Lewin standing outside. I called him over and asked him what was happening. When I understood the situation, I gave him some advice, though I can't remember what it was. Happily my words seemed to have made a difference, and as a result, Lewin was not charged.[24]

Another incident that provoked charges was when Lance Sergeant George Morrison refused a direct order to take his men through a pond. He had done a personal recce and found a route to the objective that by-passed the pond. I helped to get Morrison off this potentially serious charge of failure to obey a lawful command. My argument in his favour to Lieutenant Colonel Spragge was that Morrison had used his intelligence and initiative. At the time there was a slogan, "Sweat saves blood; brains save sweat." Morrison was following this dictum and saved his men from getting soaking wet and running the risk of becoming ineffective or even sick.

A regulation had come down from the top that any soldier caught not saluting an officer would get twenty-six days in military prison, which we euphemistically called, "the glass house." Jack Forbes, a sergeant at the time, had just come back from leave in London. He came to me and told me he was in trouble over saluting, of all things! Apparently, Forbes had been coming around a corner, and an officer came out of a building near by, and before Jack could see him and salute, this British officer placed him under arrest. The military police (red caps) cancelled his leave and sent him back to camp. My response was to give him another leave pass. Jack Forbes was a fine soldier and a good sergeant; he would never knowingly commit such a blatant breach of regulations.

I learned in 1998 that Jack Forbes was one of those Canadians murdered by the 12 SS Panzer Division troops *after* he was taken prisoner.[25] Rifleman Dave Arksey of Don Company recalls that the Germans opened fire on a group of the Canadian prisoners and that Jack Forbes was wounded in both legs as he tried to avoid the bullets.[26] Subsequently, Jack was executed. This was an entirely different incident from that of Sergeant Tommy McLaughlin and his section. McLaughlin and his men were found buried in a shallow grave about 17 June near the village of Mouen. I don't think the fact that Forbes and others like Rifleman Charlie Hood were murdered is well known even among our own people.

One of our riflemen got himself in trouble with the local police when we were stationed at Eastbourne. It seems there was some altercation in a local pub and he forcibly relieved some locals of a few pounds. I had him brought before the Commanding Officer for "summary of evidence," a preliminary to court-martial proceedings. The big, husky rifleman blurted out that he hadn't broken any military regulations, just beat up some British civilians (we called them "civvies") and relieved them of money that he felt they rightly owed him. I told the Provost Sergeant to place him under close arrest. He didn't go peaceably though, and it took three military policemen to drag him off in handcuffs. Soon he was handed over to the local police, and I forgot about him.

Several years after the war, I was walking on Yonge Street near Davenport Road, in downtown Toronto, when whom should I see approaching me but the big rifleman. I thought to myself, "Here's where I get paid back." Much to my surprise, he recognized me, shook my hand and slapped me on the shoulder. We chatted for a few minutes and then went our separate ways. As I headed to Bloor Street, I reflected on how pleasant it is to have been "born lucky," as the saying goes, rather than born rich! [27]

Liquor

What would the military be without liquor? In England, we used to get all the liquor we wanted as long as the Mess bought so much beer. There were twenty drinks to a twenty-six ounce bottle; for Mess bookkeeping purposes, it had to be accounted for at the end of each month. We received the rum ration only once a month in winter. The NAAFI (Navy, Army and Air Force Institute) ration was one bottle of liquor a month each for officers, warrant officers and sergeants. A bottle cost each of us one dollar and fifty cents and this was expensive in relation to our pay, but we had nowhere to spend our money anyway.

Clay Bell of Charlie Company was a lance sergeant, so technically he was still a corporal, and, therefore, not a part of the Sergeants' Mess.[28] I treated him as a full sergeant, however, and he got twenty cents more a day in pay. Clay used to complain that twenty-five cents a day went to the Mess so he was poorer by five cents!

We had moved from outside Hassocks to this little place with a castle, a very ritzy place called Wykehurst Park, where we spent the winter of 1942–1943. I shared a Nissen hut with Regimental Quartermaster Sergeant Gord Wice right next to the castle. The troops were further out in huts in the woods. Frank Gaines had just been promoted to sergeant, and we invited him to have his first drink in the Mess. It ended up being a first-class party! I believe that this was the night I fell into a slit trench on the way home from the Mess and got covered in mud. It was winter and the trench was half-full of water. I don't remember falling in or getting out of it. When Gordy saw me, he uttered a blasphemy and then said, "Harry, you've even got mud in your eyes." Hence my expression, "here's mud in your eye" when I'm drinking.

In some ways, I feel that I didn't have the proper background to be Regimental Sergeant Major. From the viewpoint of military discipline, I was not a "good" RSM; that is, I didn't believe in going strictly by the book.

[Despite this intelligent outlook on Army regulations, Harry Fox was still hard to please. The men had a nickname for almost everyone; for example, one officer was known as "Pills" and another was "Slit Trench." The men knew Harry as "The Long Finger," and if he pointed it at you and said, "Rifleman," you were in trouble. One young rifleman named McNabb found this out the hard way. Soon after joining the QOR in the spring of 1943, he was walking along at the time of the sunset ceremony: the flag was being lowered and a bugler was playing. Out of respect, every soldier is supposed to stop and come to attention while this is happening. Harry saw this soldier still walking and not at attention: "You," he shouted, "Stand still." McNabb said he was so scared that he nearly jumped out of his boots. Ed.]

Parades

Another of my duties as Regimental Sergeant Major was the running of battalion-level parades. There were quite a few of these held in England; every time a VIP (Very Important Person) visited, the Commanding Officer would call a regimental parade. Most parades were not very memorable but one stands out for a very personal reason. We held this one particular parade at Partridge Green for the Duke of Gloucester's visit. I had the whole battalion formed up by company and was about to turn the parade over to the adjutant. A dog suddenly appeared, from out of the ranks somewhere and ran up beside me. I think it was one of the company mascots. The dog looked up at me and then went around and lifted his leg, and peed on the back of my pant leg. I hollered out to the assembled troops, "Don't any of you laugh." The riflemen barely held themselves together without a belly laugh. I wasn't very fond of dogs at the time, and that certainly ranks as one of my embarrassing moments as the QOR Regimental Sergeant Major.

In a Rifle regiment, riflemen normally double on parade, especially when called out to the front. There was one occasion that I called out the name of a Rifleman Monday. He was a tall, gangly kid and he didn't exactly march but rather sauntered over the parade square. By the time he arrived, I was fuming and said to him, "Rifleman Monday, you're so slow, you'll arrive on Tuesday!"

Anti-tank gun used by the Canadian Army in the Second World War. (Craig Cameron)

A Bofors anti-aircraft gun. (Craig Cameron)

A 25-pounder artillery howitzer. This was the main weapon used in the Second World War by medium regiments in support of infantry units like the Hast & PER.
(Craig Cameron)

A 17-pounder used by the Royal Canadian Artillery during the war.
(Craig Cameron)

A vintage (1942) Sherman tank in use by the Canadian Army in the Second World War.
(Craig Cameron)

Some members of 14 Platoon, C Coy, QOR in England, 1942. after Cpl (later L/Sgt) George Morrison, far left, was killed in action on D-Day. Rfn Dick Ayton is at centre, second row.

German prisoners being searched for weapons prior to being taken to higher headquarters.

RSM Harry Fox and BHQ NCOs, June 1942.

Capt Hugh McRae, England, 1942. He was killed in a traffic accident in England on April 30 1943.

RSM Harry Fox and NCOs at Wykehurst Park, Sussex, UK. Front row from left, Sgt Watson, Harry Fox, Dick Bell; back row from left, Jack Wharrick, Wally Land.

Harry Fox's Italy

1 Avellino Replacement Depot
2 San Nicola + San Tommaso
3 Hitler Line
4 Pompeii
5 Florence
6 San Maria di Scacciano
7 San Fortunato
8 Lamone River
9 Leghorn

Trieste
Venice
Gothic Line
Pisa
Florence
Liguria Sea
Tiber
Via Flaminia
Rimini
Pescara
Ortona
Adriatic Sea
Sangro R.
Gustav Line
Liri R.
Rapido R.
Naples
Salerno
Potenza
Tyrrhenian Sea
Sardinia
Ionian Sea
Mediterranean Sea
Reggio Calabria

H. TORRENS

CHAPTER 3

My First Months
in Italy

Pooch Draft to Italy

The Queen's Own Rifles, along with other Third Division units, had sent selected individuals to North Africa to gain combat experience. I think Major (later Brigadier General) Neil Gordon, Major Ed Dunlop and Sergeant Earl Stoll (later commissioned and killed in action at Fort de la Crèche in northern France) were the only three selected. Of course, a number of riflemen transferred to First Division units while in England, such as Corporal Ray Skarott who was killed whilst serving with the 48th Highlanders of Canada. The Army's idea for this program was that certain key Canadian leaders should gain combat experience and then *return* to their regiments to provide a core of seasoned veterans for the invasion of France. I had earlier expressed my interest in getting some experience with a front-line unit, and the Commanding Officer could have refused the request given the important role I occupied, but he didn't. I certainly had no idea that once I left the QOR, I wouldn't see them again until the spring of 1945 in Holland. If I had known beforehand that I would be transferred *permanently* to a First Division unit, I would never have volunteered. Isn't hindsight a wonderful thing?

I left The Queen's Own Rifles on 3 October 1943 and along with a small group from the regiment, waited outside of Aldershot with a larger gathering of about four hundred commissioned and non-commissioned officers. Our contingent included: Major Sid Heyes, Captain Pat Green, Lieutenant P.C. Ostler, Lieutenant P.B. Hiscott, CSM Wils Hubbard, Sergeant Jimmy Harker, Sergeant Tommy Eastwood and myself.

These drafts were codenamed "Pooch," a North American colloquialism of the time for a dog. Everything in the Army had a name or an acronym. The code-name was for security purposes in order to confuse the enemy. We had to use words that soldiers knew and could remember easily. While in Italy, I almost got myself shot one night when I was challenged with the codeword "Delhi" and I forgot the countersign. A soldier stood there with a Tommy gun pointed right at me. It was scary. One reason for this particular password was that it was a word the troops of the Indian division next to us would remember. The same was true for radio communications. I had the worst time remembering all the various words. The officers had to remember many more than I did and I think they were smarter in this respect, than I.

Shots

Since we were headed to the Mediterranean and a combat zone, inoculations were required. I had never liked them as a child but this particular experience in England was one of the worst. One day we were told that all those in the Pooch draft had to have shots. I complained that all these non-commissioned officers had already received a full battery of shots in Canada and many of us, just a few months previous to this. I was told in no uncertain terms that everyone going to the continent had to have a full battery of six shots before embarkation. So I took the group of two hundred non-commissioned officers to the Regimental Aid Post.

My usual procedure as Company Sergeant Major and even as Regimental Sergeant Major was to be the last man in, to ensure everyone had gone through. However, in this case they were all warrant officers and sergeants from most of the regiments of the Canadian Army in England. I got tired of their grumbling and complaining and so decided that I had to lead by example.

There was a team of six doctors at different tables inside the Aid Post. Each doctor swabbed my arm and gave me the shot. I came to the last doctor and he did the same thing. This injection hurt from the base of my neck to my fingers. To make things worse, the glass cylinder broke and the green gooey liquid dribbled down my arm. The doctor wiped it off and then tried to pull the needle out but it wouldn't budge. Then he took a pair of pliers and proceeded to jerk it out. "Bloody horse doctor," I muttered, under my breath. "I heard that," he shouted. "I am going to put you on charge. Wait over there until I'm finished." I suspect that as a Medical Officer, the doctor had no idea of my rank or any clue about the military discipline system.

I went over to the corner and put my battle-dress blouse back on. I stood where everyone could see my rank badges. There are only two ways to discipline a Warrant Officer: one is simply to give him a verbal blast and be done with it; the second is much more difficult and involves a formal court-martial. I was not worried in the least about a bawling out as I was used to it by now, and it simply rolled off me like water off a duck's back. However, a court-martial was a much more fearsome prospect. I was pretty sure that my demeanour, while not appropriate to an officer, was not an offense of this magnitude.

The first few men who were behind me had heard the Medical Officer yell and knew that I was in trouble. They went past me with little grins on their faces; they seemed pleased that a Regimental Sergeant Major was in trouble! After the whole group of two hundred had gone through, the doctor started walking over to me. Before he got close enough to speak, I piped up, "I have seen Boy Scouts do a better job with a needle than you did." I walked past him and out the door. And that was the end of it.

In late October our group sailed from Glasgow in the Clyde estuary in a large convoy bound for Italy. After ten days of sailing we passed through the Strait of Gibraltar and headed into the Mediterranean where the convoy split in two; our ship went to Algiers and the rest headed to Philippeville. Our landing in Algiers was intended to confuse the Germans about our real intentions, as there was a lot of contact in North Africa with German and Italian agents. We had people from every Canadian regiment in England with us. I still had my QOR flashes and Third Division patch on my uniform. This diversion was part of the cover plan to get the Fifth Division's tanks out to Italy by December 1943, with their infantry to follow in January 1944.

Eventually our ship sailed east for the reinforcement camp in Philippeville on the North African coast. Philippeville is in Algeria right on the edge of the desert and close to the sea, about half way between Algiers and Tunisia. A short time after I arrived, a storm hit the area and virtually wiped out the whole camp. It was about mid-November by this time. As it was, we were lucky to get the men out. There are several bodies of water in North Africa that are called "schots," essentially large pools in wintertime and dry beds in summer. When it does rain, these schots become lakes and then rivers.

From Philippeville we had a rough thirty-six hour sea voyage that brought us to Italy, where we were dropped off near Naples. A truck convoy took us to the major Canadian reinforcement base at Avellino, northeast of Naples. Soldiers came there from hospitals as well as from England and were sorted out by destination. The First Division's depot for combat soldiers was farther up the peninsula, closer to the front. We cooled our heels for a few weeks here, and I still had no notion of what unit I would be joining. I began to wonder if my lot was to stay at the base camp as an unemployed Warrant Officer class one until the Army left Italy because there didn't seem to be any unit in need of an infantry Regimental Sergeant Major. There were three of us holding this rank on the Pooch draft but I was the only infantryman.

In Avellino I lived in a large building that had been bombed, and there was very little roof left on it. So a temporary remedy was to put tarpaulins over the holes and hope that it would keep the occupants dry. I suppose they assumed that infantry should be used to "roughing it." This place was known as the First Canadian Reinforcement Depot. The non-commissioned officers who came in on the Pooch draft were quartered in this building and the officers were housed in the town proper. The accommodations were all right in good weather until it started to rain and as this was December, it rained virtually every day. You could look up to the mountains from beneath the tarp and see the white clouds getting closer and closer.

There was a group of four of us in one room. The floor was not finished and rather scarred. I recall that one night, water had come through the tarpaulin on the ceiling and pooled on one soldier's blanket. He woke up rather wet and miserable. Boy, was he mad! He took his bayonet and stabbed the floor. The water ran off him "sploosh," right down through the hole he had created to the floor below, hitting some non-commissioned officers sleeping there. They came roaring up the stairs fighting mad as they thought someone had soaked them deliberately. When they saw the situation, they cooled down quickly.

There was a lot of time to kill at the depot and naturally enough we struck up conversations with others who were there. One soldier that I got to know at Avellino had been with an artillery unit in England. He told me that his former Padre, Honorary Captain Essex in that regiment had eventually been posted to the Hastings and Prince Edward Regiment of the First Division. Padre Essex was a very fine man, from the gunner's description of him in

England, but he had recently been replaced and brought out of the combat zone.[29] In addition to being the replacement depot for Canadians going up to front-line units, Avellino was also home to the Non-Effective Transit Depot for anyone no longer able to function at the front due to combat stress, and therefore with no specific position to fill. My gunner acquaintance introduced me to the Padre, and we soon became friendly, as there weren't many people around that we knew. The Padre told me a lot of little things that proved to be helpful in my subsequent job as Regimental Sergeant Major in an infantry unit, such as how to bury men. This was normally the Padre's job, but the subject was apparently bothering him and it seemed that he wanted to talk about these things.

It was while I was sitting in Avellino that the First Division was attacking in the Ortona area and it suffered terribly in the fighting there. After Ortona, the division was in appalling condition; they had 695 killed in action, 1,738 wounded and 1,773 sick, for a total of 4,206.[30] Replacements like myself didn't help very much to bring the numbers back to full strength. At the beginning of 1944, the First Canadian Infantry Division was still 1,050 below strength. General Chris Vokes, its Commander, admitted that the division had "lost its sharp fighting edge."

After yet another period of waiting, a decision was finally made and I was sent up to the First Division's depot. This was on 12 January 1944. We went by truck to the forward area, a personnel depot at San Vito, looking down on the Moro River not far from the Adriatic Sea. I made this portion of my journey with Major Harold Usher and Company Sergeant Major H. C. Usher of the Lincoln and Welland Regiment. The Sergeant Major had been a corporal in the QOR before the war. It's funny how I regularly met former riflemen while serving in Italy. Both Ushers had come out from England on the same Pooch draft with me.

It was a cold day with some rain and sleet. The main roads we drove on were fairly good but cratered. The back roads were a different story, however; they were simply dirt paths used by local farmers who mostly employed oxen. The Indian drivers of the Eighth Army with their mule trains also used these ox paths. We came to a large cliff formation made of sandstone, quite close to the coast. It was near Ortona in a valley where the Moro River runs. There was a railway that went in a tunnel under the town. I know because they used the tunnel for a mule house.

At the San Vito depot, we were made to wait in a small cave. The major sat in the one and only chair and the sergeant major and I stood. There was one table with a candle on it and we waited there for hours. Some soldier eventually brought us bully beef sandwiches, which was fine, as we hadn't eaten since breakfast. As the various staff types came and went, they gave us strange looks. I think they couldn't figure out why a major and two senior warrant officers were together in this place. The reason we three were in that cave was that we had all been assigned to the same infantry battalion. Major Usher would be placed in Headquarters Company first, and then to Able Company to replace the late Major Alex Campbell, who had been killed leading an attack on Christmas Day.[31] Officers were often moved around like this in a unit, but not the non-commissioned officers. As we worked much more closely with the soldiers, it was thought better to leave us where we were placed. Eventually they put us in a truck and away we went. We still had no notion of what battalion we were going to, and it was pitch dark by now.

I Join the "Plough Jockeys" [32]

The truck wound its way to the west and up a hill to the little town of San Nicola. It was only when I saw the Hastings and Prince Edward Regiment shoulder flashes on the men's uniforms, that I knew finally where I had been assigned. One of the first people we met was Regimental Sergeant Major Angus Duffy. I recall his first words to me as if they were yesterday: "Oh, here you are. We've been waiting for you." He took us upstairs in one of the houses where he had a place with a blanket ready for me. The village had been forcibly evacuated and taken over by elements of the "Hasty P's."[33] The people who had lived here for centuries were now refugees with no possessions and nowhere to go. To have to tell Italian people to leave their homes was an unpleasant part of advance party work that I would have to perform as the unit's Regimental Sergeant Major.

Now, it might be thought that the people would have hated the Allies for disrupting their lives but you need to remember though, that they had suffered under the Fascist regime of Il Duce, Benito Mussolini, for more than a decade. The bulk of the Italian people had no use for the *Fascisti*, the devout Fascist followers of Mussolini. We called his paramilitary types who wore the black shirts, "Musholini." The Italian people remembered the First World War when they fought the Austrians who were allies of the Germans, so we got along with them fairly well. All we knew was how the Canadians were treated.

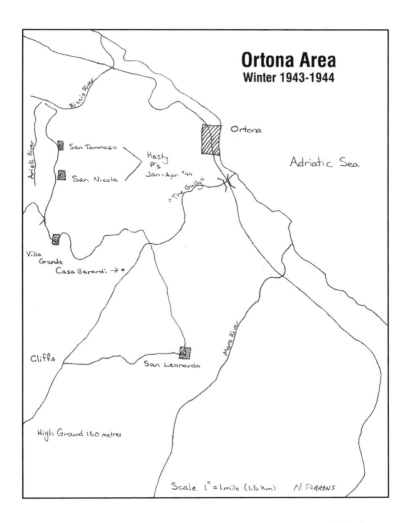

Ortona Area
Winter 1943-1944

Riccio River

Ortona

San Tommaso

Hasty
P's
Jan-Apr '44

Arielli River

San Nicola

"The Gully"

Adriatic Sea

Villa
Grande

Casa Berardi →

Moro River

Cliffs

San Leonardo

High Ground 150 metres

Scale 1" = 1 mile (1.5 km)   H. TORRENS

I did hear of some criticism of our troops and not just because of the liquor abuse problem. Our soldiers tended to loot somewhat freely, and the people may have assumed we were like the British. I know that the Italians didn't get along with the British. I think this may be a legacy of the campaign in North Africa where they were treated badly by elements of the Eighth Army.

The Americans were yet another story. There were many American GIs of Italian ancestry who could speak the language, and they were richer than us.

This latter fact seemed to endear them to their poor cousins, unlike the English who generally seemed to resent American prosperity.

In the winter of 1943–1944, the regiment was living in buildings in the two towns of San Nicola and San Tommaso that overlooked the Arielli Valley. Several rifle companies were dug in on the banks of the Arielli below the two towns. There was a rotation system in use: two companies would go out for a period of days and the others would come back to the comparative comfort of the buildings. These two towns were typically Italian, comprised mostly of low stone houses with red clay-tiled roofs. The streets were narrow and cobbled, smelled of animals and garbage and despite the evacuation, a few Italian peasants still lived there. Three times in the next three months we would leave and then return. The two towns gradually disappeared under the continual German barrages. Most buildings didn't have intact windows, and some had parts of their roofs smashed in.

At this time the rifle companies were down to about thirty-five to forty men, instead of the normal strength of one hundred and fifteen. All infantry battalions in the division were in this state after Ortona. Very few replacements had arrived to increase the numbers. Battalion Headquarters had more men in it than the rifle companies did. Headquarters Company and Support Company also had more as they didn't take the casualties that the front-line companies did. On one occasion, the Anti-Tank Platoon from Support Company was dragooned as infantry with predictable results: they went forward and got hammered.

Farley Mowat observes that the Germans knew how important covered buildings were, and they set out to systematically destroy every building in the twin towns. "It was during this winter that the men developed to an acute degree the capacity to estimate the relative strength of a building at first glance."[34] Most of the men were compelled to keep indoors. The Regimental History relates one account of a tirade by the Headquarters Company Quarterbloke, Basil Smith, who was mortared three times while on the john. He said that due to constipation, he would apply for a pension after the war.

Regimental Sergeant Major Duffy and I started a tour of the battalion lines and he introduced me to a few people, but we only had time to reach Baker Company among the rifle companies.[35] Sergeant Major Usher wound up there. I remember Usher telling me on the drive up from San Vito to walk on the side of the road in case of sudden artillery strikes, because the ditch would be ready at hand to dive into quickly. However, I never did this; I always walked down the middle of the road. My attitude at the time was, "Heck, I'm all right. If I'm going to get it, I'll get it no matter what I do." (Remember that I had just arrived and had no combat experience). About the middle of the afternoon, and right out of the blue, two shells exploded "bang, bang" above the village. Duffy said: "I don't like it." Sure enough, they were ranging on the village for a bombardment. That night when we were all upstairs asleep, the Germans whacked us with a "stonk."[36]

The Battalion Headquarters was in a big building just across the narrow street. Beside that building was a shed with a wine cellar. The shed had a big strong door and was being used to hold four or five men who were under "close arrest." A shell hit the corner of the building just as one of prisoners came out for a leak, and it smashed him to pieces. The military policeman on duty across the street was knocked on his backside but he got up, and he was okay. We saw all this from one of the upstairs windows, and we tore downstairs as someone in the lock-up was yelling at the top of his lungs. In the basement, there was a huge keg, which was about nine feet high and used for wine storage. There was someone underneath it. Apparently he had crawled into that space, thinking that it was a pretty good place to take shelter from the bombardment as the bottom of the keg was about a foot off the ground. I saw this guy with his feet sticking out, flailing away. So I grabbed him by the ankles and dragged him out. What a mess! There was nothing but red all over. It appeared to me that a piece of shrapnel had hit the corner of the building, come down through the roof of the shed, through the keg and hit him on the head. I picked him up fireman-style and carried him up the hill to the Regimental Aid Post.

After it was all over and things had settled down, Mr. Duffy and I went up the hill to visit the Aid Post. "Where is that guy I brought in all covered with blood?" I asked. There was a soldier sitting there smoking a cigarette. He said, "Hey, it was me." "You?" I replied, pointing at him in disbelief. What I thought was blood was actually wine from the cask. The shrapnel had made a hole in the cask and this fellow was choking as the wine poured out. The wine in the Ortona area is dark and quite thick, having almost the consistency of human blood. There is little in the way of water, and every family has a wine keg. (I recall that the house was perched right on top of the hill with a one hundred foot drop off the side). I had seen dead men back in Toronto, but never before had I seen anyone who looked so messy. I got over that quickly enough but I've never forgotten drawing that man out of the cellar with what I thought was blood all over him.

For 14 January 1944, the unit's war diary states: "RSM Duffy left us today, returning to England. We are all going to miss him like hell, because he is a great guy, a one hundred percent soldier, and perhaps because he seems to be the personification of the unit and its spirit." Farley Mowat commented: "RSM Duffy was gone and replaced by a different sort of man, Harry Fox, another outsider [like Lieutenant Colonel Donald Cameron] who had to make his way into the family."[37] Regimental Sergeant Major Angus Duffy went on to become the top Warrant Officer of the First Canadian Army, the most senior non-commissioned member in the entire Army. He had a journal of all that had happened in the regiment from Sicily onward, with certain parts underlined. Just before Regimental Sergeant Major Duffy left, he gave it to me as his successor.

Charles Comfort, the First Division war artist, visited one of the twin towns, San Tommaso, in early January and gives a vivid description of the desolation left after the battle. The Germans had deliberately blown up the magnificent cathedral of San Tommaso, "looking as if a mighty cleaver had struck down through the dome and split it in half like a butchered steer." In the Piazza Plebiscita, Comfort observed: "the Sherman tank *Amazing* tilted and brewed up at its center. One felt a choking claustrophobia in the place. Everywhere was misery, death and destruction."[38]

This was the place where I entered the combat zone, in the wake of one of the fiercest battles that Canadians fought in the Second World War. To make matters even less pleasant, the weather in northern Italy in mid-winter is not a tropical paradise. The 48th Highlanders' Regimental History states: "For weeks, the rain saturated everything; a battle dress was a cold clammy shroud that was often board stiff from the frost, until the heat of a man's body converted it back to a stinking mush of sodden slime."[39] I find this statement to be too extreme; things weren't quite that bad. Yes, there was wet and mud, but I only saw one dead German in the months I was there. Our men were rotated from the front line to the towns so they weren't always miserable. Tanks were still in the fields where they had been disabled. But infantry casualties were all picked up and buried, in the aftermath of Ortona.

This Drink is On Me

A Plough Jockey was standing in the doorway of a little hut on the side of an ox cart path, scowling at the rain. He was a gunner in the Anti-tank Platoon of Support Company, and his crew had just finished cleaning their gun. Suddenly he threw away his cigarette and called to his pal, who was pressing blankets. "What do you see out there?" he asked. The other man came and said that all he could see was a pile of cow manure. He had seen a million of them since Sicily. His friend said, "Sure, sure, but have you ever seen one in this country that looks like that one, all neat and tidy and level on top?" It took a minute or so for the implication to sink in, and then they both grabbed shovels and started digging.

The reward for their efforts was a cache of liquor that someone had tried to hide, totalling one hundred and twenty-nine bottles. There were no labels on them so they didn't know if they had found wine, brandy or cider. In any event, it was a real prize. The two men were generous, giving every officer and warrant officer a bottle. They went to the Commanding Officer, Lieutenant Colonel "Ack Ack" Kennedy, and asked for permission to have a party. Kennedy pondered this for a few moments and said, "Men, I know that no matter what I say, you'll drink them anyway. So, go ahead but I warn you that there is to be no loud singing or weapons firing. If the Brigadier finds out, there will be trouble." The party happened, and the Brigadier never heard about it, although the story goes that two bottles found their way to the General's bedroll.

A few hours later I was walking down a road when three Plough Jockeys came towards me. As they approached, I overheard one of them say, "It's the new RSM." When they reached me, another one asked me if I knew his brother, Yves Agasse with The Queen's Own Rifles. I most certainly did, as Agasse had been one of my regimental policemen (provosts). We talked for a minute or so about him, and then one of the others reached into his combat blouse and pulled out a bottle from the recently discovered cache. "This is yours, sir," he said. I stood there like a dummy, frozen. After all, as a warrant officer I was not supposed to drink and "fraternize" with the troops.

Put yourself in my shoes: I was the new Regimental Sergeant Major in a different regiment; I didn't know anyone here nor did I know the customs. Was this allowed in a combat zone? The fellow piped up, "Well, are you gonna taste it or not?" I took the cork off and took a swig. It was great liquor, nice and sweet, the way I like it. But it burned all the way down, just like drinking a liquid mustard plaster, and I made a face. The soldier then said, "You'll have to learn to hold your liquor (he pronounced it *likker*) better than that if you're going to be a Hasty Pee." I replied, "Is that so? Well, if you can take a drink from this bottle without making a face, I'll give you one hundred lire." He didn't say a thing but reached over and took the bottle. We could hear the liquor gurgling down his throat. His face never changed, not even a smile, so I handed him over a brand-new AMGOT note for one hundred lire.[40] The three soldiers walked away laughing as they had pulled a fast one on the new Regimental Sergeant Major.

Later that year at the Hitler Line, the same fellow, Private Bernard May, was acting as an ambulance driver and rescued a number of wounded men from burning tanks. He was awarded the Military Medal for his bravery. Some years after the war, my wife and I were returning from a day trip to Niagara Falls. As we were leaving the bus depot on the way home, a bus passed us and then suddenly the brakes squealed and it jarred to a halt. The door opened and out rushed a man who came over and put a bear hug on me. I had no idea why this stranger was acting like a long-lost brother, until he opened his mouth and said, "Sergeant Major, have you had any good liquor lately?" I remembered the distinctive accent and the face: it was Bernard May, the soldier who took me for one hundred lire when I was new to the Hasty P's. In the two decades after the war, I was constantly meeting men in Toronto that I had known in the Army.

Combat Stress

"Ortona scarred men, both physically and mentally. One quarter (484) of the Canadian sick were cases of exhaustion."[41] The Army recognized that many soldiers were suffering from what was officially called "battle exhaustion" and appointed an Army psychiatrist to deal with the issue. The First Division had been in action since July and there were many cases of soldiers who were at the end of their rope. In his interviews with combat soldiers, the First Division's psychiatrist found every example of psychological disorder among combat soldiers from "gross hysteria with mutism, paralysis to the inadequate personality who showed little outward evidence of anxiety but said simply 'I can't take it'."[42] Farley Mowat's description of the combat faced by the First Brigade in Sicily, and especially at Ortona, in *And No Birds Sang*, shows graphically how the strain of combat literally wore men out. Countless other books on soldiers in the Second World War bear this out. One book that I read about British soldiers in North Africa shows how one young lieutenant simply came to the end of his powers of endurance after six months of fighting in that environment and died.[43]

We had some cases in the First Division, but my impression is that it was more noticeable during the second winter (1944–1945). Most of the worst cases would likely have been evacuated by then. One example of a Plough Jockey whom I know was suffering from combat stress occurred later in the spring. We'll come to that when I talk about the Hitler Line offensive.

During the winter of 1943–1944, the Adriatic front had turned into a kind of Passchendaele, that memorable horror of a battle from the fall of 1917 in Flanders. General Crerar concluded that this war was so much like the last war "it's not even funny," and yet he instigated a policy of aggressive patrolling because of his memories of the First World War. "It was one of the most controversial decisions of his brief tenure in command of I Canadian Corps."[44]

Patrolling

There were three basic kinds of patrols that we did that winter. The first type was a reconnaissance (recce) patrol with an officer and three or four men. Its main purpose was to gain information and to study enemy positions. The idea was to avoid contact and trouble. Then there was the standing patrol with up to a platoon in size, whose intent was to ambush Germans. Finally, there was a fighting patrol in which the idea was to draw the enemy into a firefight and capture German soldiers so as to identity their formations.

The Hasty P's were very good at things like night patrols. Many of the Plough Jockeys were outdoor types, comfortable in the woods in all kinds of weather. Many of them came from little towns in central Ontario like Maynooth and Tweed. One group would go out three or four miles and come back a totally different route so as not to be picked up by the enemy. The papers at home during these winter months simply stated that the Italian front was "quiet."

Patrolling is a constant activity for the infantry in a defensive setting. It is dangerous but important work and takes great skill. The primary mission while in a defensive position is to gather information. In an infantry battalion you spend months training men to do a patrol. However, one frustration for us was that if the information gathered does not coincide with what the higher-ups think, they just "chuck it out." Occasionally, they made us repeat patrols and the men absolutely hated this order. They felt, quite rightly too, that their *lives* were on the line to satisfy the whims of some paper pushers at higher headquarters.

Soon after I had arrived at the unit, there was a prime example of this kind of thing. We received orders from First Brigade to send out a patrol. Lieutenant George Hopper, age 32, from New Liskeard, Ontario, led the patrol on the night of 28 January. He almost reached the objective and then decided to turn back just short of it. Lieutenant Colonel Kennedy interviewed him and asked why he stopped. "I just had a feeling there was trouble ahead," Hopper said. The Commanding Officer told brigade and they replied that it had to be repeated. So the same men were sent back the very next night to do the patrol again! The patrol advanced about *fifty feet* beyond where they had been the night before and walked right into an ambush. Lieutenant Hopper was hit when a German machine-gun opened up on them. He was killed, and Private Thomas was badly wounded, dying a few hours later.[45] Someone up at Brigade had had an idea; they needed information for some unknown purpose and were not satisfied until they got it. When the Padre buried Hopper, I was with Lieutenant Colonel Kennedy at the graveside service. After it concluded, he said to me, "RSM, I'll never do that again. If Brigade insists, I'll tell them to go whistle."

When you got close to the Germans you could smell them. It was a combination of smells comprised of their uniforms, soap and different food. Some men swore they could smell the presence of the enemy from the odour of leather, German tobacco and their rations, which gave them a distinctive body odour. Once we had several Jerry prisoners at Battalion Headquarters and we couldn't get them back to Brigade for more than twenty-four hours. As soon as I came in the room, I knew they were still there without seeing them, simply because of the smell. On the opposite side, they could smell us easily too. Our men often smoked cigarettes in the line, even though this was not permitted. We used different tobacco from the Germans. Some men used cream on their hair, and this had an odour. Even our toothpaste had a distinct smell. There were always one or two men who were obsessive about their teeth and were always brushing. The Germans were just as clean as our troops but more disciplined.

Lieutenant Hopper was an experienced combat officer, so he may have felt by some slight smell in the air that there were Germans there. He had done his job the first time. So he died, but what did it accomplish except to satisfy the curiosity of someone at Brigade?

Morale and Medals

The day I was enroute to the Hast & PER, the Army in Italy began publishing a weekly newspaper called *The Maple Leaf*. One of the features the men really loved was the cartoon "Herbie" by Bing Coughlin. Coughlin had Herbie address things that actually happened, from the soldier's vantage point. We obtained more information from *The Maple Leaf* about what was happening than from anywhere else, except for month-old newspapers that came from family in Canada. Within the military chain of command, we were only told what we needed to know. This is something that doesn't change in the military. Humour was, and is, essential to survival in the Army and especially in combat. In order to retain some semblance of sanity in this kind of environment, if something unfortunate happens to a buddy, you laugh at him.

About this time they also gave out the Canadian Volunteer Service Medal (CVSM) to Italian campaign veterans. We laughed because it was known familiarly as the "Surrey & Sussex Border Star." This was the soldiers' cynicism. The same rules applied as in the peacetime Army: you had to serve twelve years to qualify. The only exception to this rule was that being on "active service" every year of service was counted double. I got the CVSM and clasp for volunteering *and* for service overseas in England. As I had joined the militia in 1932, I also got the Efficiency Medal. At one time this decoration was called the Volunteer Decoration (VD) but as you can imagine, many people didn't want this after their names with the stigma of the other VD (venereal disease) so prevalent in wartime. So after the Second World War it became the Canadian Forces Decoration.

The medal parade was held in a gravel pit outside of Ortona in the last week of January. Two companies of the battalion paraded while the others held the line. No brass showed up but there was a band. It was not the regimental band as all unit bands had been broken up in England. When the QOR band was broken up, the buglers became stretcher-bearers. Some of the musicians who wished to be combatants were placed in the Anti-Tank Platoon, and the rest of the musicians were seconded to the Third Division Band.

Liquor: Second Installment

I've already talked about soldiers and drinking. In Italy there was plenty of wine and the local vino was stored in the cellar of each home. There was a story about Regimental Sergeant Major Duffy, that he would go around and shoot the wine barrels with a Tommy gun because liquor caused disciplinary problems. Soldiers would trade cigarettes for vino. Some enterprising types even made their own liquor. We Canadians weren't that heavily disciplined, unlike the Germans. We would go into places where wine casks had never been touched, yet the Germans had been there before us. We had the attitude that the Germans and Italians started the war; we didn't. "So tough on you, Willie." If some of our soldiers saw liquor, they would just go crazy and drink, "glug, glug." The Commanding Officer said it was okay to drink as long as they weren't hung over the next day and were able to soldier on. Inevitably, there were charges laid, and men were regularly in detention (close arrest) for drunkenness.

The abuse of liquor by soldiers was the reason that the British Army introduced the "slow march" every morning. A regiment would be formed up on the parade square with the non-commissioned officers in front, while the officers walked around in pairs. In the slow march one didn't use his arms, just his legs. If he was able to march straight, fine, but if he fell out or wobbled, then that was proof he had been drinking. I believe the Duke of Marlborough introduced this in one of his campaigns on the continent in the early 1700s. Prior to this, the British Army had not been in Europe since the end of the Hundred Years' War (1453), and the abuse of liquor by soldiers was not a huge problem. "Johnny Cope" is played at reveille first thing in the morning. This is a reference to the English General John Cope, who was defeated at Prestonpans in 1745 by the Jacobites under Charles Edward Stewart.

The Regimental Sergeant Major's Job in a Combat Zone

The Regimental Sergeant Major's job in a front-line situation is rather different than it is in garrison where the emphasis is on drill and deportment of the men and on training. There were five duties that I performed in the combat zone as Regimental Sergeant Major with the Hastings and Prince Edward Regiment:

1. Taking care of Prisoners of War (POW's).
2. Protection of Battalion Headquarters (BHQ), including set-up and

security and especially protecting the Commanding Officer.

3. Evacuation of the wounded.
4. Traffic control, including vehicular traffic in the headquarters area.
5. Ammunition supply.

Prisoners of War

My main job with regard to prisoners of war was to make sure that they got out of the Battalion Headquarters area as soon as possible. The infantry companies take prisoners on the attack and they get frisked and then turned over to the Intelligence Officer, who is supposed to question them when they arrive at headquarters. Quite often he didn't talk to them, so we just shipped them back to Brigade as soon as possible. First Brigade staff were always complaining to us when prisoners of war arrived there. They would say things like, "You didn't search them properly; he had a knife on him." We never could get them to understand that with thirty or forty Jerries at Battalion Headquarters and only one or two men to look after them, we couldn't afford to take the risk of searching or even questioning them as thoroughly as we might have liked. What would happen if the guard was overpowered? There would then be thirty or forty enemy soldiers in the middle of headquarters and this would be a big security risk. One of my jobs was to ensure that nothing disrupted the command and control element, particularly anything to do with the Commanding Officer's personal welfare. What was I supposed to do? I was responsible for the headquarters' security. We didn't give a hoot about pencils or pocketknives but those were the very things that Brigade complained about. I could never make them understand that it was dangerous and we had to get them out of there as quickly as possible. The higher staff always had "ideas" and they didn't want reality to change their theories.

I understand that the subject of shooting prisoners in the Second World War is a contentious issue. Some people, including a few well-known veterans of Normandy, insist that it isn't believable that Canadians shot German prisoners. I don't know why they think it's unbelievable. If your blood's up, you'll do anything. We are human beings after all, and many things can make us fighting mad. Quite often, the front-line officers didn't know what happened once the prisoners were taken to the rear. We would ask one or at most two soldiers to take prisoners back to higher headquarters. What can you say to the soldier if he returns and says that the prisoners tried to run so he had to shoot them? There are too many stories about Canadians retaliating for the shooting of their men by the Germans to simply dismiss it, as one well-known veteran does in a video done in the nineties. I know several Sherbrooke Fusilier veterans who still get angry today when the subject comes up. One reason for these veterans' anger is that 12 SS Panzer Division troops shot Honorary Captain Walter Brown, their Padre, and his driver just after D-Day about 7 June 1944. When the Fusiliers found this out in early July, they quite naturally wanted revenge on the Germans.

I think I can see a few reasons why some people deny that such retaliatory shootings took place. However, it just does not square with the stress of a combat situation and with human nature. Our passions are easily aroused, especially by injustice and to find your own men shot in cold blood whilst prisoners of war, would make the meekest man, who had decent sensibilities, angry. In fact, if one didn't get angry and desire retribution, I would wonder what was wrong with him. I experienced these very same feelings myself in September 1944 when I heard that a good friend, formerly with The Queen's Own Rifles, had been killed under questionable circumstances. I know the Hasty P's shot a few prisoners during a desperate situation while fighting near Ortona. They had taken these prisoners on the offensive, and then a German counterattack was launched before they could get the prisoners to the rear. What the Sam Hill are you going to do? When you're in a situation like that, only one thing matters, survival. War is utterly unlike anything we experience in our normal civilian lives. It's a brutal reality: kill or be killed. We certainly believed ourselves as Canadians to be decent, honorable people and we adhered to the Geneva Convention. But here was a situation where the prisoners of war were just sitting there waiting. If the attack had overrun them and picked the prisoners up, then the enemy would have been twice as strong. So they shot them before the counterattack could come through. What are you going to do when you're between the Devil and the deep blue sea and you can't swim?

Battalion Headquarters: Set-Up

The usual procedure for the Battalion Headquarters set-up was that the Commanding Officer would get his map and tell me where he wanted Tactical Headquarters to go; his small-scale map showed minute details, like specific buildings. In the advance, the Second-in-Command of the battalion would normally go up just behind the rifle companies. This was a new tactical development that came after an incident in Sicily where the

Commanding Officer of The Royal Canadian Regiment was killed because his headquarters was ambushed during a night move.

An order was given that the Second-in-Command was to be able to run the battalion from the Fighting Echelon. This way, there would be two men in the regiment who had experience and would be able to command the unit in action. It made sense, really, because if the Commanding Officer was knocked out, the Second-in-Command would generally not be experienced enough at handling the battalion in combat, as his was largely an administrative job. This had actually happened for the Hast & PER when Lieutenant Colonel Bruce Sutcliffe was out on a recce and the sun shone off his binoculars or something, and a sniper shot him. The other commanding officers in our brigade refused to comply with this order but our Commanding Officer saw the sense of it and used it.

There could be up to a hundred soldiers at Battalion Headquarters. There were always soldiers on the radios because they passed the time by chatting with one another. They used a "charley horse," a little electric motor, to keep the radios running. There was always activity at headquarters because food had to be cooked by the kitchen staff, the medics at the Regimental Aid Post had to be instantly available for the wounded, and the Intelligence section was always making maps, and so on. We tried to keep the different sections separate, but it was difficult to find the needed accommodation. The Germans knew our need and consequently continually hammered buildings with artillery fire.

As we moved into a new location, my dealings with the Italian people consisted largely in telling them to get out of the buildings. I normally led the advance party for the regiment on the move. I took this job over from the Second-in-Command, Major Ketchison, when he was required to lead the battalion's rifle companies into action. So they sent me out, and I'm happy to say that I never lost a man or vehicle, even during the last battle of the war in Holland when we were quite close to the rifle companies. As soon as things were quiet, I would go about another of my jobs, helping the padre and stretcher-bearers carry out casualties.

LCol A.A. Kennedy, DSO. (Hast & PER)

CSM George Ponsford, MBE, MM. (Hast & PER)

LCol Cameron, DSO & Bar, ED, CD. He later became Brigadier General. (Hast & PER)

Army cooks with their "dixies." The cooks are called "pot-wallopers" in Harry's stories.

Capt. J.F. Goforth, MC, CD. He was later Senior Chaplain (P) of the Canadian Army. (Hast & PER)

CHAPTER 4

Sketches of the Italian Campaign

A Full-Fledged "Plough Jockey"

The first big step to being accepted by the Hasty P's came a few weeks after I had arrived. It was hard coming in as an outsider and especially hard to fill the shoes of someone like Angus Duffy. I don't think I ever filled his footsteps completely, but I tried. I'm a quiet guy; I don't argue too much. Duffy was the opposite; he was a small Irishman, somewhat boastful and argumentative. He would tell people off if he thought they needed it. Duffy told me that he had to take several guys behind the headquarters building and "beat the hell" out of them. I would characterize this as "old school" non-commissioned officer style, leadership by physical aggression and mental intimidation. My style was different; I tried to lead by reason and example.

Some people wondered at Regimental Sergeant Major Duffy being replaced when he was such an integral part of the regiment. I ran into a major from the Royal Canadian Regiment two weeks later who was surprised to hear that Duffy had left the Hasty P's. He asked if I was specifically chosen for the job, as I had been the QOR Regimental Sergeant Major in England. I told him that I had volunteered to get battle experience but that there had been no thought of any specific unit, let alone becoming a permanent replacement."[46] I can tell you that when it became clear I wasn't going back to The Queen's Own Rifles, I was royally cheesed!

The process of being accepted by the Plough Jockeys began during the Tolla Road attack at the end of January. I had twenty men who were designated to go forward as stretcher-bearers to get casualties and I personally led them up to the river to get the wounded men. I think that once the men saw I wasn't a rear-echelon type, that I wasn't afraid to get dirty or be shot at, they began to accept me. There were other tasks I performed too, such as helping to carry rations and bottles of rum up to the companies. Members of the regiment slowly began to realize, I think, that I was a soldier even though quite different in personality and style from Regimental Sergeant Major Duffy.

I never had a map or radio although I had repeatedly asked the Intelligence Officer for one. I never got one, by the way, throughout the whole war! I wasn't interested in hanging around Battalion Headquarters, so I regularly went around to the various companies and visited the soldiers. They had lots of questions about the tactical situation, but more often than not, they asked about more mundane things like rations, cigarettes, mail, news from home, and fellows they knew in the different companies. Some of them would talk to me just to be able to say to buddies, "I argued with the RSM." I found it worked well because some of their complaints were reasonable, and I would go right to the Commanding Officer rather than their Company Commander. There are a lot of things happening among the soldiers that the officers don't know about. I think a good Company Sergeant Major and the Regimental Sergeant Major should be in tune with these things. We all had a job to do which was to assist the Colonel in running the battalion.

The Hasty P's gained a new commanding officer, Lieutenant Colonel Donald Cameron, three months after my arrival. Lieutenant Colonel "Ack Ack" Kennedy had been wounded by a mine during the fighting at Ortona after Christmas. Cameron had come to the regiment as a volunteer company commander from the Stormont, Dundas and Glengarry Highlanders of the Third Division in England, due to the shortage of officers. He was promoted from command of Don Company to battalion upon Kennedy's evacuation. As he was in command throughout 1944 and into early 1945, naturally he was the commanding officer I worked with and knew best. The Hasty P's had good commanders, men like "Ack Ack" Kennedy and Cameron. Their attitude was that the men were to be looked after; that they weren't just cannon fodder but men.

The Higher-Ups

Unfortunately, from the ordinary soldier's viewpoint, once officers were out of the fighting battalions and working at higher headquarters, a strange kind of craziness seemed to set in. You can call it a loss of common sense, I guess. You can't tell generals or their staff anything, and I'm not referring simply to policies like the one that took me to Italy for combat experience and then kept me permanently away from my own regiment. Take Operation Market Garden in Holland with the British Red Devils and American airborne troops in September 1944 as an example. The generals had been itching to use their air-

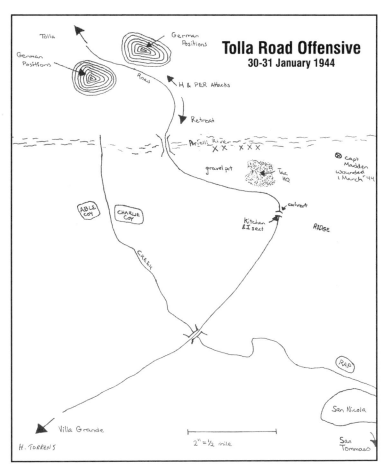

Tolla

German Positions

German Positions

German Positions

Road

H & PER Attacks

Retreat

Tolla Road Offensive
30-31 January 1944

Arielli River

X X X X X

⊗ Capt Madden wounded 1 March '44

gravel pit

Tac HQ

culvert

ABLE COY

CHARLIE COY

Kitchen & I sect

RIDGE

CREEK

RAP

Villa Grande

San Nicola

H. TORRENS

2" = ½ mile

San Tommaso

borne army all summer and had been frustrated by the rapid advance across France and Belgium. The Drop Zone for the British jump at Arnhem was too far away from the objective because the Royal Air Force was worried about a flak battery on their return trip to England. There was only one narrow dike road for the British tanks to advance on and all the supplies for the whole column had to be brought up along it. The plan was to advance seventy-eight miles on this narrow road in *two days*! As American military historian Stephen E. Ambrose observes in *Band of Brothers*, only a commander (Montgomery) guilty of gross over-confidence could have planned such an operation.[47]

Furthermore, the airborne troops had to capture *all* the bridges, from those near Eindhoven (101st Airborne) to the crucial one at Arnhem in the north (British 1st Airborne), or the entire operation would be a failure. General Browning knew from Dutch intelligence reports that there were seasoned Panzer troops in the Arnhem area, but simply dismissed the concern and fired his intelligence officer to boot! There were serious concerns with the radios before the jump occurred, but no one took steps to rectify the problem. I think these different points support my general contention about the "higher-ups."

There were some priceless cases in our experience in Italy too. The two events that stand out in my mind are the Tolla Road attack in late January 1944 and the Lamone River crossing in early December 1944.

Tolla Road Attack

One event that we could see no sense in at the time was the attack on the Tolla Road that was launched on 30–31 January. This was the day before General Crerar took over First Canadian Corps because General Chris Vokes was on leave. The higher-ups rationalized the attack on a tactical basis by saying that if we attacked, the Jerries would move their reserves, and then we would be able to defeat them as we had control of the air. If the Germans moved in daylight, they would be hit. One other factor to take into consideration is that the Americans had landed at Anzio on 22 January in an attempt to outflank the Germans and get to Rome quickly.

Brigadier Dan Spry gave the regiment the Tolla Road job because they had been "so reliable many times before."[48] Our battalion was to push forward along the road at right angles to the road that went from Villa Grande to Tolla. The Calgary tanks were to go up the Tolla Road with the infantry on the verges. Backed by the Calgary tanks and Canadian, Indian and British artillery, we jumped off at 1600 hours. The two companies out front had things go well for a while, and then the lead company ran into a huge volume of fire from German mortars and at least fifty machine-guns firing from the hills one hundred feet above the valley. The two companies were forced to draw back several hundred yards to a shallow gully, where they dug in for the night. In three hours, we had lost forty-eight men killed or wounded. The Padre needed the assistance of much of Support Company to carry out the wounded.

Our Battalion Headquarters moved up to a gravel pit in the lee of a hill. A little creek ran by, and the hill went up about eighty feet for a hundred and fifty yards. After we had been there for a few days, the staff went into a house and remained there for ten days, as it turned out. The Intelligence section and the kitchen staff lived in a culvert under the road! The two forward companies dug in on the banks of the Arielli River. The riverbanks were almost perpendicular, and the Jerries had already dug holes so our troops took advantage of them. The reserve company was in buildings behind them. In the distance we could see our old homes, San Tommaso and San Nicola, on their two hills. The ground sloped down to the Arielli River and the valley was three-quarters of a mile wide. The Tolla Road was just a mile or so away. The forward edge of the battle line was the river, with the Germans on the north side and us on the south side.

Lieutenant Colonel Cameron received orders to continue the advance the next day, 31 January. A third company tried but the result was the same; forty-three additional casualties were taken on our second attempt to get up the Tolla Road. The First Brigade diary noted that this was "a very heavy price to pay for the knowledge that the enemy is holding the approach to Tolla in strength." Thankfully, it was the last major action of the winter for our brigade.

These two days on the offensive were costly: the Regiment lost twenty-four men killed and sixty-seven wounded out of a total strength of three hundred and fifty. Among the dead were Lieutenants Douglas and Thompson and Lance Sergeant Matthew. Farley Mowat writes, "In many ways this was the Regiment's most terrible but greatest hour."[49] I don't understand this comment because there were far worse battles and trials ahead for the Hasty P's. Physically, yes, it broke the Regiment's strength, yet that futile and sacrificial battle did not abate the spirit of the unit nor weaken its morale. Much anger did ensue, however, as a result of this action. There has been much criticism of Brigadier Spry for ordering that attack, and some commanders, most notably the Commanding Officer of the Calgary tanks, were infuriated at the waste of their tanks and men.[50]

The trouble with fighting in Italy is the hills: the infantry can go anywhere, but they can't be supplied. We had Indian mule drivers, but they weren't of much use because this method of transport was slow and had a limited capacity. So it was the roads, and the Germans knew this.

Harry, the Army Mule

It was a few days after the Tolla Road attack, in early February 1944. Tactical Headquarters was located in another gravel pit, down the steep road that ran from Villa Grande to Tolla. To get to the Regimental Aid Post, which was located in a tent in the woods, about a hundred and fifty yards from the bridge that ran across the Arielli, I had to cross the Bailey bridge over the small creek and then go up the hill. Incidentally, the Aid Post should have been at least two hundred and fifty yards from the bridge, as it was a legitimate military target for the Germans.

After I had been to the Aid Post, I headed back to the bridge, where I came across a group of six men in a huddle. I asked them what was wrong, and they said there was no trouble except that they were one man short for their Baker Company ration party. I said that I knew where Baker was located and would help them. They were pleased with that, and we all grabbed a load and took off. My burden was a dixie full of hot tea.[51] It was easy to carry, though heavy, and covered with soot from the fire. It left a mark on my battle-dress trousers that I could never get completely clean.

Two nights later there was another ration party, and I once again volunteered. My load was different this time, not heavy but very awkward to carry. It was almost cube shaped, about three-feet square and made of tin. There was something loose inside that continually rattled around. I could not get a grip on it with just one hand and so was forced to use two hands. Eventually I gave up on this and put it on my head, where it occasionally clanged against my helmet. The noise brought muttered curses from the other bearers, and I gradually dropped about a hundred and fifty yards behind them so as not to be a hazard. When I finally got to Baker's lines on the banks of the Arielli, I was totally cheesed off and glad to be rid of this burden. I asked with some exasperation what was in this container, and I was told that it was an oven; the cooks were going to bake pies the next day. The cooks really did a fine job looking after the men. Later in the fall of that year, I recall seeing the kitchen truck pulling a trailer that contained hens and geese that had been scrounged from local farms by the pot-wallopers.[52] Whenever the kitchen crew got a chance, they served the soldiers hot meals with fresh meat.

The next morning the Adjutant told me to bring more men up and clean up the Battalion Headquarters area as we were going to be there for at least ten days. I figured that I must have been the last man in the unit to find out.

No Watch for Harry?

A few days later I was once again on the path from the Aid Post to the little bridge, and I passed an officer standing beside a jeep. It was Captain Baldwin, the Regimental Quartermaster, and so I asked him if there was any trouble. He said, "Yes, I have four rum jugs to deliver to the rifle companies, and no way to get them there." They had to be carried on foot from this point, and he could only handle two. He was concerned that if he left two in the jeep, they would surely go "missing" by the time he got back. I too could see that and so I agreed to help him by taking the other two jugs. Captain Baldwin declared that he would see to Able and Charlie if I looked after Baker and Don.

I grabbed two jugs and away I went, up past the Aid Post, and then left up the hill, going overland to these two companies. I stayed off the road for two reasons: first, the Jerries often swept it with machine-gun fire, and two, it was mined. The Second-in-Command, Major Don Cameron, and I had already mined it using a dozen No. 75 grenades (anti-tank weapons). It suddenly dawned on me that I was going to the forward companies, and Captain Baldwin to the reserve ones. Certainly not an equal distribution of work, not to mention the danger! In any event, I reached Baker and Don with the rum jugs, seals unbroken.

Several days hence I found myself once again on the same, very busy path from the Aid Post, and I met Captain Baldwin a second time. I saluted him and stepped off the path to make room for him to pass.[53] He stopped and asked me the time. I pulled out my trusty Ingersoll two-dollar watch (one dollar at the beginning of the war) and told him. In reflecting on this encounter, I now think it was his way of finding out if I had a watch. He said that he had three watches to distribute to deserving members of the regiment, and as Regimental Sergeant Major I qualified. He went on, "But as you already have a watch, you don't really need one of these, do you?" What could I say? If he had not asked the time, I could have accepted the watch. There is a saying in the Army, "Never volunteer for anything." It seems that I didn't pay attention to that dictum and got royally shafted as a result.

We had been in the Tolla Road location for more than ten days when the order came for First Brigade to be relieved on the frontline by Third Brigade. It was a miserable February night with rain and sleet and a raw, bone-chilling wind. Everything was proceeding smoothly: the Forward echelon vehicles had departed along with one of the rifle companies. First Brigade had successfully pulled back to First Division lines and then to the Corps position.

When the troops started arriving at the latter location, the Corps Commander hit the roof. He said in no uncertain terms that there had been a mistake: it was not just First Brigade alone that was being relieved, but the whole First Division. We had no business doing what we were doing, and everything had to be reversed. All the battalions, including ours, had to return immediately to their previous positions as soon as possible. It was extremely fortunate that the Germans did not get word of the move or we would have been royally hammered. Thankfully, no one was hurt or a vehicle lost.

The first rifle company to depart its slit trenches on the Arielli was marched back into the line, none too happily, I might add. Some of the men had managed to secure vino, and I watched them go by Tactical Headquarters; one rifleman in particular was making a loud noise, singing his head off.

His platoon commander saw me and asked me if there was anything I could do to get the man to settle down. The lieutenant said he did not want to put the man under close arrest, and could I suggest an alternative? In these situations, as Regimental Sergeant Major, I had to use my wits and find a quick solution to the problem. I walked over to the noisy soldier and asked him if he would like a drink. Naturally enough he said he would, and I took him over to the kitchen, which was located in the culvert under the road. I asked Basil Smith, the Quarterbloke for one of the rum bottles. Basil looked sideways at me but handed me three glasses of rum. We all took a drink, and the drunken rifleman was out like a light. The hard liquor on top of the wine he had already consumed had the effect that I wanted. I shoved him under the tarpaulin that was used to cover the Commanding Officer's carrier. Several hours later, I heard this same man grumbling. "Why did someone throw water on me?" I went over to him and made sure he was fully awake. "Where am I?," he asked. I told him that he was at the Tactical Headquarters. "I shouldn't be here. Where's my company?" We indicated that Charlie Company was back in its old position, and he grabbed his rifle and staggered off. This just goes to show that regardless of the tactical situation or miserable weather, a soldier wants to be with his pals.

Padre Goforth

I've mentioned several times Padre Jack Clough who served with The Queen's Own Rifles of Canada in England. For non-military readers, "Padre" is the Canadian Army colloquial term for a chaplain, originally adopted by the British Army while fighting during the Peninsular Campaign of the Napoleonic wars.[54] The Hastings and Prince Edward Regimental Padre when I served with them was Honorary Captain, the Reverend J. Frederick Goforth, M.C. He was well known and respected in the unit, just like Regimental Sergeant Major Duffy.

Padre Goforth was about forty, the son of Reverend Jonathan Goforth, a Presbyterian missionary in China at the time of the Boxer Rebellion in 1900. In Italy, Padre Goforth often assisted at the Regimental Aid Post as he was trained in first aid in China, and was nearly as good as our doctor at treating wounds. His fame in the regiment dated from December 1943 at Ortona when he went out to the front and under fire dragged two wounded men to shelter and remained with them for several hours until help arrived from the Aid Post. He was awarded the Military Cross for that act.

Casualty Evacuation

The normal procedure for evacuation of casualties was for the Company Commander to radio back that he had so many wounded. The code word for dead soldiers was "Goforth," the name of the Padre. There was also a code name for wounded soldiers, which would tell how many men we had to bring out on stretchers. I would usually get the bearers from Headquarters Company and occasionally from the mortar platoon. Those men who were wounded badly but who would likely recover were taken from the field hospital, which was located at division, and evacuated to the British Army hospital at Bari, further south on the Adriatic coast.

The most dramatic case of casualty evacuation in my first few months with the Hasty P's occurred at the beginning of March 1944. The worst of the winter weather had ended and the first signs of spring were beginning to show. Captain Bernard Madden, age twenty-eight, from Ottawa, was Second-In-Command of Don Company. He had been going between the platoons, which were dug in on the banks of the river, checking on his men. The three platoons of the company were spread out over a quarter-mile front. Most of the soldiers were resting or snoozing in the sun. A German saw him and fired a rifle grenade. It exploded right above him, and Captain Madden was badly wounded by shrapnel in the chest. I was back at Tactical Headquarters and the military policeman was there with three men who were under arrest for minor crimes and in the "digger" (gaol) as the actual lock-up was in Ortona itself. We used these men in the daytime to clean up the area around the headquarters. The Adjutant came running up to me, saying that an officer was badly wounded and we had to go out and get him.

One of the men argued that I had no right to take him into a forward area as he was under the provost's authority. I replied that I had authority to make him do anything I wanted within the battalion's boundaries. As we stood there scowling at one another, one of the other three men asked who was wounded. When I said, "Captain Madden," the first soldier said, "Oh, he's an all right guy. I'll go with you."

We went to the Aid Post, and they grabbed the Red Cross flag. This would be a signal to our people but, more importantly, to the Germans, who would notice the movement, to communicate that we were picking up wounded. So the five of us went down into the valley. We started to run, with one of us holding the flag. There were no buildings and few trees, just low-lying scrub, and not a sound to be heard but our feet hitting the wet ground.

The banks of the Arielli River are about ten feet high and made of hard clay. We ran towards the company's location where a flag was displayed to indicate the casualty's location, and we threw the stretcher over the bank. They handed the stretcher back up to us over the bank with Captain Madden on it. Five of us began to run back as fast as we could, four bearers plus one with the flag so the Germans wouldn't shoot at us. When one got tired, he could be relieved. This is pretty tricky on the run while trying to administer first aid to a wounded man, but we did it.

I happened to be the extra man, and one fellow suddenly said, "Stop." So we put him down. "What did you say that for?" one of them asked. "He died," was the reply. "He died?" "Yes, I felt it." I looked at another fellow on the end, and he just nodded. Then I remembered talking to a fellow I knew at Eaton's in Toronto who had been a stretcher-bearer in the First World War and he had said the same thing. There is a tremendous difference between a living man and a dead one. It is easier to carry a living man than a dead man. Alive he is a man, but dead, he is just a lump of flesh.

The bearer had felt a jolt or something. So we checked his pulse and breathing, and Captain Madden was indeed dead. We walked, from then on. Everyone could see us, and they knew the officer was dead. All the time there was not a sound or a shot fired, yet there were dozens of our people in the open.

I'll make a few observations about the weapon that killed Captain Madden. Unlike the Americans and Germans, we Canadians didn't have rifle grenades. One reason for this deficiency was that the Army had brought out a new type of rifle and the barrel would not take the appliance that fit on the end. The device was a steel nose cap to place the grenade on. The grenade needed to be fired at an angle of about forty-five degrees and supported by your foot. It would put a hole in two inches of armour and is also a very good weapon to fire against men in trenches. You fire it; it then explodes above the trench with the shrapnel showering downward. This is what you practised in training in order to gauge distance.

So why had a German soldier fired this grenade in a quiet sector? Normally, combat veterans adopt a "live and let live" attitude during quiet periods. Perhaps he was a replacement who was trying to prove something or perhaps he was ordered to do so by a replacement officer. I can only speculate. Captain Madden was dead and so we buried him in a temporary grave up in the town near the headquarters.

We usually buried soldiers close by the side of the nearest road so they would be more easily picked up later for transport to a larger cemetery. All the fatalities from this period were eventually buried in the Moro River Canadian War Cemetery near the town of Ortona. We put a proper white wooden cross on it with name, rank and number. However, we couldn't always include the date, because there was only so much room on the piece of wood. There were records kept at headquarters of the names and dates of men killed in action.

Normally the Sanitation Corporal in the regiment digs the graves and the Padre performs the burial service. I took the burial job on to help the Corporal who was in charge of all the sanitary arrangements. During action he couldn't go up to the front-line troops and normally he was located at BHQ. Our Commanding Officer wanted as few people as possible at headquarters; he preferred most of the men to be with the rifle companies. As a result, the

Hasty P's didn't have a platoon of men available to draw on for this duty. There were four regimental policemen, two pot-wallopers, two men in the Intelligence section, and two drivers who were borrowed when necessary. I couldn't take anyone from the Signal Platoon for other duties.

Artillery: "The Bane of the Infantryman's Life"

No matter how long a soldier is exposed to shellfire, he never develops immunity to the fear of it. Machine-gun fire can be terrifying and cause men to freeze in action. But the really terrifying fire was artillery, the bane of the infantryman's life. One American paratrooper wrote to his parents from Holland, "Artillery takes the joy out of life. [It] is a terrible thing. I hate it."[55] In particular, the high moaning whistle of the German multiple-barreled mortars, called *Nebelwerfers*, which we dubbed "Moaning Minnies." Oh, what an unearthly, screaming sound they made as they came over. If men were exposed to that kind of bombardment for too long, their nerves would give way. I know from talking to many QOR riflemen after the war, that they were under almost constant bombardment for four days at Carpiquet airfield, 5–9 July 1944. It was a true nightmare and ranked among the worst combat experiences they endured.

Soldiers being human beings and needing to cope, some would make a game of the peril. One solder devised a game of Dots and Spots in an attempt to guess where the next round would land. There were even wagers taken as to whether someone would be hit. I guess we would call this "gallows" humour.

One of the most memorable casualties of shelling occurred on 7 February when several rounds with phosphorous came down, burning some of the men horribly. A phosphorous shell hits the air and starts to burn, providing a smoke screen, usually for an attack or a diversion. This was about the time that the German First Parachute Division was pulled out to go to Anzio. One of the men hit by the spray was Sergeant Hollingsworth.[56] Even though he was in agony, he told his men not to touch him. It was a very brave thing for him to do. We did not have the suits available to us in the Second World War that the Army uses today, which would have protected us from such chemicals.

I only saw one German 88-millimetre gun during my year in Italy, and that was in the Po Valley in northern Italy, where it had been used as a self-propelled gun. The 88 was very versatile; it could be used as an anti-aircraft weapon, for airbursts against infantry and as an anti-tank weapon. This gun was the best

German artillery piece of the Second World War. Normally you can't tell from an explosion what kind of gun has been used unless it is very big. A six-inch shell makes a larger hole and noise than an 88 millimetre shell. We used to come upon ammunition dumps regularly but we never once came across a supply of 88 millimetre shells. There were 75 millimetre and 100 millimetre gun ammunition and all types of mortar bombs. We didn't find any 88 shells in Italy because I believe the Germans didn't use them there. In contrast, we saw millions of these shells in Holland, where the flat terrain is ideal for such a weapon. In Italy, with all the hills, the 88 was not an effective weapon and having a long barrel, it was harder to conceal. We had many planes, and they would be able to spot guns like that. In those hills and valleys, the mortar was the artillery weapon of choice because of its high shell trajectory.

From what I'm able to gather, the British 25-pounder gun, with the Field Artillery regiments that directly supported the infantry battalions, was the best artillery piece of the war. It could be swivelled to fire 360 degrees because it rested on a large metal plate. They brought out a fifteen-hundredweight truck specifically as a tractor for the artillery to carry this huge plate. It was a heck of a job to get it off and on. Originally the plate was about four hundred pounds and it had to be offloaded from the fifteen-hundredweight truck and then set up to provide a firing base for the gun. I understand that during training in England, some Canadians from a Second Division artillery unit accidentally found a better way to mount the gun. They just hooked it underneath and hauled it away. Even though the troop commander got royally chewed out by his superiors, this became the standard procedure for setting up the guns. The gunners could unlimber after a drive and be firing within a matter of minutes of receiving a fire order.

Another piece of equipment that we used was called the Very pistol. It was about one and a quarter inches in circumference and had been an effective device in the First World War for firing flares to illuminate objects at night. The only drawback was that you had to extend your arm straight up in the air to fire it in order to get maximum height and benefit. Our troops kept complaining about it not being effective. We found it rather difficult to use, especially on the offensive, as the man firing it would be in the prone position. When you put your arm up, you are a target. So we fired it lying down, and it went on an angle and, therefore, went too low, illuminating very little of what we needed to see. In the Hast and PER we used our two-inch mortars at night for illumination. We would fire an illuminating flare behind the object we wanted to see, and it would be silhouetted, thereby allowing us to detect any movement, and then we could fire on the enemy.

Food

We tried to feed the rifle companies twice a day. Those in Battalion Headquarters and Support Company basically suited themselves. Most of the Tactical Headquarters' personnel got three meals a day. You have to remember that each company is a largely autonomous body in action. Even in rest areas, the companies are all on different timetables for meals and are bivouacked separately. One of the tough things about being at Battalion Headquarters was that we were only issued so many rations and we never knew until mealtime who was going to be there. Take the stretcher-bearers, for example; there were thirty of them attached to our headquarters. The Forward Observation Officer (an artillery captain) was always there along with several artillery representatives. There would normally be several representatives from a tank regiment, several military policemen, engineers, signallers and so forth. Sometimes the meals were pretty skinny if all these people were around.

Shortly after I arrived, the regiment was down to skeleton strength with not enough men to go around the rifle companies. What one particular company did at night was to pull every man that could be spared from the outposts and the front line. The kitchen was left empty too for the night as the cooks were pulled out to get some rest. One morning they returned to discover all the food supplies for the company had gone! Vanished as if by magic, not a crumb of bread was left. It was initially blamed on a German patrol, but it could easily have been some troops in our Brigade, or even the Indian soldiers who were beside us in the line at that time. We never did find out who did it.

Every man was supposed to carry a chocolate bar in his pocket but I think most of them ate it first. Often you'd just give them bully beef and biscuits at the side of the road, and that provided meals for the next two days.

British "compo" (17 in 1) rations went out of style the first winter. The British composition ration package came with food that was supposed to provide three meals (one day's rations) for seventeen men. Most of our troops found items like the meat and vegetable stew, known as "muck and vomit," virtually inedible. So our Canadian units took to preparing their own food. This was normally done at the Advance echelon, which was behind the Fighting echelon. A jeep or a fifteen-hundredweight truck would bring up the meals

98

contained in dixies, and they would be placed on the fire. We usually made stew and tea and would bring the food to the Company Quartermaster at last light. The British and the Germans had the same customs; as soon as it was dark, the sick and wounded were taken out and the meal was brought up to the troops. This custom had begun in North Africa and had become an Eighth Army tradition.

British tanks from the Seventh Armoured Division, the famous "Desert Rats," usually supported us. After Ortona, every chance they got, the tanks would pull back when it was dark. This was British Army doctrine. In Italy there was more to be afraid of at night than in North Africa, as there was no continuous front line here. The forward edge of battle might be a village or a group of farmhouses and often a river. There was normally quite a lot of space, and if the enemy wanted to take the chance, they could get through.

The Germans: Tough Adversaries or Savage Barbarians?

I've had arguments over the years with other veterans who say that all German soldiers were barbarians. The Italians had a term for the Germans, *Tedeschi*, meaning "uncivilized," which many of our men adopted. In *And No Birds Sang*, Farley Mowat refers to one notable example in December 1943 when the Germans retaliated against a village because a group of partisans had killed some of their men.[57] The Germans dumped the bodies of the captured partisans in the village square and set them on fire. As horrible as it was, you have to understand the German way of thinking. Partisans were simply murderers as they were not uniformed or formally recognized combatants. In the German mind, such fighters had no rights and could be treated in an inhuman fashion. Other soldiers tell stories of hospitals and trains with Red Cross markings on them being attacked by German planes.[58]

The truth is that *all* German soldiers were not Nazis and they were generally very good soldiers who followed the rules of warfare. Perhaps their only serious failing was their rigid adherence to orders and rules. Flexibility is essential to being a successful combat soldier. The paratroopers were their best soldiers, and although very tough fighters, they were not killers. We fought the German airborne troops repeatedly in Italy. Their officers were very professional and arguably the most capable officer corps of any army. They made sure that the Geneva Convention was strictly adhered to, as you might expect from such a disciplined group. I encountered an example of this attitude during the fighting at the Lamone River in December. Their stretcher-bearers and medics even helped our guys on occasion, as we'll see later in the story of Corporal Playfair at San Maria di Scacciano. Once you're wounded you're out of the fight. You drop your weapon and don't do any sniping after that. That was the implicit understanding that all soldiers in combat had. Occasionally, we encountered Germans who did not abide by this convention but these exceptions did not mean that all Germans were barbarians.

The same was not true about the SS troops. Their fanatical Nazi beliefs and personal allegiance to Hitler made them into killers in uniform. The veterans whom I know that fought in Normandy encountered mostly SS troops, at least in the initial few weeks of fighting. Just look at the trouble our soldiers of the Third Division had with the 12 SS Panzer Division under Kurt Meyer. I found out in 1998 that my cousin, Sergeant Bill Simmons of the 1st Hussars, was one of those captured Canadians who were murdered by the 12 SS Panzer soldiers.[59] I knew he died in Normandy, and had always assumed that he was killed in an encounter with one of the superior German tanks. According to writer Howard Margolian, after their tank "brewed up," four of the tankers abandoned it. Simmons was the tank commander and he saw a Panther tank coming at them. He ordered his men to flee and then, to save their lives, he ran directly towards the oncoming tank. Sergeant Simmons' body was later found in a ditch on the grounds of the 2nd Panzer Grenadier Battalion headquarters. The nature of his wounds indicated that he was probably executed.

Sickness

During this winter period there were still casualties but more soldiers were sick than were wounded by enemy fire. In First Canadian Corps there were 120 killed, 585 wounded and 3,466 sick in February and March.[60] I think it varied greatly from unit to unit. The Hasty P's didn't have a lot of colds or flu, primarily because they were countrymen and used to living an outdoors life, and I think they were hardier on average than city folk. There were cases of malaria, jaundice, hepatitis, and the ever-present venereal diseases. There were many skin problems such as "desert sores." These were great big ulcers that would develop all over your legs, from living in the muck. For things like lice, there was a powder available in a four-pound container called AL 63.

I think a part of the sickness issue had to do with the fact that the First Canadian Corps had just expanded in number. The Fifth Canadian Division (called "Big Maroon" from their divisional patch) had just come out from England and was only fully operational on 17 January 1944. Their soldiers had not had time to adjust physically to a combat zone or an Italian winter, so I suspect a majority of those sick were in the Fifth.

Harry Gets the Blame

It was late March and I was doing my usual walk-about when I came to one of the mortar sections. I knew Sergeant Morris but his crew members were strangers. I had been with the regiment nearly three months by this time, but I still had not been able to meet all the men. So we stood around visiting for a while. The field telephone buzzed and a fire order came from the observer, who at this time happened to be Lieutenant Wiese, one of the platoon commanders.

The ground sheet covering mortar was whipped off and it was set to fire on the coordinates that had been given. A bomb was dropped in and nothing happened. It was a misfire. In order to fix it, the mortar had to be stripped down, the barrel tilted, and the bomb caught at the muzzle by one of the crew. He then had to gingerly move it off to the side for eventual disposal. The mortar was then reassembled.

I admired the efficient way those four men went about clearing the mortar; they were a good crew. The fire mission still waited so another bomb was dropped in the tube with the same result, a misfire. Once again the teardown drill was followed and the bomb removed from the mortar.

The telephone buzzed and the observer wanted to know why they had not fired. The sergeant said, "Sorry, sir, we had two misfires." The lieutenant replied," Oh, well, the target has gone. Over and out." The four mortar men just stood there and glared at me. Sergeant Morris said, "Sergeant Major, your ammunition is no good. You've got to do better than this."

The sergeant's remark got the wheels turning in my mind. I recalled a comment made by Sergeant Sharpe of the same platoon, a few weeks back, that I should be more selective at the divisional ammunition point. As ammunition supply was one of my primary responsibilities, the soldiers were, in effect, blaming me for the misfires!

I asked Sergeant Morris why he thought the ammunition itself was at fault. He replied that I should try my best to get New Zealand-made bombs as they are the very best made. In descending order of priority, Canadian-made was next best, followed by British ammunition. "But whatever you do," he roared, "do *not* bring us any more of that crummy American stuff."

This comment set off another train of thought taking me back to my pre-war militia days when we trained on the World War One vintage, Lewis light machine-gun. Our sergeant-instructor, a First World War veteran, told us that they had used American ammunition occasionally and they found that ten per-cent of it was defective. This was apparently the reason that "immediate action" was done when the Lewis gun stopped firing. "Immediate action" was simply to re-cock the weapon and press the trigger. At least half the time, a dud round was the cause of the stoppage.

Another experience came to my mind from the previous year when we were on the rifle range in England. I was doling out ammunition for the Lee-Enfield .303 rifle from cases that were marked "Made in the United States of America for the Royal Air Force." However, stenciled overtop of this in red, diagonally, was the phrase "NOT TO BE USED IN SYNCHRONIZING GUNS." Over that, in black and going diagonally the other direction it read: "TO BE USED FOR GROUND PRACTICE ONLY." So apparently the British had already discovered some flaws with the Lend-Lease program.

The four mortar men were still giving me the evil eye when one of them said, "Hey, I just thought of something." He went over and examined both misfired bombs. Then he went to the bag holding the cleaning equipment and spare parts, which was hanging in a bush to keep it off the damp ground. The mortar man then turned to us with a big grin on his face and a firing pin in each hand. It wasn't the ammunition after all. The crew had cleaned the mortar that morning and had forgotten to put the firing pin back in its proper place.

So they set to work to replace the firing pin, laughing as they worked. This little episode had broken the monotony of standing around waiting for a Fire Order. I said "So long" and headed out, as I did not want to wait around for something else to go wrong and get the blame for that, too.

CHAPTER 5

Rome and Beyond

I Try My Hand at Mountain Climbing

We moved out of our winter quarters at San Nicola and San Tommaso on 21 April and moved back to Campobasso along with the rest of the division. We were engaged in mountain-climbing training for about a week until the beginning of May.

The trip down the mountains in an open-air vehicle was miserable. I believe this may have been the coldest I have ever been in my life, worse even than when I was in Sussex, New Brunswick in January 1941 and the South Downs of England in January 1942.

We went south to Lucera, on the Foggia plain, where the Americans had an Air base. We did a week of training with the tanks, and then went over the mountains again to camp at the foot of a large hill. I guess we were bored because a group of us in headquarters started discussing why there was a huge cross on the top of this mountain. In such a poor country we just could not understand why they would go to such lengths for a religious symbol. I don't think any of us really understood the Italian people, however. Italy was an officially Roman Catholic country, and in many places the people expressed their devotion through erection of statues and crucifixes. In discussing this with Padre Craig Cameron in more recent years, I have come to a better understanding of religious piety and spirituality that I lacked in 1944.

The talk then shifted to how long it would take to get to the top of this steep hill. I asserted that I could make it in two hours; wagers were laid, and the Quarterbloke Basil Smith said he would come along with me to show them it could be done.[61] We got to the top with a few minutes to spare, and I had a notion to shoot off a flare to show the fellows down below that we had made it in time. I took the gun out, loaded the flare and was about to fire it off when it suddenly dawned on me that this was not a smart move. We had travelled in secrecy across the Apennines and had taken down our shoulder flashes and obscured the numbers on our vehicles. Here I was, the Regimental Sergeant Major of one of the infantry battalions, about to demonstrate to friend and foe alike our exact position from the top of the largest eminence in the region! In retrospect, if I had done so, I'm quite certain that warrant officer or not, I would have been convicted in a court-martial and likely still be in gaol for that one.

It was some time later that I heard of the death of Captain Pat Green, a Queen's Own Rifles officer serving with the Princess Patricia's Canadian Light Infantry. He had come out on the same Pooch draft as myself along with Sergeant Jimmy Harker and Company Sergeant Major Wils Hubbard. Pat Green was a fine athlete, a boxer and a skier. Apparently, he fell about thirteen feet while doing mountain operations training on 1 May and died of a broken neck.

Another Dose of Medicine

Just a few days after my mountain climbing adventure, the battalion was camped near the town of Limatoga, doing river-crossing drills on the Volturno River about thirty miles north of Naples from 6 to 11 May. On schemes like this, the troops were fed in a long chow line at the company kitchen. As we were a long way from the frontline, there were no problems in feeding everyone in the open like this. I had come up to oversee the process when the Quartermaster, Captain Baldwin, came along and handed me a large bottle of pills. "Make sure everyone gets one of these," he barked and walked off.

They were anti-malaria pills, know as Atalgrin and Mepacrine, and it was once again mosquito season in Italy. We were to take one a day until the cool weather returned. I had a cook take the dixie with hot tea down to the start of the food line (normally at the very end of the line) and had someone instruct the soldiers, "No pill, no dinner."

One young fellow saw me standing nearby and asked why he had to take a pill. I told him that I wanted to see his eyeballs turn yellow, which is one of the side effects of the treatment. This got a bit of laugh from some of the men in the line. Some wiseacre chimed up, "That's about the only thing yellow

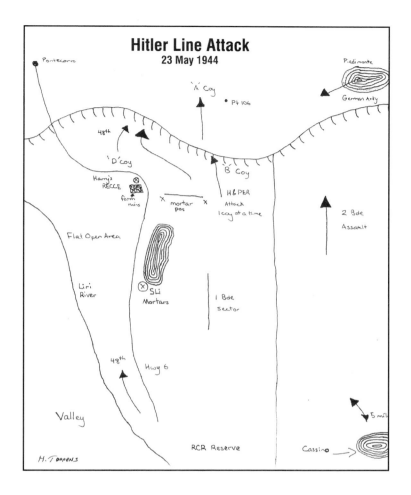

Hitler Line Attack
23 May 1944

Pontecorvo

Piedimonte

'A' Coy

• Pt 106

German Arty

48th

'D' Coy

B Coy

Harry's RECCE

farm ruins

H & PER
Attack
1 coy at a time

mortar pos

2 Bde
Assault

Flat Open Area

Liri River

SLI Mortars

1 Bde Sector

48th

Hwy 6

Valley

5 mil

RCR Reserve

Cassino

H. TORRENS

about a Hasty P, his eyeballs." This retort got a louder response than my quip, and the men seemed in better spirits to take their medicine, for which I was thankful.

Little did I know that the Medical Officer was standing not far away under a tree. When the last man had got his meal, he came up to me and said, "That was quite well done, Sergeant Major. I was quite amused to hear what some of the men had to say." Then he grinned and said, "Here's your pill." There was no way around it but simply to scoff it down in front of him.

Dr. Eshoo then went back to Battalion Headquarters to report that all the men had been given their anti-malaria medicine.[62] They relayed the message to Brigade and they in turn passed it on to Division. It just happened that we were the first to report, so "good one on the Hasty P's." The higher-ups loved to get little snippets of information like that. It gave them things to put in their reports and justify their existence.

Close Calls

I was down on one knee checking a soft spot in a gravel road using my fingers to check for any trace of a mine. Suddenly, "crack," a bullet whizzed by me, and I was so frightened that my bowels moved involuntarily. Despite the discomfort and embarrassment, I ran like Billy Stink. The enemy soldier fired four more times, but he was a rather poor marksman as none of them hit me.

A few days later, I was on one of my usual strolls to visit the rifle companies when suddenly mortar bombs started landing around me. I turned and once again ran like Billy Stink, taking shelter in a patch of trees. This was not the best place to be, but, basically, I wanted to be out of sight. I wondered how the Germans could see us and then realized we had forgotten to clear the mountain immediately behind us. The Germans must have had an artillery outpost up there. I helped get the casualties out and started back to Tactical Headquarters. As I rounded the corner of a farmhouse, I saw a man sitting down with his back against a tree. I said, "Hello Corporal Castle. Enjoying the sunshine?" He replied that he was enjoying himself much more so than those guys on the hill. As I turned to watch, there was a line of explosions on the hillside moving up to the top. The corporal said that he was stationed there by the tree with a radio to alert the battalion if the Jerries attacked down the hill, because they could reach the river and cut us off. I wandered back to the farmhouse, where about thirty of our men had been for four hours. A young Italian woman came along and stepped on a mine, and was badly injured. Good luck seems to ride on some people's shoulders, but not on others.

Hobnobbing in the Liri Valley

The Americans were still fighting at Anzio on the coast, and our division was to advance around Monte Cassino and attack the Hitler Line, which was behind it. First, we had to advance up the Liri Valley, where we launched a series of attacks on 17 May from Pignataro. Even before we actually assaulted the Hitler Line, which was a series of built-up defensive positions with machine-guns and artillery pieces in concrete bunkers, we took a number of casualties. One of the men I remember was a Lance Sergeant Tom Graves from Belleville, C 4365, a 1939 original volunteer. He was killed when a mortar round landed right inside his slit trench.

One day on our way through the Liri Valley, I was back with Advance and Forward echelons, getting them settled for the night. As I lay under a tree for a sleep, it suddenly occurred to me that my place was at Tactical Headquarters, not back here in the boondocks. So I got up and headed to the forward area. The night was as black as the inside of a quartermaster's hip pocket, and I realized that I was acting rashly, going forward alone at night. Besides, I was tired, and so I decided to bed down for a few hours in a little barn that I had come across. When I got going again, it was a little foggy with visibility reduced to about thirty feet.

Soon I met the Commanding Officer and the Intelligence Officer heading back to Brigade for a conference but I didn't go back with them. I decided to follow their footprints in the wet grass. After following them for some time, the tracks suddenly disappeared. I had missed a turn somewhere because I was so tired.

I then came across the tracks of two men in the grass, and I felt better about this and picked up the pace. Soon I saw another pair of prints joining the track from the left, and then another two hundred yards further on, a set of prints joining from the right. I thought about what this might mean and came to the conclusion that the Germans were pulling in their outposts. I had the vague notion of trying to follow and perhaps learn their challenge and password. Soon I came to a spot that looked as if a platoon of men had been tramping around, and there was a dead German under a blanket. I knew I was on the right path, and as I walked, the sun suddenly came up and the fog disappeared.

Not far ahead was a tower, at least fifty feet high, and I thought I'd better have a look. I had checked out two rooms when an older Italian man came up to me with the usual greeting, "Mussolini, SOB." I agreed with him and he asked if I was *Englesi* (English). "No," I replied, "I am *Canadesi*." He told me that he knew Canada as he had worked in Detroit for thirty years before the war, and had been in Windsor many times. The man then went on to say that there were two *Tedeschi* in the cellar. He took me downstairs, pointed out a room but refused to go any further.

I stamped heavily across the dirt floor to a hole in the ground, with a ladder in it. Cocking my Tommy gun noisily, I called out, "Anyone down there?" A voice answered, and two Jerries came up the ladder. They just stood there, and I asked them if they had any weapons. They stared at me until I made a gesture with my thumb and finger, pointing at the Tommy gun. "*Nein pistolen, machine pistolen,*" one of them replied and pointed down the ladder. I wanted a Schmeisser machine pistol but didn't think it a good idea to go looking for one, so I waved them to come with me.[63]

We walked along for a distance and then came to a wood, where a group of men jumped out in front of us. Lucky for me, it was a recce patrol from Able Company. When I said that the Jerries had not been searched, the men took care of that job quite quickly. One of the Germans had a set of binoculars round his neck, and they were passed on to me for a souvenir.

When we arrived back at Tactical Headquarters, the Intelligence Officer questioned the two prisoners, and I was ready to take them back to Brigade, when the Forward Observation Officer asked if I could do him a favour. He had a battery that was nearly dead. Could I take it back to his gun position where the gunners would look after recharging it? As the artillery location wasn't too far out of my way, I said, "Sure."

The sight of two German prisoners created quite a stir at the gun position. Before you could blow a whistle, about fifty men congregated around the three of us. These gunners had never seen a live German prisoner before, and they were impressed. The two Germans asked for a cigarette, and I agreed as they had carried that heavy battery over a mile of rough ground.

A brigadier came by and asked about the prisoners; I told him all that I had seen on my personal recce. He was pleased and said that my information was more accurate and up-to-date than his morning situation report. As we talked further, it turned out that I knew his brother, General Gibson. After I had finally delivered the prisoners and was back at the Tactical Headquarters, I thought, "How many RSMs have captured two of the enemy right out of their own lines and had a conversation with a brigadier, all before breakfast?"

A few days later, as we sat in front of the Hitler Line, I decided that I was going to do a personal reconnaissance of the area with one of the sergeants from Headquarters Company. One of the pot-wallopers asked if he could come along too and I agreed. So the three of us walked up the road (Highway 6) that runs to Pontecorvo and stopped at a bend in the road by the ruins of a house. The sergeant took a look and said that he wasn't sure why but he didn't like the look of things. I decided to venture over to take a closer look, and the cook came along. Normally when an Italian house was hit by artillery, the corners remained intact because they were made of large slabs of brick. What I saw confirmed the sergeant's suspicions. The bricks of the house had all been dragged away from the house, and nothing remained even a foot high, providing no cover whatsoever. On the other side was an absolutely flat area devoid of vegetation, which was a perfect killing zone. The cook realized the danger we were in and started to run. I said, "Willie, don't. They'll see sudden movement." So we walked on eggshells back to the road and then, once out of view of the Germans, we took off running. I reported this back to the Commanding Officer and when the initial assault was made, we went to the right of Highway 6 and kept well away from that killing zone.

I mentioned that the regiment sat in front of the Hitler Line for two days while our guns were being brought up. Sergeant Jack Morris, in charge of one of our mortar sections, was talking to his counterpart from the Saskatoon Light Infantry. It was our support unit with 4.2-inch mortars and Vickers machine guns. Morris asked him where he was placing his mortars, and he was told, behind the hill. Our sergeant then ventured his view based on long experience, that this was a bad place. "No," the Saskatoon guy said, "It's a good place." Sure enough, once the fight began and the counter-barrage came in, the Jerries hammered them.

In 2000, during the Fifty-fifth Anniversary of VE Day trip to Holland, I ran into a man who was the Forward Observation Officer who called in an artillery strike on the day the Second Brigade attacked the Hitler Line. The Second was attacking to our right and as they approached the line proper, they were hit by artillery fire from the town of Piedimonte. The artillery veteran was standing chatting with Lieutenant Colonel Steve Brand,[64] a former Commanding Officer of The Queen's Own Rifles, who turned to me and said, "Harry, is that so?" I confirmed that what the former artillery officer was saying was correct as I was there, and had seen the German artillery fall on their troops. This artillery officer then called in a "William" strike, which to the best of my knowledge, was the only such call made during the Italian campaign by a Canadian.[65] This "stonk" allowed the lead elements of the Carleton and York Regiment to penetrate the line.

German battle doctrine dictated that as soon as the enemy attacked, they were to respond as soon as possible with a counterattack. In Italy, due to the limited number of troops, this usually consisted of mortar fire. Artillery guns are hard to conceal, but mortars are easy to conceal and move. The *Wehrmacht* had a heavy company attached to their infantry battalions, the same as we had, but they had more mortars than we did, some five and even six-inch.

The Hastings and Prince Edward Regiment was quite clever in their use of mortars. I don't remember any mortar men getting hit but the Hasty P's didn't exactly go by the book. The Army manual said that mortars were to be located behind a hill where they couldn't see you. We didn't stick to this and the enemy knew it. This was the reason that Sergeant Morris advised the Saskatoon Light Infantry mortar crew against locating there.

While we were fighting on the Hitler Line, I was leading a ration party up to Baker Company, and we heard some mortar rounds coming in. We all dropped our loads and hit the ground. One round landed three feet away from me but on the other side of a low hedge. The mound of dirt at the base of the hedge was a foot high, and it absorbed the concussion of the round and the shrapnel. The men behind me were amazed to see me walk out of that cloud of black and dirty grey smoke.

About the same time as this close call, I was on my rounds and came to the mortar platoon. There was a great big tree, about one hundred and fifty feet high right in front of their position. The mortar sergeant said, "Damn that tree. If it wasn't there, I could really paste those guys." It was just high enough that they had to fire around. I suggested knocking the tree down but he demurred, saying that then Jerry would know for sure we were there. They would have it marked already as a possible spot for an enemy position. If you can believe it, they never got hit, sitting right in the open.

Some of the other brigades, especially the Second, had a very bloody battle to break through the Hitler Line. It all depended upon which unit you were fighting against. The First Parachute Division and the Fifth Mountain Division were hard nobs, tough as nails, and always gave ground very grudgingly. In fact, the First German Parachute Division was considered the finest fighting division in the world. They had twice the number of machine-guns per company we did. Our troops who attacked Monte Cassino found out how tough these German paratroopers were. They were handpicked and extremely well trained soldiers. For another example of the

German paratroopers' fighting ability, just look at the trouble our Canadian soldiers had in February 1945 during Operation Blockbuster when they invaded the Rhineland area of western Germany. A platoon of German airborne troops at Mooshof and Steeg inflicted one hundred and one casualties on The Queen's Own Rifles in a fierce morning of fighting. This was where Sergeant Aubrey Cosens won the Victoria Cross. Only on D-Day, with its one hundred and forty-three casualties, did the QOR have a higher number of casualties.

The Germans on the Hitler Line that the regiment encountered were third-rate troops. We went through them like "shit through a goose." The 1027 Panzer Grenadier Division was a collection of draftees from all the nations the Germans had overrun in Europe. We breached the Hitler Line on 23 May with Don Company making the assault on the left and then Baker attacking at 1500 hours on the right, with the aid of British tanks. Farley Mowat eloquently expressed the regiment's success:

> It was probably the most brilliant single action fought by the Regiment in the entire course of the war. For a total cost of eight men killed and twenty-two wounded, the Regiment has smashed through the Hitler Line, taken more than three hundred prisoners and had killed or seriously wounded another hundred. Later looking over the enemy fortifications with their prefabricated steel pillboxes, 75 mm cannon in ground mounted steel turrets, mine fields, wire entanglements, camouflaged mortar and machine-gun positions, the achievement took on a new luster.[66]

Despite the quick victory we still took casualties and lost some fine men. This is the price of war; even a successful battle like the one we celebrated that beautiful spring day in Italy. One of the casualties was Lieutenant Ken Smith. Mowat describes Ken Smith as "bespectacled, small and scholarly and strictly temperance," who led his platoon of Baker Company that day. He got caught in the wire in front of one of the German positions and was wounded by machine gun fire in the right knee. I came up with the stretchers-bearers and helped carry Smith out under fire. Back at the Aid Post, Padre Goforth persuaded Smith to accept a shot of rum but he spat it out, commenting, "People actually drink this stuff?"[67] Smith survived the war and wrote a book about Regimental Sergeant Major Angus Duffy, entitled *Duffy's Regiment*.

German Defences

After the First World War, the German military gave a great deal of study to the subject of why they lost that war. They convinced themselves that they were too good a military to lose to amateurs. They prided themselves on being successors to a long line of professional soldiers. Prussian militarism stretched back, in their minds, to the Teutonic knights of the Middle Ages, who incidentally, were one of the main military forces used in the Crusades.

So they made many adjustments, such as increasing the number of machine-guns per company and platoon. The Spandau MG-42 was one of the best and most feared weapons of the Second World War. It was durable and could fire nine hundred rounds a minute, a much higher rate of fire than that of our Bren gun. The Germans also increased artillery coverage for each battalion, especially mortars.

Wire construction became a key part of the German defensive strategy. Barbed wire is really awful stuff, but the staff seemed unaware of how difficult it was when troops were on the offensive. No one would jump onto German barbed wire the way you see portrayed in certain Hollywood war movies and Canadian Army training films. We were trained that way in England because of the way the British did wire. It was four feet high and six to eight feet deep. A rifleman would run up and throw a blanket over it, and then jump on it to push it down and allow others to go over him. The Germans had wire that was eighteen inches high and twenty *feet* deep. Yes, that's right, twenty feet! You put one foot in that mess and if you put your other foot down you would never get out. They had their wire taped for mortar and machine-gun fire, so getting stuck on wire was a sure way to halt your attack and take casualties.

Despite the unqualified success of the Hitler Line assault, there was one very regrettable incident. It happened following the second attack of the day; a group of German prisoners had been collected and were waiting to be taken to the rear. A German sniper shot and killed Lieutenant Peter McGovern of Don Company who was guarding the prisoners. He was doing my job really, which consisted of rounding up prisoners after an action and taking them to headquarters for interrogation. Apparently, McGovern was walking up and down in front of them with a Tommy gun, when the sniper shot him in the back from the bushes a short distance away. The sniper then ran up and joined the other prisoners. The men in the company didn't know who it was because the second soldier guarding the Germans was looking the other way. Those prisoners were very lucky because if the Company Sergeant Major had been there, he would have turned his Tommy gun on the lot. At least that's what he told me that he would have done had he been there. The remaining guard didn't want to shoot them as they might jump him before he got them all.

I was up visiting Able Company one day. We were behind a house and a Churchill tank pulled up, just a few feet away. I recall that the tank had a red phone on the back for infantry leaders to talk to the tank commander without him having to unbutton the hatch. A captain jumped out to use the tank phone and an MG-42 opened up, cutting him down. The Company Sergeant Major and I ran out and grabbed him, pulling him behind the house. As we picked the officer up, I could see the tracer rounds hitting the track in front of us. The German gunner fired another burst and missed us.

I mentioned earlier the subject of men suffering from combat stress. During the attack on the Liri Valley just before the Hitler Line, I knew one soldier in our unit who suffered from combat stress. He was my batman for a long time.[68] During an advance on a village one day, a mortar bomb exploded beside him and actually blew him up in the air but didn't hurt him. He was quite scared and he got up and ran. Who can blame him? He was a good man and that was why they kept him with the unit. Actually, he didn't do much "batman-ing" for me as he was a pot-walloper. This was his job and he accepted it. He knew he couldn't go back to one of the rifle companies. He wasn't frightened, but it seemed to me that his nerves were shot. In the First World War they labeled this as "shell shock." So he stayed at Battalion Headquarters and was a good worker as long as rounds weren't coming down.

A Light in the Night

It was the night after we had cracked the Hitler Line. The Commanding Officer, Lieutenant Colonel Cameron, called me in and asked if I knew where Able Company was located. I said, "Yes, sir, they are about three hundred yards behind where they have been for the past two days." He replied that they had in fact moved forward and had not reported being in their new position. He pointed to a spot on the map and said that he was sending Major Kethison and myself to find them as they may be in trouble.

The major and I headed out. Part of our route was along a road that at one place was sunk down about ten feet below ground level. We kept on for what seemed like an eternity. This was a strange experience because just hours before thousands of men were trying to kill each other and the noise was deafening. It was so quiet now you could feel your ears listening.

In the end we did not find Able Company and decided they must have found a hole and crawled in. We turned around and headed back to headquarters. As we passed that sunken portion of the road, an aircraft came overhead. The major said, "Don't look up, your white face will show." Incidentally, we never bothered about camouflage paint on our faces at night. The plane flew ahead of us a distance and then dropped a chandelier flare. We froze. The yellow light from the flare showed everything clearly. The flare popped and crackled and seemed like it was going to come down right on top of us. Fortunately, it came down about two hundred yards away, and believe it or not, the heat from that flare made us turn our faces. After it was finally extinguished, Major Kethison pulled a pack of cigarettes out and offered me one. I told him, "No, thanks. I am a Baptist and don't smoke." He claims that I took one and puffed away like a veteran. We've met many times after the war and he still insists I smoked a cigarette that night.

A Salute to the Hasty P's

During the fight for the Hitler Line, 2nd Field Regiment, Royal Canadian Artillery, fired support missions for all the attacking units of First and Third Brigades. They decided that the Hasty P's had done the best job in the division as the regiment had put in *three* successful attacks. Second Field fired a twenty-one gun salute to us the next day. It was rather nice to know that the gunners thought that much of us in the infantry.

We had a week of rest after the Hitler Line attack and then were put into the advance to pursue the Germans who were trying to escape westwards. The plan was for the Americans to break out at Anzio and head east, thus cutting off the escape of the divisions we had been facing. However, General Mark Clark, Commander of the Fifth Army, directed his troops to Rome, as the Germans had declared it an "open city," not to be fought over. The Americans wanted to capture one of the capitals of the Axis Powers, and the British let them "liberate" Rome. So the pursuit was called off, and we halted at the town of Anagni.

All the news reports placed great emphasis on the Americans' capture of Rome, and we were royally cheesed about this. We knew that those German divisions who had escaped because of the Americans' "grandstanding" would have to be fought again further north at the cost of some of our men's lives.

Then came news that D-Day had occurred on 6 June 1944 with considerable success, though the casualties were high. I wondered how the QOR had fared and if any of the men from my old Charlie Company had been killed. It turned out that five Charlie Company men had died, including Corporal Rob Drew, one of the 1940 "potato sackers." I heard from one of the platoon sergeants after the war that a German half-track, with troops from the 12 SS Panzer Division, approached the company position, flying a white flag. As the non-commissioned officers moved out to organize their men for a prisoner detail, the Germans opened up with a machine-gun killing several and wounding a number of others.

We were pleased to think we weren't fighting the Germans alone. However, we soon realized after a few months of listening to the BBC and reading *The Maple Leaf* that the campaign in Northwest Europe would totally eclipse our efforts in "sunny" Italy. It *was* sunny now, not like in January when I had arrived, but it was also unbearably hot and dusty.

"D-Day Dodgers"

The term "D-Day Dodger" comes from a term used by Lady Astor (an American who had married an English lord) in a speech in the British Parliament. She suggested that those of us fighting in Italy were deliberately avoiding the "real" war in Normandy. Her biographer argues that it was an entirely innocent reference and that the actual term came from an Eighth Army veteran's letter to her. He maintains that the term was along the lines of "Desert Rats" and not a criticism at all. Anyway, someone composed a song to mock her sentiments and honour those in Italy. It was sung to one of the war's most popular and evocative tunes, "Lilli Marlene," that both armies knew well.

> We are the D-Day Dodgers out in Italy,
> Always on the vino, always on the spree.
> Eighth Army skivers and their tanks
> We go to war in ties and slacks.
> We are the D-Day Dodgers in sunny Italy.
>
> The Moro and Ortona were taken in our stride,
> We didn't really fight there, we went there for the ride.
> Sleeping until noon and playing games,

We live in Rome with lots of dames.
We are the D-Day Dodgers in sunny Italy.

We hear the boys in France are going home on leave
After six months' service, such a shame they're not relieved.
We were told to carry on a few more years
Because our wives don't shed no tears.

We are the D-Day Dodgers in sunny Italy.
We are the D-Day Dodgers way out in Italy.
We're always tight, we cannot fight.
What bloody use are we?

You sense an undercurrent of bitterness in the song, and I guess many soldiers felt that way. They also took a kind of perverse pride in the term "D-Day Dodger." For those of us who had come from Third Division units like The Queen's Own Rifles, there was a strange feeling that perhaps the term hit too close to home. By the end of 1944 we wondered why we weren't fighting with the rest of the Canadians.

While we were at Anagni, the mail caught up with us with the usual letters from home and care packages. My mother used to send me parcels with socks and toiletry items but mostly cigarettes, even though I didn't smoke. I gave them away to others who did and kept the boys in the Regimental Aid Post supplied. The Aid Post had to be manned twenty-four hours a day and it seemed that most of the medics always had a cigarette hanging out of their mouths. Cigarettes were like money and were very inexpensive for the folks at home; on the black market, however, a thousand cigarettes sold for twenty-seven dollars, almost a month's pay for a private. We read of the booming war economy where everyone had a good paying job and our peers were going dancing, skating and to movies. Rationing was a slight hardship for the folks at home and one of the reasons I sent money home regularly. But those sacrifices were nothing compared to the sacrifices our soldiers were making. I think especially of the men who died, buried in the dark Italian soil, never to return to Canada.

Leave

After the Hitler Line offensive, leave became an irritating issue once again for the troops. The higher authorities deemed that sending troops to Rome would undermine morale! Can you fathom the logic? This decision of the higher headquarters only shows how different a world the staff inhabited from the world of the front-line soldiers! Some secured transport to the Eternal City, anyway, and saw the sights, but this wasn't communicated very widely. A decision was made that we needed to get ready for battles ahead, so the brigade was moved south to a barren spot in the hills near a disreputable little village called Piedimonte d'Alife. We were housed in two-man tents, which were unbearably hot in the heat of an Italian summer. For the old soldiers, the most disconcerting development was that the Commanding Officer ordered us back to basic infantry training. So many new soldiers had come to us as replacements that this work was essential if we were to maintain our fighting efficiency as a battalion. However, it was not enjoyed. My duties as the Regimental Sergeant Major returned to those of the garrison role, that is, primarily dress, deportment and discipline.

Many men felt they deserved a break after a year of combat, and ended up playing hookey from their army duties. There were charge parades that I had to organize, and a number of quite severe punishments were awarded to those who were guilty of being away without official leave or simply of shirking their duties during this six-week period at Piedimonte. This wasn't my preference as I knew what our men had been through and I felt they deserved kinder treatment.

The leave centres for the division were first at Bari on the southeast coast and then at Rome. The Americans had claimed Naples and a host of other towns on the western side of Italy. There was a complete Army facility at Bari because it was the only port not damaged, and there was a major hospital there. Many of the soldiers felt it wasn't worthwhile going to Bari as all you could do was drink. The American flyers had garnered all the local women, and there was precious little else to do for diversion. You would spend two days in a truck banging along the cratered roads of Italy and then two days coming back. For many of us, this wasn't our idea of a leave. Many of the soldiers did eventually get leave in Rome after things had settled down later in June.

We All Need a Hero

My military hero was a man named was George Ponsford. He was from New Zealand and was travelling around the world when the Second World War broke out. Ponsford happened to be in New York City and he surmised that the United States would wait to fight, so he hitched a ride to Canada to

117

enlist. The first recruiting station he came across was in Picton, Ontario, one of the Hastings and Prince Edward Regiment's depots.

He was the finest fighting man that I ever met, a great leader, and a top-notch all-round man. Ponsford became a Warrant Officer Second Class and Company Sergeant Major of Charlie Company. He was awarded the Order of the British Empire (Member) and the Military Medal for his leadership and courage.

We had cracked the Hitler Line, lost the race to Rome and were pulled back into General Headquarters reserve at Anagni. The battalion was brought up to strength with replacements, and basic infantry training began. This particular day, the regiment was doing a live fire exercise with armour support. I thought it would be interesting to watch and was on my way there when I noticed Ponsford on the road ahead of me. He heard me coming and waited for me to catch up. I noticed that he had a bloody bandage on his left forearm. I asked if a mosquito had bitten him, and he said, "No, it was this," and pulled a chunk of metal out of his pocket. I couldn't be certain but it looked like a piece of shrapnel from a six-pounder antitank shell. I asked him who was going to take over as Sergeant Major, Jack Hill or Red Ducharme. Ponsford said no one was taking over; a scratch like this was nothing.

The policy was that anyone with a wound was supposed to go to the hospital because living in the dirt the way we did, infection was quite common. I asked him what the Medical Officer would think about his decision, to which he replied that he didn't care what the doctor thought. George Ponsford *hated* doctors.

Ponsford's antipathy to doctors dated from an event in England in 1942. All our Canadian troops had a Sports Day on 1 July and he had decided he was going to enter and win the twenty-five mile cross-country run. Although he had never been athletically inclined, he decided this event would separate the men from the boys. So he began rigorous training for the event, running in the morning and sometimes for an hour at night. George Ponsford was not a slender man, and did not have a runner's physique, but this did not deter him; he was going to win that race!

Three weeks before the race, he came down with a terrible pain in his abdomen and was rushed to hospital, where they took out his appendix. He still competed in the race on Sports Day, finishing a very respectable third.

Ponsford was convinced that the doctor was to blame for his not winning the race. Did I mention that Ponsford was tough?

I Play Tourist in Pompeii

It was while we were in Piedimonte that I decided to go down to visit Pompeii with a group from Corps Headquarters. I don't recall the exact date but it was summer and quite hot. We spent the better part of a day there and we were all quite impressed with the place. One fellow did a watercolour drawing of a street with the Temple of Good Fortune, which I still have. I feel that I've been blessed with good fortune, having almost shaken hands with a mortar bomb several times and been missed by a sniper several times. The town of Pompeii was buried in ten to fifteen feet of ash when Mount Vesuvius erupted in A.D. 79. At the port, the water level is fifteen feet below the dock. I think there had been an earthquake too. While we were in Italy in March 1944, there was another eruption of Vesuvius. A veteran of the Devil's Brigade wrote: "A lot of ash rained down on the surrounding countryside covering many square miles of vineyards, olive groves, towns and villages, we felt the shock wave which ripped through the country."[69] Peter Cottingham was with the First Special Service Force in the Anzio Beachhead when it erupted. I personally heard news of the earthquake from my old Company Commander, Major Gianelli, a former Queen's Own Rifles' officer, who was given the job of "town major" of Rome. How a Canadian got such a job with all the Americans around, I can't tell you. He was chosen for a job at Eighth Army Headquarters in Sicily after coming out from England. The Italian government subsequently decorated him for his work with refugees of the lava flow from Vesuvius. This was a different occasion than the actual eruption in March 1944.

Touring Sunny Italy: Florence

From 25 July until 7 August our northward journey took us through Rome, Assisi, Perugia and eventually Florence. We had to take down our cap badges and take off our shoulder flashes and all vehicle identification. The strategic purpose of moving the whole Eighth Army all across Italy was to mask our real intentions and confuse the Germans. Many of our men remember this period of the war fondly, especially our two days in Florence, that jewel of a city. Once we got near to Florence, we restored our flashes and cap badges.

Several memories stand out from our brief visit to that city. I had just picked an old school for Battalion Headquarters and once everyone was settled in, I went over to the Intelligence section and looked at the battle board. I noted where the different companies were bivouacked and decided to walk down to the Arno River, which intersects the city, to visit Don Company. On my way there, I happened to see a British fifteen-hundred-weight truck coming up the street, pulling a six-pounder gun. As the truck came opposite me, the trolley wire above it came off and fell on the truck, setting it on fire. The driver bailed out and, seeing me, came running over. When he saw my rank badges, he asked me what to do. I gave him some advice to reassure him that he wouldn't be charged, though I didn't know the repercussions or how the British did these investigations. I decided to be on my way, as I didn't want to get caught in the middle of a British military police investigation.

I finally arrived at the area near the Arno River where Don was supposed to be. The Arno reminded me of the St. Lawrence River below Montreal, a very dirty river. There was no sign of our troops anywhere. I thought this was curious, and investigated the streets in the immediate vicinity. There was no sign of sentries, and I wondered where the Sam Hill was Don Company? By this time it was dusk, and I realized it wasn't too prudent to be out walking alone in Florence at night because the city had a reputation as a "hotbed" of Fascism.

I later learned that the company had never appeared at their assigned bivouac location. Don Company had been the last in the battalion order of march that day. They had been stopped by the military police at a crossroads near the city to let a column of tanks go ahead. Tanks always had the priority when the Army was on the move. Don Company was held up a long time and then, as so often happened with the "meatheads," they sent the company down the wrong road. They came to the top of a hill, and the road ended. They could see Florence below and where they needed to go, but dark was fast approaching. Their major decided to stay put for the night rather than go traipsing into a strange city in the dead of night.

The next day they marched into the city and were cheered by the crowds as they passed by a section of the city not yet visited by any Allied troops. Reports were circulated that great numbers of Canadian soldiers were going into Florence. This is exactly what higher headquarters wanted!

A Matter of Judgment

Later that same day in Florence, an altercation occurred between two of our regiment's leaders. The battalion had been issued two Vickers machine-guns, which were not normally part of a Canadian infantry battalion's weaponry. One of these machine-guns was set up in a waterfront position, on the Arno River. The corporal in charge had been with the Toronto Scottish Regiment, a machine-gun unit, before being transferred to the Hasty P's. It seems that he and the officer in charge of the detachment disagreed about the positioning of the gun. The officer had warned the corporal that he would be charged with insolence and refusal to obey an order if he persisted; the gun was to stay where the officer located it. He then gave the order to open fire, which was done.

In less than a minute, the German answer came back, and the gunner was hit. As the officer and the corporal looked at the dead man, the corporal said something to the effect of "*Now* will you let me put the f _____ gun where I wanted to in the first place?" The officer understood he was responsible for the death of the gunner, and backed down.

This wasn't the end of the problem in that platoon, however. Several days later the same corporal came to me as Regimental Sergeant Major saying that he had lost all confidence in this officer, and was being ridden unmercifully. He was considering giving up his stripes and requesting a transfer to another company. I told him that I had a better job for him; he could come and be the corporal in charge of my little provost section at Battalion Headquarters. He took it and was a great success as Provost Corporal. He proved to be a good organizer and though he cursed everyone he dealt with, most of the men just laughed. At this point, we all needed to laugh and so Fred Crompton proved to be the answer to a Regimental Sergeant Major's prayer for the men's morale. I think it was the best personnel decision that I ever made in the Army. Now mind you, I am a little biased because Fred Crompton saved my life, not once but *three times!*

The Allied strategic focus at this point in the war definitely emphasized the campaign in Northwest Europe so it was important that Field Marshal Kesselring's twenty divisions remain in Italy. If they had been released to fight on the Western front, it could have spelt disaster and defeat. The breakout from Normandy didn't happen until the third week of August, and so the Eighth Army's task was to continue to engage the Germans in Italy and thus dilute the German military effort.

Fred Crompton Saves My Life

The first time that Fred Crompton saved my life happened not along after I appointed him Provost Corporal in August 1944. I wanted to go back to Advance Echelon and I told Freddie to get ready to take me there. He asked if I was going to ride pillion (behind the driver) on the motorcycle, as was my habit, and I said, "Yes." He replied, "No way." As you can infer from this remark, Freddie was a bit weak on respect and military protocol, but he was still a good man. Pillion riding was strictly prohibited as too many men had been killed and injured doing it. Crompton explained that he would gladly take any message I wanted to send to any location, but he would not take me pillion. One of his reasons was that he was just learning to ride a bike and didn't think it wise to take me along.

I jotted down the message I wanted to send, and away he went. A few hours later I saw Freddie limping along the road, his riding britches torn, bruises on his face, covered in dirt and cursing louder than usual. It turns out that he had delivered the message and was heading back to our lines at about fifteen miles an hour, enjoying the sunshine. Suddenly a British half-track armoured vehicle appeared from the middle of some bushes at the side of the road and ran right over the bike. Fortunately one of our fifteen-hundred-weight trucks was coming along and picked him up. Freddie showed me the motorcycle in the back of the truck. The Norton bike had a large metal luggage rack over the rear wheel, and that was where I would have sat. The track of the armoured car had run right over the back wheel and luggage rack, twisting them into a hunk of metal. If I had been along riding pillion, I would have been killed. I was scared and it was about a week before I got up the nerve to go riding again.

Rider Down: Harry to the Rescue

It was a pleasant evening after a hot August day as we rolled through the Italian countryside north of Florence. The route was a twisting, narrow mountain road with a valley on one side. The only lights showing were the housing lights under the truck ahead. There were no white lines on the road, or guardrails, so the drivers had to be alert.

A motorcycle came into view ahead of us and then suddenly just disappeared. The only place he could have gone was down into the valley. Our driver braked, and we got out, went over to the edge and looked down into the black. We couldn't see a thing but heard some sounds so we proceeded carefully down the hill. About thirty-five or forty feet down a thirty-degree slope, there was the motorcycle rider, flat on his back, head to the valley floor. We hoisted the big Harley-Davidson off his chest, and in a few moments he sat up and said he was okay.

The hard part was getting that large bike up the hill to the road. We pushed and pulled and shoved and swore that machine to the road. Someone asked the rider how he had come to miss the road. He replied that he didn't know what happened, he just went blank. We told him to go to the head of our column and get in behind the Commanding Officer's jeep and stay there. If anyone enquired about who he was and why he was in the column, he was to say that he was the Commanding Officer's mobile orderly. I knew nobody would want to bother the Boss Soldier on an important move, and things worked out fine.

A couple of years after the war, the Ladies' Auxiliary of The Queen's Own Rifles Sergeants' Mess asked me to go with them to hand out Christmas presents and soldiers' comforts to veterans who were in Sunnybrook Hospital in Toronto. They felt the presents would be better received from someone like me, whom so many former riflemen knew. We were going along one corridor when I heard a voice call out "Sergeant Major Fox," so I headed over to find out who had called my name. It turned out to be the man whom we had picked up from the crashed motorcycle in Italy. I shook hands with him, and the ladies gave him some gifts. As we were leaving, he said to the woman with me, "Hey, Mom, this is the man who saved my life in Italy."

Naturally, this piqued her interest and she wanted to know the details. This fellow spun a dandy yarn for her, laying it on thick with gestures and everything.

In his rendition of the story, the truck driver didn't exist and the bike wasn't just a few feet down the slope, but at the bottom of a steep ravine. It seems that I picked him up, slung him over my shoulder like a bag of apples, grabbed the motorcycle in the other arm, and waltzed up that cliff as if I did this kind of thing every day before breakfast. After we finally left, the woman turned to me and asked if it had really happened like that. All I could say to her was, "Sort of."

Queen's Own Rifles Warrant Officers: Wykehurst Park, Sussex, England, October 1942. Back row left to right: CSM Ted Hartnell (later RSM Hartnell), CSM Davy Giffen, CSM Wils Hubbard and CSM Tom Chivers. Front row left to right: CSM Bob Hess, RSM Harry Fox, CSM Jack Bray.

Here's Mud in Your Eye: a farewell pint with HQ Company NCOs to honour Captain Warde "Foxey" Taylor, RCAPC, QOR pay officer, as he left the regiment, May 1942. RSM Fox on Capt Taylor's left.

Temple of Good Fortune, Pompeii, Italy. It was visited by Harry Fox on leave in the summer of 1944.

CHAPTER 6

Gothic Line Offensive

We moved south and then northeast in order to prepare to attack the German defences that barred our advance into the Lombardy Plain. These defences were a series of fortifications called the Gothic Line. Unlike the Hitler Line, it was a series of strong points positioned in depth at various key locations. First Division and our First Brigade would be engaged in penetrating the Gothic Line from 26 August until 20 September 1944.

The 48th Highlanders and The Royal Canadian Regiment did the opening attack on 26 August to Momboroccio, while our unit was in reserve. I had yet another "close call" on that first day of the Gothic Line offensive. Tactical Headquarters was in a big church and we came under a heavy artillery "stonk." I was outside, and dove under the only available cover, a half-track armoured vehicle. I wasn't hurt, but the armoured car did a St. Vitus's dance throughout the bombardment.[70]

We went through the other two units on the attack the next day taking Points 268 and 146. The Hasty P's operation drew fierce resistance from the German defenders and there was a very fluid situation with the forward edge of battle moving several times. It was very hard for the respective commanding officers to keep their units and companies straight. Among the casualties were: Sergeant Desjardins; Lance Corporal Edwin Hanson, son of Lieutenant Colonel Hanson, DSO, of Montreal; and Private Ron Smith, MiD.

Aircraft Alert

Tactical Headquarters was set up in two houses of a little village. As I left one of the buildings, I heard an aircraft and looked up. It was bright yellow, one of ours, so there was nothing to be concerned about. Then I saw it drop a bomb. The bomb stayed close to the plane and then dropped its nose and picked up speed. As I watched, it seemed to be falling right on top of me. This was a perception that was common to soldiers on the ground. I craned my head back as far as I could and almost lost my balance. I rubbed my neck and heard the bomb explode about a mile away.

Then I recalled an incident with a captured German paratrooper a few weeks previous to this. He had been standing near me and heard a tank rumbling along in the distance. One of his men said, *"Panzer."* He made a face, spat on the ground and said something about the tanks that made his men laugh. He then pointed to the air, said *"Flugenwaffe"* and cringed down, holding his arms in front of his face. He rattled off a long sentence to which his men nodded agreement. I took all this to mean that he was not afraid of tanks, but he was scared of aircraft. I then knew what he meant.

The Pot-Walloper Takes Off

On 30 August we were on a hilltop and Jerry hammered us with artillery fire. We got the casualties squared away, and then the kitchen trucks came up to give the men a hot meal. A favourite German tactic was to wait five or ten minutes after an initial bombardment and then send in a second one when we thought it was all clear and had resumed our activities. So the second barrage of shells came in, and the pot-walloper, who had cracked during a mortar barrage in the spring, as I mentioned earlier, tore right past me away from the shelling. I decided that he needed to be stopped, so I grabbed another cook who was near by and we chased after him. If he had bumped into anything, he would have hurt himself.

He didn't know where he was going and so we ran like "merry hell." The only reason we caught him was that he ran into a patch of bush and fought furiously to try to get through it. The two of us went around the bush and then knocked him down and sat on him. We had to slap him and say, "Andy, wake up, you silly b___." He was still trying to get up to run even with the two of us sitting on him. The power of fear is amazing!! After a minute or two he calmed down and then said somewhat belligerently, "Why did you slap me?"

About one hundred fifty yards away, there were some Baker Company men who had seen us chasing him and, in soldier fashion, took bets over whether we would catch him or not. They thought it was great fun, especially when we sat on him. It wasn't so exciting for us when a few minutes later we got him on his feet and turned to head back. The slope was almost forty-five degrees and one hundred and fifty feet in length. So up we went, huffing and puffing. I recall going up that particular hill three times that day. When we'd come down, we hadn't noticed it because the adrenaline was flowing.

Keep the Bullets Coming

Ammunition supply was the last of my five major responsibilities, and it was not as hard in Italy as in other fronts. We would attack and capture a hilltop and then supply the rifle companies. When our unit captured a position, the Germans would counterattack with artillery. The reason for this was that the Allies had more artillery and soldiers than they did. When a battalion takes over a new position there is a certain degree of disorganization. If they hit you then, you take more casualties, and further confusion sets in as you try to find

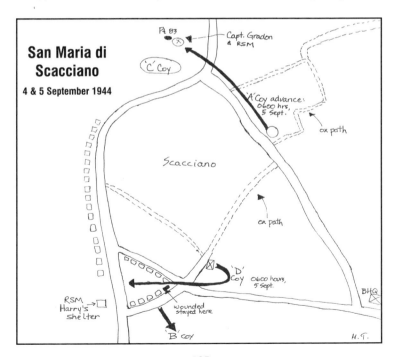

San Maria di Scacciano

4 & 5 September 1944

Pt. 83
Capt. Gradon & RSM
'C' Coy
'A' Coy advance: 0600 hrs, 5 Sept.
ox path
Scacciano
ox path
'D' Coy 0600 hours, 5 Sept.
RSM Harry's shelter
wounded stayed here
BHQ
'B' Coy
H.T.

cover and then evacuate the wounded. I went up as close as possible in the ammunition truck and I usually got there. In summertime there wasn't much water in the valleys to slow the truck down; during the fall and winter it was much more difficult. The Company Sergeant Majors did the actual distribution of the ammunition to the soldiers in the platoons.

San Maria di Scacciano: The Most Interesting Day of My War.

I call 4 September 1944, "the most interesting day of my war." It was especially memorable for getting twenty-six wounded men out of the small town of San Maria di Scacciano, which was part of the Gothic Line. At this particular time, the British division on our left was lagging behind because the going was tough in the hills. The push up the Adriatic coast road was expected to help the situation, and as the Hasty P's were known to be the best unit in the brigade for night marches and sneak attacks, this job was given to us. As I mentioned before, many of the men were country folk, used to operating in the bush of Ontario. However, when we were repulsed in our first attack on San Maria, and the whole Eighth Army was held up for twenty-four hours, it had a terrible effect on the campaign.

When the San Fortunato Ridge was captured at the end of August, patrols went to the river beyond the ridge and it was a gentle stream, easily crossed. However, that same night a huge rainstorm occurred, with the result that the gentle stream became a raging torrent and it took the engineers three days to get a bridge across. This gave the Germans time to bring up reinforcements. Even though the Lombardy Plain is good tank country, the mud forced us to the ox roads, and as in earlier fights in southern Italy, each river became a set-piece action.

In the meantime Baker Company had been house clearing, and they suffered four killed, nineteen wounded and four missing. Fighting in built-up areas is one of the toughest and most costly jobs the infantry has to perform. The fight for Ortona by the Loyal Edmonton Regiment and the Seaforth Highlanders in December 1943 demonstrated just how tedious and costly it could be. Baker took twenty-five prisoners as they cleared the houses at the edge of the town. The companies then pulled back later in the day for an artillery bombardment. Most of the British tanks were out of action by this time. New tanks hadn't come up yet and the attack was postponed until the next day.

I wrote the following account for *The Plough Jockey*, the regimental magazine of the Hastings and Prince Edward Regiment, in 2001. This version highlights very well two aspects of my job as Regimental Sergeant Major: the move and set-up of Battalion Headquarters, and the evacuation of wounded.

The CO later in the day called an Orders group and explained the task given to First Brigade. The RCR would go down the road Via Adriatica, as far as they could. The Hasty P's would follow up, swing left and capture a hilltop village. The 48th would follow through, then swing right, get behind the enemy facing the RCRs and so force Jerry to retire.

We were to pay no attention to what was going on to the right of the road. A few heads came up at that, but no questions were asked. The CO wound up by saying that there would be no forward move before 1600 hours. A hot meal was to be served and the men were to get some sleep, as it would probably be twenty-four hours before they got a chance to get their heads down again.

The meeting broke up, and I was the first out and stood beside the sentry to make sure he gave the proper salute to each officer coming out. The CO was the last out, and he asked if I was doing anything. I said, "No, sir." He said, "Come with me," and we got into his jeep. We were going to an area that had been declared clear at 1000 hours but nevertheless we kept our eyes open. So the Commanding Officer, his driver, Private Orval Wiese; and I headed out. We didn't dawdle at 12 MPH (the prescribed speed) but closer to 50 MPH. We had been warned to stay on the left-hand side of the road because two Royal Navy destroyers were cruising up and down the coast and had orders to engage "targets of opportunity" between the road and the sea.

We turned onto a side road, drove along and turned into a lane and stopped. The CO and I went down the lane to locate Tac HQ on the Brigadier's instructions, so he would know where to find the Commanding Officer when he came forward. The Brigadier was new, this being only his second attack, and he was not used to the way our regiment did things. We were walking through a forest that must have been 100 years old as the trunks of trees were nearly 3 feet thick, and with the branches arching overhead, we were moving though a green tunnel. The road eventually divided and became a circular driveway with a large house on the other side. In the centre was a plot of ground, likely once a garden of some sort, but now just an empty bit of grass. The CO and I split up, and I followed a number of smaller outbuildings and began to plan where to put everyone. One shed had a good strong door and could be used for a lock-up. In another there was a large doorway which the kitchen truck would fit into and where they could have a light on all night and play cards or whatever they did to kill time.

There was an open area, called a *palazzo*, full of bushes between this building and the main house (*casa*). I was curious to know what was behind the bushes, so I slowly parted the branches and all I saw was blue sky. However, when I looked down, I could see the valley floor, likely 100 feet or more below. As was so often the case, we had chosen a site on a steep prominent hill with a main building right at the crest. This seemed to me to be a poor choice as it was a very visible target for the enemy. As I retraced my steps, I noticed several bomb craters in the grass and the tails of several German mortar shells. On an impulse, I gave one of them a good football kick and immediately wished I hadn't as it flew up and just missed LCol Cameron, who was standing a short distance off. I went to him and told him in no uncertain terms that I didn't like the place. He agreed, saying it was a shell trap.

We came to a hollow in the ground with a gravel pit a short distance away. The CO crawled to the top, took out his binos and began his appreciation. I did the same, drawing little sketches in my notepad for each of the BHQ sergeants, who were anxiously awaiting my return. Their company commander had given them a rather vague heads-up about the move but needed a more detailed plan for the new Tac HQ. After the CO and I returned, driving a little less quickly this time, though no less wary of those destroyers, I gave the sergeants the plan but cautioned them that we didn't have time to check the rest of the road for mines, so to be careful.

When the move was actually done, it was the best move of BHQ that we did in the war, as a regiment. Everyone knew exactly where their section went and the ensuing speed and efficiency greatly pleased the CO, though it would be one of the last things he was happy about during the ensuing fight for San Maria.[71]

After the Brigadier approved our move, he then told Lieutenant Colonel Cameron that we would be supported by a squadron of the 44th Battalion of the Royal Tank Regiment. The Commanding Officer replied that he had not asked for them and felt he didn't need them. The Brigade Commander replied that he knew how Cameron felt about British tanks but he (the Brigadier) had received comments from Division Headquarters that the British were tired of Canadian complaints about the battle performance of British tanks. It was a law now that Canadian infantry would have veteran British tank units in support, not our own. The Commanding Officer was royally displeased, but what could he say to this?

The attack began well on 3 September with the three assault companies getting into place. Don Company got right up to the foot of the hill but due to lack of cover, they had to hunker down and wait. Able Company got to the edge of a rocky spur and then stopped. Charlie Company took cover where they could in the rocks and trees, and Baker Company, acting as our battalion reserve, went off with the tanks.

The assault was supposed to start at 0001 hours the next day, but the British tanks made so much noise moving into position that they decided it was futile to function at night. So a platoon was left as a guard, and the other two platoons of the company went forward without support. The Jerries now had a pretty good idea where this company was, and the element of surprise was lost. In Able Company's sector, the tanks crept along and took an hour to cover ground that Sergeant Major Ponsford and I had walked earlier in twenty minutes. Very soon the tanks were out of action, having been hit by machine-gun fire directed at the company behind them. In Charlie Company's case, the tanks turned right too soon, with the result that they collided with a platoon on the ground, running over and killing one soldier.

I got tired of sitting around Battalion Headquarters and so I was just lollygagging around. I didn't have a radio set or a map. Perhaps the Intelligence Officer thought the Regimental Sergeant Major should always be in the rear? In any event I was up with Able Company at that point and was being shot at. There were tank tracks in the ox-cart road, and MG-42 bullets were landing around us, knocking sparks off the road. I came across the Able Company Commander, Captain Bill Graydon, MC, who was standing alone behind a building but he had no signaller. He was talking to the tanks and getting quite exasperated. Soon after this, Graydon was hit in the left ankle by six machine-gun bullets, and I helped dress his ankle wound. He refused to be evacuated for two hours, until the battle was under control.[72] The Commanding Officer's after-action report stated that the Able Company Officer Commanding was wounded while trying to communicate with tanks after Able had advanced across country in the face of stiff mortar and machine-gun fire.

I wrote the following account for the history of the regiment in the Second War World written by Farley Mowat in 1955. It picks up the narrative after I leave Able Company's location.

It gave me a nice feeling to be walking over those sunny fields munching some figs I had picked. Breakfast had been quick, skimpy and long ago. I crossed a deep drainage ditch and went along for a peaceful mile, as if there wasn't any war at all, through vineyards, orchards and ploughed fields. Finally I reached the foot of the hill from the far left and I started up it, keeping my head down to look for mines. Then CRACK and a bullet snapped by my head so close I smelled it. I did not wait to see if I was hit, but made a flying leap for a deep ditch fifteen yards away. I landed crawling and must have looked comical, all arms and legs, Tommy gun dangling about my neck, jumping along like a bear with a burned backside. It was comical for the joker who had fired, and he whanged away four more rounds but missed with all of them.

Finally, I moved off up that ditch and pretty soon found two lost men from Baker Company. I pointed them to the rear and crawled on, only to bump into four nuns. They had pillowcases full of stuff and lost no time in social visiting but disappeared down the hill.

For a while I crawled on the road, on my belly, checking it for mines, then I cut straight up the hill and ran for it through an old orchard. I carried on, huffing and puffing and wondering where the house was, when a Jerry popped out of a bush and ducked behind another one. He had an MG-42 in his hand but his back was to me. I dropped behind a convenient tree and started to breathe again.

As I lay there wondering if it was any use praying, a voice in unmistakable Canadian Army language hailed me, so I upped and ran to the left to a seven-foot stone fence that I cleared without touching anything but the top row of stones. I landed in a lean-to at the back of the Baker Company house, and the guy who yelled at me gave me almighty hell. He said he was one of the few men still standing, and would I please not call attention to the fact by wandering around that hill and getting Jerry to start the war up all over again. At the house I found Captain Lazier and Sergeant Major Forshee. They were somewhat surprised to see me and borrowed my water bottle. While they were drinking, a Jerry stretcher-bearer came bustling round the corner, waving his Red Cross flag. I was startled but unconcerned. They told me he had been around most of the day and had arranged a kind of truce at the moment, and was making sure everybody abided by it. The situation was such that Jerry couldn't throw Baker out of its houses, and Baker couldn't move the Jerries with the few men it had left in one piece.

I walked over to the Jerry and asked him if I could bring a vehicle to evacuate the wounded, but he wouldn't hear of it. It was a pretty wild conversation since I spoke no German and he spoke no English; all we had was vino-Italian. While we argued a broken-down Sherman tank about a hundred and fifty yards off cut loose with its machine gun.

Everybody cursed and got a horrified look on their faces, particularly the Jerry. Then there came an almighty BANG as a *Faustpatrone* exploded on the tank and two Jerries popped out of a bush and charged the tank head-on, firing machine pistols. One of them hopped on top and emptied his mag down the hatch, and the two hauled a wounded man out, and still at the double, carried him fireman fashion over to us and plopped him down before dashing back to their bush.

The place was full of our wounded and there was no time to waste so I said goodbye, and took off down the hill, staying under cover pretty well, and getting back at last to Battalion Headquarters. I told Colonel Cameron the story and he suggested I might borrow an armoured half-truck from the tank medical section and try to rescue the wounded.

Off I went again and bumped into a platoon of 48th Highlanders under Sergeant Jim Harker. He and his platoon razzed me cheerfully for going the wrong way, but I told them that this was the usual thing for a Regimental Sergeant Major, and when we parted they wished me the best. Too bad they couldn't have used it for themselves; they ran into trouble that night, and Jim and most of his men never came back.

A flock of 75 millimetre shells straddled the road, and I dived for the ditch again. Something banged me on the shoulder, and I grunted, sure I had bought it. Then a very haughty Limey voice asked what I was grunting for. The voice belonged to a tank officer who had leapt for the same ditch, gouging my shoulder nicely with his big boot.

He told me where his Regimental Aid Post was and when I got there and explained my needs, the Limeys jumped to help, only they insisted in stripping me of my weapons and equipment and tying a Red Cross brassard on my arm before we started.

The trip back up that hill was pretty quick. I rode on the outside to con the way and wave the Red Cross flag. I held it in my teeth, and it at least kept my teeth from chattering as we approached the place where I had seen the Jerry machine-gunner. He was still there holding a *Faustpatrone* in his hand at the "ready" position and staring at us as if he didn't believe his eyes. We went past fast, and he never budged. We swung into the village and up the main street to the Baker Company house.

In no time we had a load [of wounded men] and were heading down the hill, feeling a little naked with our back to the Jerries. But nothing happened, so we unloaded and came back up, this time with an ordinary ambulance following.

We were met at the top of the hill by a Jerry corporal looking pretty mad, and waving his gun at us and yelling *"Kaput!"* It was pretty clear we weren't welcome. But our driver had a spare pack of cigarettes, and I passed these to the corporal. He was looking at my rank badges the way corporals always do, in that "you've got nothing on me this time" sort of way. The cigarettes mellowed him a bit and he let me into the big house, but what was left of Baker Company seemed to have vanished.[73]

San Maria was memorable for other things as well. It was on this same day that, while evacuating the wounded, I received the best compliment I ever had from a soldier. Baker Company's wounded men were lying up against a wall in the village. I saw this fellow whom I recognized right away from The Queen's Own Rifles in England. His name was Glen Love and he had been a corporal in the Mortar Platoon. His brother, Stan Love, was a sergeant in the same platoon. Here he was, lying wounded as a private with the Hasty P's in Italy. Love saw me coming and I greeted him. Though he was still dopey from morphine, he reached up with one hand, grabbed my arm and said, "Harry, I knew you would come and get me." I was so overcome with feeling that I didn't know what I should say. Apparently, he had been sniping through a wall, and a German blew the wall down on top of him with a *Panzerfaust* (an infantry anti-tank weapon). I asked a stretcher-bearer about his condition and he said that Love's back was broken and that he would never walk again. Despite this pessimistic prognosis, Glen Love made a complete recovery, though he was always quite skinny after that.

I brought all the wounded out by vehicle, and it took three ambulance loads. The Jerries would only recognize the Red Cross ambulance for wounded. These German paratroopers recognized and respected medical personnel.

The following account by Corporal Ray Playfair of the Hasty P's illustrates the point about German soldiers respecting the wounded and acting in a humane and civilized manner.

> The fighting stopped and people came out to pick up the pieces. The Germans took our wounded back to our lines and those not wounded were taken prisoners. I regained consciousness to find myself being dragged, my arms around the neck of two Germans, their hands grasping my belt, and my feet dragging on the ground. THE STRANGEST THING WAS THAT German medical personnel dressed our wounds. Our stretcher-bearer had been killed earlier in the day. I seem to remember that the German medic spoke English and did an excellent job with limited resources. Our people could not get ambulances up to us because the Germans controlled the roads. After some time, we were able to get the tank group to send up their ambulance half-track to pick us up.
>
> They loaded us like sardines in the half-track. It was then that I found out the shells that ended our activities in the house were fired by our [own] tanks. The gunner related the story to me by saying he saw nothing but enemy around the house so he fired his last 75 mm shell at them. I'm afraid I was not too complimentary with respect to his parenthood. Today they call this 'friendly fire.'[74]

Almost all the casualties were from Baker Company. San Maria had the second highest casualty rate for the regiment in a single engagement during the Second World War, with eighty killed or wounded. Among the dead officers were Lieutenant Charles MacDonald, age twenty-nine, from Hamilton, and Lieutenant William White. Among the dead enlisted personnel were

Corporal Walter Cork, twenty-nine, of Brampton, and Private Jim Staats, nineteen, from Niagara Falls.

When a regiment is defeated, there is usually an inquiry and the Commanding Officer is replaced. Fortunately this did not happen for the Plough Jockeys this time. The fault was plainly the British tanks in support of our attack.

The Day I Lost a Friend

About a week after the San Maria fight, the kitchen truck had just gone up the hill to set up for a meal. A corporal from the 48th Highlanders came over the same hill with two Jerry prisoners and asked if I could take them over so he could go back to his unit. I said, "Sure, have them sit down over there," pointing to a spot about twenty feet away. "They can't run anywhere." He then proceeded to tell me that these two Germans were thought to be responsible for the death of a soldier who was well liked in their regiment. So the 48th corporal said, "Hey, RSM, weren't you Sergeant Harker's friend in the QOR?" "Yes," I replied. "He was killed last week."

Sergeant Jim Harker joined The Queen's Own Rifles in 1940 as Rifleman James Harker, B 63775, and he had initially been in Baker Company. He was a very good sergeant, and I picked him to go with us to Italy to gain battle experience. I had asked Lieutenant Colonel Jock Spragge, the QOR Commanding Officer, if the sergeant could go on this Pooch draft to Italy with the rest of us and he agreed. Sergeant Jim Harker was killed on 4 September, the same day I had passed by him and his platoon on my travels at San Maria.

When I heard this bit of bad news, something inside me snapped. I was furious at the two Jerries. I started to walk over to the prisoners and I brought my Tommy gun down. Thankfully, the artillery captain attached to the regiment saw this and came running after me. "Remember where you are, Sergeant Major. You can't do this." He knocked my Tommy gun away and stood in front of me. This allowed me to cool down a bit and think more rationally about the situation. The incident gave me a personal glimpse into what many Canadian soldiers felt in Normandy when they learned their friends had been shot by the 12 SS Panzer troops while prisoners of war.

I recall that prior to the San Fortunato attack in mid-September, I was out one night doing a turn of sentry duty, watching the horizon, when suddenly there was a large yellow flash of light. It was obviously an explosion, but there was no sound and the earth didn't shake. I thought this to be odd. It was a huge flash that covered a large area, about six feet across from my vantage point. A thirty-foot dike or wall requires a breach at least twice the width, sixty feet or more. So I went inside and told Lieutenant Colonel Cameron that the Germans were doing demolitions. He was rather skeptical and came out to have a look. He stood there watching for about five minutes and was about to turn away when there was another similar flash of light. He went in and called the Brigade Commander who just laughed at him and said it wasn't possible. We only realized the results of this demolition a few weeks later after we had secured San Fortunato and were advancing north in October.

San Fortunato

The Hasty P's along with First Division, continued the advance toward the Po River Valley in September. The next objective centred on a ridge called San Fortunato, a high hill that we attacked on 20 September. This was the final battle in the Gothic Line campaign. The German paratroopers put up their usual fierce resistance, and it took hand-to-hand fighting by the men of two companies to capture the position. We took about forty casualties that day, most in Charlie and Don Companies. The lieutenant and sergeant in one platoon went down, and Lance Sergeant Marcel van Hende took over, leading the men into a large building near the top of the ridge.[75]

Van Hende led his men inside the old *palazzo*-style building and came to a porch type of arrangement looking over a broad, paved, inner courtyard about one hundred feet across. He noticed three Jerries running across the square, and his men shot two of them, but a third escaped into a well that was in the centre of the courtyard. Van Hende jumped down the ten-foot drop into the courtyard and ran over to the well. He threw a grenade and went in after the Jerry. The bold lance sergeant noticed a light and then he came across an underground barracks where he shot a number of the Jerries who were there. By this time the room was smoking because the straw in the mattresses had caught fire from the grenade's hot shrapnel. It was still burning when I came up about two hours later. I stood on the veranda and looked down into the courtyard where the well still smoked. Lance Sergeant van Hende received the Distinguished Conduct Medal for this initiative because those soldiers could have attacked us unawares and created havoc. He acted bravely but also took a real risk; he had no idea what he would find down that well.

Among the nine Hasty P's killed at San Fortunato was Lance Corporal Tom Leatherbarrow from Quebec. I recall coming across his body along with several other men from his section, lying in the ditch where they had been killed. As I went over to get their ID disks, a captain called out to me "Get lost." He was sitting there smoking a cigarette, apparently unconcerned about his dead men.

That night, the Commanding Officer sent me out to find Baker Company. It was dark, and the Germans fired an MG-42 at me; the tracer rounds showed that they were coming too close for comfort, so I hit the deck. I stayed there for a few seconds and then moved out. After about fifteen minutes I was fired on again, this time by three Lee-Enfield rifles and a Bren gun, so I knew I had found Baker Company. Each weapon has a distinctive sound, and in the dark, with hearing as one of your main senses, you got to recognize the differences quite quickly. My "luck" continued to be good as neither the Germans nor our men managed to shoot me.

While we were still near San Fortunato, I was taken prisoner by soldiers from the Seaforth Highlanders. I had been doing my usual wandering about to see the troops and I got lost. I did not have the correct password and my uniform had no rank badges or regimental shoulder flashes in case of capture by the enemy. These soldiers thought I was a spy and they planned on executing justice right then and there. I was extremely scared and somehow managed to convince them that I was a Canadian soldier and the Hasty P's Regimental Sergeant Major. I'm not sure what words I used, but I think someone at a much higher headquarters than the Army interceded on my behalf. I consider this incident the closest I came in the war to getting my soldier's white cross.

CHAPTER 7

War in a Forgotten Theatre

The Replacement Crisis: "Zombies"

The regiment was soon pulled out of the line and into a reserve position at Miramare, a former resort town, from 22 September until 10 October. Despite the barren white-washed villas that we were to inhabit, the Canadian soldier's endless ingenuity eventually made them livable temporary residences. The first few days were a pleasant respite from the stress of action, but trouble soon joined us there.

Hopes were high that other units of the Eighth Army could soon break through the hills in Italy's northeast and drive into the Lombardy Plain. However, because of the topography, with the Apennines on the west and the low-lying marshy ground south of Rimini near the coast, there was only one clear area for an advance. It was along Highway 9, the *Via Emilia*, and then across the famed Rubicon River, so well known in Roman history. The hopes of a quick victory were cruelly dashed with the onset of miserable fall weather at the beginning of October. The temperature dropped, the rain turned the countryside into a bog, and streams and canals overflowed. The offensive ground to a complete halt.

In a rear area soldiers do a lot of talking, and the rumours were flying concerning the fighting in Northwest Europe and about things at home in Canada. One story had us home by Christmas and all veterans being replaced by conscripts! The talk became so incessant that the "higher-ups," General

Vokes and General Burns, the Divisional and Corps commanders, felt it necessary to come up to talk to us and tell us why we were not getting trained reinforcements. I recall that during General Burns's visit, all First Division officers and non-commissioned officers were gathered in a theatre in Miramare. The General's staff went along the aisles carefully scrutinizing each one of us. Then one of them called out, "You there," meaning me. I had brought my drill cane, and the general needed a pointer for the map, so they borrowed it for him to use during his briefing.

Mr. Ralston, the Minister of National Defence was visiting the European battlefields to assess the situation first-hand, and he paid us a visit. The Minister was personable and genuinely interested in the soldiers' views and promised to see that something was done. He was shocked to see how weak the regiment was at that time. It seems that his senior staff had deliberately kept from him the news of the actual condition of our infantry battalions. We were once again down to about three hundred all ranks, with each rifle company being the size of a platoon. Some replacements came in, but they were mostly old soldiers back from the hospital.

The conscripted soldiers in Canada were called "Zombies" by those of us overseas. The term "Zombie" was taken from a silent movie made during the early 1930s starring Bela Lugosi. It refers to mythical creatures that are the "living dead," mere automatons, not truly human. It seemed like an apt metaphor for the conscripts who had to serve in the Army in time of war but not obligated to go into combat. The commitment to excuse conscripts from having to serve overseas was made by the Liberal government despite the fact that our country was engaged in *total war*. In Italy and Holland our infantry battalions were chronically undermanned. Perhaps the politicians had forgotten what had happened in the First World War when whole battalions were wiped out in single engagements.

Of course, there were genuine conscientious objectors, mostly from groups like the Quakers and the Mennonites, and many of them had to do "alternate service," as it was called, in remote areas of the country. The term "Zombie" would never be employed today, but we lived in a different time then. Those of us who had volunteered and sweated through training and now in combat didn't care if the term offended others. All we knew was what we were going through and these healthy young men in uniform were not there helping us out! The war was being won on the battlefront, or so we thought.

In actual fact, it was a war of production just as much as a war of combat and the Allies won that fight on the home front.

One scheme that the Mackenzie King government used to try to appease combat veterans was the Tri-Wound program. Every soldier who had been wounded three times was to be returned to Canada. A decoration (such as the Military Medal) counted as a wound. There were about sixty soldiers in the Hasty P's that qualified. However, only three men per battalion were allowed to go, due to the chronic manpower shortage!

The regiment was placed back on the offensive on 10 October and had stiff fighting to take the town of Savignano and then to cross the Rigosa River.

Late one afternoon, I heard that the rifle companies had reached the river, which was our final objective. I set out to visit them and came to a flat open field, a good half-mile wide. In the middle of it my attention was drawn to an object because of some movement on it. As I've mentioned, I'm rather a curious person so I decided to investigate. When I got closer I realized that the object I had seen was a cattle-watering trough and the movement was one of my men having a bath. The soldier had filled the trough full of cold water and was sitting in it, cursing his head off. He had nasty desert sores on his legs, and he was using a small scrubbing brush to clean the scabs off. Painful? Yes, indeed!

The man asked me if the final objective had been taken, and I told him, "Yes," and that the recce parties from Third Brigade were already coming up to check for crossing points on the river. The situation could have become quite awkward for me as Regimental Sergeant Major if I had chosen to ask him if he had permission from his platoon commander to be away from the line. If he had said, "No," then he was technically Away Without Leave. As the chief disciplinarian of the regiment, it would have been my job to do something about it. However, I sympathized with the poor fellow. He was doing his best about field hygiene and remaining an effective infantryman, ready for action. Another route would have been for him to go to the Medical Officer and then be out of the line for several weeks, not only that, but he would be among strangers. So I carried on, leaving him to his scrubbing and cursing.

On the Trail of the "Ortona Express"

We had been out on a rest and now had moved forward close to Sant Arcangelo. The engineers had trouble getting a bridge across but managed to install small foot-bridges, which the regiment crossed in the dark and we moved to our allotted positions.[76] In the morning, the Intelligence Sergeant showed me the battle board, to give me an idea of what was going on. Then I went across the bridge and eased over to the right and followed the railway line. This ran straight as a die for several miles and was built up about four feet above the level of the land, which was as flat as a pancake.

After going some distance, I noticed a spur line coming from a wooded area on the left. It was not shown on the map, and being a nosy fellow, I followed the line into the woods. It changed from being a well-built track to a poor one. The cross ties were not regularly spaced, some being three feet apart. The longer logs were in a diagonal manner and had no ballast at all. This was what we used to call a "Jerry-built job." There were three big shells on the ground, and measuring with my hand, I calculated that they were for an eleven-inch gun. I concluded that this spot must have been a firing position for the so-called "Ortona Express" that picked at us all the way through the Gothic Line, firing only at night. I passed the information on to the Commanding Officer, who in turn passed it on to the Brigadier, as the brass liked to have such snippets of information. It gave them an opportunity to put a colored flag or pin in a map and make it look good.

Later that evening, I was told that a couple of very senior artillery officers would come up tomorrow morning to inspect the site. I started to do some thinking: they would want me as a guide; after inspecting the site, would probably take a minute, and then would say to me, "Sergeant Major, have these shells picked up and taken to this location. Make sure they are there by 1300 hours sharp." I would only be able to salute and say, "Yes, sir."

In the infantry battalions, we had no winches or hoists capable of picking up a five hundred-pound load, and then placing it in a truck four feet above the ground. Nor did we have planks or timbers or ropes with which to wrestle it into a truck. The job was just impossible, but how could I tell a general that? So, next morning, I suddenly and very conveniently remembered I had some unfinished business in the forward area. I headed out without leaving any notice of where I was going or where I could be found. To this day I do not know if those officers found and picked up their precious shells. I did not know nor did I care; I was in the same happy position as the Scottish paratrooper who jumped out of the plane and as his parachute opened properly, said, "This suits me right doon to the groon."

If we had been able to get out of the hills and into the Po River Valley, our armour would have allowed us to get up into the north and then out of Italy.

One of the geo-political problems in the post-war era was the Soviet control of most of Eastern Europe and the Balkans. We could have gone through Austria, and once onto the Hungarian plain, our tanks could have cut off the Balkans and ensured Allied control of that portion of Europe.

As we moved north toward the Po Valley, the Germans contested each river crossing and it became a major offensive action for the attackers. To impede our progress, the Germans blew up the dikes surrounding the (normally) small rivers. An order was given that no vehicle was to drive off the road. The water was hub deep on the road, but often there was *seven* or *eight* feet of water in the surrounding fields, much like the conditions faced by the Third Division who at the same time were fighting in the Scheldt area of Holland. The rainy season started in early October, and the vehicles were often up to their axles in mud. Incidentally, this is very good farming country. The thick black soil grows grapes, olives, almonds, figs, fruit trees and grains. But heavy soil made the going very tough for the Army at that time of year. Most of the roads were ox-cart paths as the local farmers used bullocks for agriculture.

Bridges

There are rivers everywhere in Italy, and the engineers always had to construct their Bailey bridges to get our vehicles across. Each bridge would be given a name by the company that had built it. I saw so many bridges but can only remember two of the names: one which I will talk about later at the Lamone River was known as "Grief Bridge." The other one that I recall was over a small stream. The recce party had picked the best place for a bridge and found three dead German soldiers there. This was a good landmark for the engineers. When they had finished the bridge, they called it "Three Jerries Bridge" and painted three green chamber pots on the sign. Every soldier that crossed this bridge got a good laugh from the sign: in war, a good laugh is nearly as precious as a letter from home.

Shelter in a Stable

The engineers had finally got a Bailey bridge over the river, and I moved the Battalion Headquarters kitchen truck into the battalion area. This truck fed all the men at Tactical Headquarters, which could be as few as the Commanding Officer, his signaller, driver and myself. I recall one day, however, when there were twenty vehicles present and almost one hundred men. As I had overall responsibility for the feeding and movement of Battalion

Headquarters, I bunked with the kitchen staff and usually located the kitchen close to Tactical Headquarters.

At Sant Arcangelo, the battalion area extended from the railway track on the right, also the right boundary of First Brigade and First Division, about a mile and a half over to a road on the left that ran parallel to the rail line. Beyond the road was the 48th Highlanders' area, and it was all hills and dales. This kind of terrain was very difficult to advance in quickly as every hill and re-entrant had to be carefully checked. Our area, in contrast, was flat with trees and orchards that provided excellent cover, so we advanced more quickly than the 48th did.

As we went to set up the kitchen, I had Basil Smith, the Quarterbloke, two cooks, two pot-wallopers and the driver. I elected *not* to place the kitchen in a building that looked as if it had been a jam factory, now lacking all the necessary machinery. As the Germans tended to shell large buildings, I chose instead the stable across the way.

Fortunately everyone in the kitchen gang was in the stable when a sudden artillery barrage was unleashed on the town. The first shell exploded as we dove into the stalls where the oxen had lived. The walls of the stall were built of terrazzo and concrete, so they were strong enough but they had no overhead cover. The stable emerged unscathed, but the main building and the courtyard were thoroughly hammered.

At this point I recall that a canary flew into our stall and landed with an audible clank, right next to the cook. A "canary" is what we called a very small piece of shrapnel, from the sound it makes going through the air. A horrible expression came over the cook's face, and he went a pasty whitish yellow. After a minute or so, we asked him if he was okay and he said he didn't know. We checked him over, and he wasn't hit, apparently just scared.

I decided to check on the gun crew from 5 Platoon who were manning the crossroads, covering the stable area. About halfway there I met one of the anti-tank gunners coming my way. He was coming on the same mission, to see if all of us were all right. This little incident shows how closely knit the regiment had become, with everyone looking out for his comrades. This man was risking his life, coming down a road that had just been shelled, just to check on us.

That same night the New Zealand Division on our right put in an attack. It beats me why they waited forty-eight hours to attack, but doubtless some general knew why. It's hard to describe the noise the Kiwis made as they attacked. It started about a mile behind us and continued until they had passed by our lines. The Maoris of New Zealand have a tradition of entering battle yelling slogans at the top of their lungs. The shouts, curses and screams of their troops kept us wide awake all night.

In the next few days during the fighting at "the Hamlet" and Bulgaria, 13 to 14 October, we lost a number of good men, including Corporal Huron Brant, who had won the Military Medal in Sicily. Brant was killed with his whole section by enfilading machine-gun fire.[77] This was a few days before Private Roland Nahwegezhic was killed in action. Roland Nahwegezhic was the younger brother of Rifleman Charles Nahwegezhic, MM, from Manitoulin Island, Ontario. Charles was a rifleman in Charlie Martin's Able Company of the QOR and succumbed on 28 February 1945 to wounds received near Mooshof, Germany.

More Lucky Stories

While on the road to Bulgaria on 13 October, I had still another close call. I was in the Commanding Officer's jeep, and we were crossing a small bridge, at the foot of a steep hill. The Jerries threw a salvo of four rounds at us. The rounds were right on line for the bridge, but fortunately, the wind caused them to drift over to one side, and they landed about fifty yards away.

Sergeant Major George Ponsford of Charlie Company later told me how he came to be wounded during the advance on Bulgaria. The company was moving along a road at night in an attempt to skirt the village and come at it from behind. It just so happened that a platoon of Germans was coming along the same stretch of road from the opposite direction and the Germans were taking a break in the ditch. Their sentry could not have been paying attention because the lead platoon of Charlie Company walked right by their position until someone spotted the sentry and opened fire. The Canadians had the advantage as their weapons were at the ready, and they used them before most of the Germans got theirs in action. One of the Germans did have time, however, to fire his rifle at Ponsford, and the round went through his hip and came out his backside, making a hole as big as your fist. As he was only about six feet away, he was thrown back. I asked him what he did then and he said that he got up, aimed his Tommy gun and took out two of the enemy with it. Inspired leadership by the Company Commander, Captain Max Porritt, in that attack earned him a Military Cross.

One day a reporter from the Army newspaper, *The Maple Leaf* came to visit the unit. He had been sent up to interview the Commanding Officer about an engagement we had just finished where we had successfully beaten off thirteen German counter-attacks in twenty-four hours. The fourteenth had been too much for us and we had taken a beating. It was my job to make sure that the reporter got back safely to Advance Echelon. The only transport available was a very small armoured car with no room for passengers so we had to sit on the roof. It was a miserable night, wet and cold with a thirty mile per hour wind. There was neither protection nor anything to hold on to as we bounced along the ox-cart path back to Advance Echelon. We heard a pinging noise, and then it stopped. After a time we heard it again. The reporter, who had glasses like Coke bottles, asked what was making that sound. I told him that they were German machine-gun bullets hitting the car: he was so frightened that he almost fell off the car.

Another night, when it was very dark and moonless, I decided to catch a lift with one of the vehicles by standing on the running board. This was strictly against regulations. Suddenly we heard this rumbling, and a tank drove by us, nearly squashing me against the truck. I had had another lucky escape.

One miserable night that same fall of 1944, I was out checking on the sentries. I had visited them all and everyone was fine except me. I was soaked, cold, tired, and thoroughly cheesed off by the time all these visits were concluded. I was still a long way from Tactical Headquarters so I decided to take a short cut (avoiding the track plan) across an open field. The mud was only three or four inches deep and all the fences and ditches ran parallel to my course, so it was a fairly easy walk. I jumped over one ditch and landed on the shoulder of the road. My hobnailed boots made a sound as they hit the gravel, and the sentry at a building about one hundred yards away called out a challenge. I was in no mood to humour a sentry so I ignored him. Another challenge was issued, and then he fired a short burst from a Tommy gun. I knew he would miss me at that distance, but it was certainly a peculiar feeling to hear those big slugs coming my way.

A few weeks later, when it was still raining, I had an overloaded carrier almost turn over on me. I had one heck of a time keeping it straight on the steep hillside.

A Rifleman's Loyalty: A True Band of Brothers

Unless you have served in a combat zone you can't really understand the deep personal ties with others that are established when you share the horrors of action together. One might naturally think that everyone would simply want to shoot himself in the foot and get out of the action. For the most part, however, exactly the opposite was true. The men wanted to stay in the front-line as long as possible, even when they were sick and miserable. This testimony is true of soldiers in most armies, I think. The recent mini-series, *Band of Brothers*, about American paratroopers in Easy Company, 506th Parachute Infantry, portrays this well. At Bastogne, one of their sergeants voluntarily returned to the front line from the Aid Station despite suffering from trench foot and a shrapnel wound in his arm. Only when he was hit again and had his leg chewed up was he evacuated for good.

Our experience was that a sick man would hang on until the very last moment. As soon as the objective was taken, if he knew it was okay, then he would agree to be taken off the line. As long as there was a chance that his platoon was going to see action, however, he wouldn't agree to leave; and the only ones he knew in the Army were his friends in the company. So soldiers stayed with their battle buddies as long as possible. I think that is what kept soldiers going, this commitment and loyalty to friends in the section and platoon, this true comradeship. I know some soldiers didn't want to wait around in the replacement depots and somehow found their way back to their parent unit. I'm told that later in the war, Lieutenant Ken Kavanagh went Absent Without Leave in order to rejoin the QOR in Holland. Kavanagh had been in my Charlie Company as a rifleman. Sadly, he was killed in action at Rha on 6 April 1945 just a short time after rejoining The Queen's Own Rifles.

Replacements came to the Hasty P's from the reinforcement unit. Whether they were straight from basic training in Canada or drafted from other trades, they often had a difficult time. Every regiment prefers to get its old soldiers back, but the manpower shortage was so bad that units would take anyone who was available.

In late 1944 the Hasty P's got a draft of forty men who had served with the Cape Breton Highlanders of the Fifth Division before being wounded. Lieutenant Colonel Cameron asked me what I thought of this particular group, and I said I didn't think much of them. This was the only regiment that I had had any trouble with in Canada. Despite the fact that many of these men had been in combat, done well and then been wounded, they didn't really gel with the regiment. I know many of them spoke Gaelic, and they just didn't seem to fit in with the other men in their platoons. "Capers," as they were known, like their Scottish forebears were rather clannish, and I think this quality somewhat hindered their effectiveness in a new regiment. However, the main reason they didn't work out was that they had been in combat too long and were now no longer effective. Even their sergeant would cry at difficult times.

Very few soldiers who have been in combat are cowards; this bunch had just had enough. The higher-ups never seemed to accept this reality, even when Army psychiatrists told them about the problems. Within three weeks virtually all these replacements were either casualties or returned to the transit depot in the rear. Studies of combat stress in the Second World War indicate that ten percent of soldiers were immediately impacted negatively by combat operations.[78] The longer troops were exposed to this strain, I think, the greater the number that became ineffective. Their effectiveness was eroded by the combined effect on the body and spirit of powerful emotions like terror, panic, guilt, anger, sorrow, bewilderment, helplessness, despair, and so on. Even when all the time in the rear is subtracted, the Hasty P's had been in the combat zone more than one hundred and eighty days.

Prisoners of War

The ammunition truck was at Tactical Headquarters and we needed to get about a dozen German prisoners back to Brigade. The Intelligence Officer had questioned this group and had got nothing but name, rank and serial number. There were about fifteen men from our headquarters just standing around watching to see what would happen. One of the drivers, Private Billy Mansfield, was from Kitchener, Ontario, and as his maternal grandparents spoke German, he could speak a little. Mansfield had been awarded a Mentioned in Dispatches for some smart work with a jeep at the Moro River in December 1943.

A Jerry said something, and Billy swore, stepping forward as if he were going to hit the German. I stopped him and he said to me, "He called me a *scheisse* and I don't take that from anybody." One of the Germans who spoke English piped up, "He did not call *you* a *scheisse* but merely asked for permission to go take a *scheisse*." That was certainly a different matter, and so I told Billy to take him out to the latrine. When they came back, they weren't exactly friendly but they were at least telling each other about their respective grandparents.

The prisoners were loaded into the back of the ammunition truck. I turned to one of the corporals, and told him to get into the back of truck; he was to be the guard for the group. This fellow started to shiver and said, "Oh, no, not me." He was scared stiff. This put me as Regimental Sergeant Major in a difficult position. I had given an order to a non-commissioned officer and he had refused to carry it out, not only in front of our own men, but in front of twelve well-disciplined German soldiers. So I snarled, "Get in the bloody truck and shut up." The man got up on the tailgate, one leg in and one leg out. He had to hold on to the tailgate with both hands. He just looked so ridiculous that everyone started laughing, even the Jerries!

A Lesson in First Aid

Most military people have heard of Private Ernest Alvia "Smokey" Smith, who won the Victoria Cross for single-handedly destroying several tanks in the Seaforth Highlanders' attack on the Savio River on 22 October 1944. It was sad to hear of his death on 3 August 2005, as "Smokey" Smith was our last surviving Victoria Cross winner. Nothing quite so dramatic happened on the First Brigade front that day, but it was an interesting night for me, nevertheless. I recall that it was a night not fit for man or beast. It had started to rain in the afternoon, and by evening it was a full-fledged downpour. Third Brigade was to pass through us and go over the Savio. There was a long line of Van Doos (Royal 22nd Regiment) soldiers trudging down the hill with their heads down, trying to keep the rain out of their faces. With the British style "tin pot" helmet, you had a choice: you could either turn it to one side to keep the moisture out of your face or you could tilt it back and keep the water from running down your neck and under your clothes.

> Our Regimental Aid Post was located behind the shelter of some leafless trees. The Commanding Officer and I had come up for a visit and we were standing off to one side, talking with the Medical Officer, when suddenly a salvo of mortar bombs exploded not far away. It's hard to estimate distance on a miserable night like that, but I figured they were about a hundred yards away, so we were okay or so I thought.
>
> One of the Van Doos who happened to be going by us at that moment gave a grunt and went down in a heap. The Medical Officer

pointed at the man and then at his two stretcher-bearers who were in the process of getting a stretcher out to come to his assistance. They ran over to the man and put him on it while the marching column simply moved around them. They threw his rifle and webbing in the ditch and then brought the stretcher over to the doctor. The soldier had a small puncture hole, high up on the right side of his chest, but very little bleeding. The Van Doos' man had been directly in front of Lieutenant Colonel Cameron, so it's fair to surmise that if he had not been in that spot, the Colonel would have been hit.

The Medical Officer said nothing, just pulled out a cigarette and lit it up. The Commanding Officer scowled at him but he didn't say a thing. Once the smoke was going well, he bent down and stuck it in the man's mouth. The soldier said "Merci" and puffed contently on the cigarette as if he didn't have a care in the world.

The Medical Officer then turned to Lieutenant Colonel Cameron and me with a wide smile on his face. To this day I can still see his shining white teeth in that dark night. He said, "When a man is hit in the chest, give him a cigarette; if he coughs, he is hit in the lung. This fellow didn't cough, so his wound is minor and he'll be back with his company in four or five weeks." The Commanding Officer got a message from his signaller and decided it was time to go. I got into the back of the jeep and crawled under the signaller's ground sheet, which he had over the radio to keep it dry. It was warmer under the sheet out of the wind, but not much drier. There was about an inch of water sloshing around in the back of the jeep, and that's where I had to lie down. Remember that standing in the rain is much more comfortable than sitting in it![79]

Anger and Alienation: No "Zombies" for Italy

We were taken out of the line once again and placed in reserve from late October until the end of November: first, under canvas outside of the town of Sant Arcangelo and then back to our former quarters at Miramare. We bivouacked in the trees and bushes near a large open area that the Commanding Officer declared would be suitable for a parade. He told me that the men were getting sloppy and needed smartening up. I agreed, and so we planned a parade. Lieutenant Colonel Cameron saw no point in bivouacking in the open area, however, as a British battalion would have done, because there was no cover and concealment and this was still a combat zone. The area was about one hundred yards by three hundred yards and any long line of tents would have been visible to aircraft from thirty thousand feet.

The first night there the rain began, and it absolutely poured for three straight days without let up. The "parade ground" turned into a huge swimming pool overnight, and the Commanding Officer called the parade off because the men were simply too uncomfortable and there was mud everywhere. Each day that it continued to pour, more men reported in to the Regimental Aid Post with head colds and other flu-like symptoms.

Normally the damp brought out the bugs as well as sickness. I recall that in one place we bivouacked right behind a field that had been recently fertilized with human waste. The insects were terrible, as you can imagine, and we took to using a grey powder called Anti-Louse 63 (AL 63). When it was dry, we would place a two-inch high pile of AL 63 all the way around our tents to stop the little creatures from invading our space. At Sant Arcangelo, it was simply too wet for it to be effective.

An Italian civilian who lived in a house near my tent came out after the rains stopped and started dismantling the ten-foot stone bridge that went over the water near his home. The low footbridge was displacing the water, and so he removed it to lower the water level and to prevent flooding. When the water subsided, he proceeded to rebuild the bridge.

It was at Miramare on 19 November that we learned just how far the government of Mackenzie King had failed those of us who had volunteered in 1939 and 1940 to serve overseas. The manpower shortage in our units had created a political crisis for the Prime Minister.[80] Colonel Ralston was forced to resign, and General Andrew MacNaughton took his place. The soldiers felt that he would treat them right, but, in truth, MacNaughton was just a pawn in a larger chess game. The "Zombies" (National Resources Mobilization Act men) who were trained as infantry were *not* compelled to go overseas. They tried to solicit volunteers among the conscripts, but very few agreed. The three men scheduled to leave the regiment under the Tri-Wound plan were to have a thirty-day leave in Canada, to be followed by *a return to front-line duty.*

Farley Mowat points out in the Regimental History that the soldiers' anger and indignation were something to behold. Even mild and even-tempered men were incensed at what they felt was the King government's betrayal. The

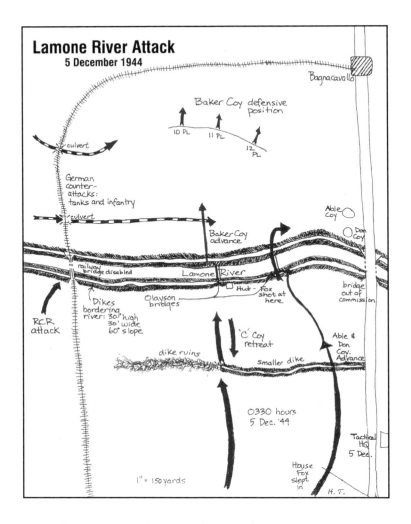

Lamone River Attack
5 December 1944

Bagnacavallo

Baker Coy defensive position

10 PL 11 PL 12 PL

culvert

German counter-attacks: tanks and infantry

culvert

Able Coy

Don Coy

Baker Coy advance

railway bridge disabled

Lamone River

Hut - Fox shot at here

bridge out of commission

RCR attack

Dikes bordering river: 30' high 30' wide 60° slope

Olayson bridges

'C' Coy retreat

Able & Don Coy. Advance

dike ruins

smaller dike

0330 hours 5 Dec. '44

Tactical HQ 5 Dec.

1" = 150 yards

House Fox slept in

H. T.

soldiers knew there were thousands of trained infantry soldiers at home, about 60,000 in 1944. However, because of Mackenzie King's earlier promise, these troops would never be forced to serve outside of Canada. I think this was the last straw for many of our men, who were already worn perilously thin inside because of all they had been through. Although the government soon relented and released 16,000 conscripts to go overseas, not one arrived as a reinforcement for us in Italy!

Saved by a Beret

My Provost Corporal, Fred Crompton, and I were hiking up a broad four-lane highway from Advance Echelon to Tactical Headquarters when a Baker Company ration party in a jeep overtook us. They picked us up and we whipped along until we came to the top of a hill, where there were two concrete blocks, about twenty feet square and slightly offset, with only room for a jeep to get between them. So we slowed down and then went down the hill, across an old stone bridge (which had been half blown away) and up another hill in low gear. At the top was a long straight stretch of road, and the driver accelerated. Freddie was sitting at the back of the jeep, and I was on the right side, legs dangling pretty close to the rear wheel.

As the driver hit the gas, a sudden gust of wind blew Freddie's beret off. He yelled, "Stop! I've lost my louse cage." We stopped and immediately a German MG-42 opened up with a long burst. We could see the line of white tracers going up and up and then crack across the road about twenty-five feet in front of where we had stopped. If we had kept going, that burst would have hit us and probably killed most of us.

Up to that point we had been a happy group, chattering like starlings. Now, as we started off, not a word was said until I called for a stop at the house where Crompton and I were staying. The next morning I thanked Fred for saving my life, and he just stared at me and replied, "What the hell are you talking about? I was there and nothing happened." Two days later when chatting with some Baker Company men, he was also thanked by one of them in the ration party for saving his life. Then it dawned on him about the beret and how that decision to stop had saved us.

"Bloody" Lamone

After our month-long rest, First Division was scheduled to be part of the advance on Ravenna and the drive for the Po River valley. We were told to cross the Montane River and then the Lamone River before capturing Bagnacavallo.

The plan for the First Brigade attack on the Lamone River was to get six of our Royal Canadian Regiment and Hasty P companies across the river by first light on 5 December. Six companies would have given us a strong position to fend off the inevitable German counterattacks. The Lamone is normally a small creek that a man can jump across easily in the dry season. At this time of year it was much wider because of the rain coming out of the mountains. Charlie Company of the Royal Canadian Regiment was to cross the river starting at about 0000 hrs, on our left, and they made it successfully, as far as we knew. It turned out that the platoon from the Royal Canadians assigned to take up a defensive position on our left flank didn't make it. As they went across the blown but not totally demolished railway bridge, they were fired upon; some men were hit and fell in the river. The ones who reached the German side had two choices: keep fighting and be killed, or surrender.

Major Ketheson pulled out a map and showed his batman a house on the right side of the road to Bagnacavallo (Horse's Bath), not far from the Lamone River that he would use as a Tactical Headquarters. All the civilians were to be cleared out, and the place secured for Battalion Headquarters' arrival. Several hours later our group moved down the road and met the batman, who informed Major Ketheson that the Italians refused to move. The major replied, "Too bad, we'll use it anyway. And by the way, private, you will be sentry until midnight for refusing to carry out my instructions."

Tactical Headquarters consisted that night of eight of us, including two signallers. We moved into this tiny house, not more than twelve feet square. It had one table half the size of an ordinary card table, one chair and a bed; that's all. In the bed was a very good-looking young woman. She lay there looking petrified and I imagine I would have been too if I were in her situation. I don't think she moved an inch during the whole night!

The Signals Officer and the Intelligence Officer each put a candle on the table for illumination. The two signallers sat in a corner on the mud floor, and the three officers sat on the side of the bed. No words were spoken in the dimly lit room, and it soon filled with the blue haze of cigarette smoke.

One of the radios buzzed, and a message was passed to the Signals Officer who put it in his log and swore, then gave it to Major Ketheson. He read it aloud: "Private Smith (not his real name) has been awarded the Military Medal effective 5 December." As you could expect, the room exploded with very uncomplimentary remarks about higher headquarters sending such a message when an offensive was about to begin. Incidentally, the next day First Brigade denied having sent such a message.

Sometime later, someone poked me as I had apparently fallen asleep in my spot on the floor and was snoring. Major Ketheson asked how much sleep I had had the night before, and I told him about an hour and a half. He said that things were going to be quiet for while and that I should go back and get some down time.

I walked back up the road about three hundred yards in a fatigued daze to a building where I had placed the kitchen. I didn't want to disturb the kitchen staff and the Italian family who were asleep, so I went into the front room and flopped down on the couch with my feet hanging over the end to keep the mud off. It wasn't a very secure place as it was in direct view of the Jerries, but I was so tired I didn't care. I needed some sleep!

Sometime later, the Sergeant Major of Charlie Company rudely awakened me. He was crying his eyes out over what had just happened to his men. I asked him to tell me, and he blurted out that all his boys had been killed by the terrible shellfire. I put my arm around his shoulders, and he laid his head on my shoulder and wept like a lost child. It took ten minutes for him to regain his composure. Here is what had happened:

At about 0330 hours, our Charlie Company was ordered to lead the way across the river. However, there was to be an artillery barrage preceding their advance. Normally the medium guns fired at targets closest to the infantry and the 25-pounders engaged targets further back. In this engagement the order was reversed, as they were to take out German positions on the north side of the Lamone. The Intelligence people told us that there was a preliminary dike about six feet high before they came to the thirty-foot dike on the banks of the Lamone. The Charlie Company Officer Commanding was new, a major who had arrived just a week before from First Brigade Headquarters' staff. There was a policy that in order to be eligible for promotion to commanding rank (lieutenant colonel), all senior officers had to have a least one-month in combat. This officer had been on the staff most of the war, so he was inexperienced.

Charlie Company was told to go up to the six-foot dike and wait for the artillery barrage that was to come down. The major discovered that the six-foot dike petered out on his front, and he told his men to go forward to the dike by the river. He was keen and wanted to be on the start line early, which is how commanders were taught; always be early, never late! Even though the barrage was supposed to be on the German side, the first few rounds landed on our side of the river. Charlie was already down to a two-platoon organization, and when the 25-pounders fired on the south side of the river, a number of his men were hit. Baker Company was also up at the dike helping put together the Olayson equipment for crossing the river. Major Cliff Broad, in charge of Baker, had half his men become casualties in a matter of a few minutes. Both companies had to be pulled back without getting across the river.[81]

I maintain that the reason they were hit by the opening rounds of the barrage was that the first round or two were a little short of the targeted objective, as well as the fact that the Officer Commanding had advanced the company several hundred yards beyond where they were thought to have stopped. The 25-pounder guns fire on a flatter trajectory than the medium guns, and the margin for error in this kind of close support operation is much smaller. One reason for our guns firing short is simple physics: the guns don't fire as accurately when the barrels are cold as when they are warm. The same principle applies to rifle shooting. They always used to give us two application rounds to allow the rifle to warm up and for the shooter to adjust accordingly. Normally there was a safety margin of several hundred yards for an artillery barrage, and this inexperienced officer, through his concern to be on the objective early and not late, moved his men into an exposed position.

Several hours later, Able and Don Companies moved over the river on the Olayson bridges. The better-known Bailey bridges were much larger and used for vehicular traffic; though prefabricated, they took many hours to assemble for a river crossing. The two companies moved to their right to secure the right edge of the axis of advance, which was a road that ran from Bagnacavallo to Russi. Baker Company then followed them over the river, taking a position a few hundred yards from the dikes on the north side of the Lamone. The river was about ten to twelve feet wide and the dikes were about thirty feet high and thirty feet wide with a sixty-degree slope.

Sometime about first light, the Germans launched a counterattack around the left flank of Baker Company, crossing under the railway bridge through two underground culverts. They attacked in battalion strength with infantry and Mark V tanks. Baker's Officer Commanding later told me that he heard a noise and turned around, only to see tanks and troops coming out of the culverts. This came as a total shock because the area was supposed to have been secured by the Royal Canadian Regiment platoon. The major found his company in imminent danger of being cut off from the other companies and the Lamone. He ordered his men to get out fast, not a tactical withdrawal but a sprint back to the Olayson bridges. This was a good decision as the men arrived at the bridges individually, so there was no bunching up and they were able to get across.

Word was soon communicated back to the Second-in-Command that they were under attack and they were withdrawing across the river. Major Ketheson came out to check as he couldn't believe it, and this was when he was hit by mortar fire. This prompted the other two officers in charge of Don and Able to order their men to head for the safety of the south side. Meanwhile the Germans were not idle but were firing on the troops as they departed. Men were hit, and fell all along the route back across the Lamone and as they crossed the dikes on both sides of the river.

Captain Porritt was in charge of Able Company, and as he was pulling out, one of his men was hit badly and cried out, "Don't leave me." Porritt assured him they would be back for him.[82] He got the rest of his men across the river and then grabbed two stretcher-bearers and headed back across to pick up the wounded soldier. By this time, the Germans had advanced and overrun the old position occupied by Able. There was a German soldier guarding the man, and when he saw the three Canadians, two with Red Cross brassards on, he waved them to pick their comrade up. Just then an officer came up and he demanded to see Porritt's papers, saying, "Papers, please" in German. The German officer had seen his rank badges and wanted to ascertain if he was either the Medical Officer or the Padre, both officers considered non-combatants under the Geneva Convention. Porritt indicated he had none, and despite a lengthy argument with the officer, he was taken prisoner.[83]

The Hasty P's Honour Roll indicates that they took fourteen killed in action on 5 December 1944. It was the costliest day of the War for the regiment, with more than eighty casualties.

Captain Oscar Christiansen was one of the casualties when the initial advance to the Lamone was made on the previous day. Christiansen, age thirty-six, was from Waterloo, Ontario, and his father was a Lutheran minister. He joined the Hasty P's as an inexperienced infantry officer in late October or early November. When someone told him that we had a former Sergeant Fox of The Queen's Own Rifles as Regimental Sergeant Major, he said that he trained in Canada with a Sergeant Fox of the QOR at the Horse Palace, Canadian National Exhibition, and then at Camp Borden. I was able to tell him that it was Eddie Fox, who had been seconded as an instructor early on in the war before joining us in the QOR. Eddie was a small-arms expert.

To make matters even more confusing, there were three others Foxes in the QOR. Gordie Fox became the Regimental Quartermaster Sergeant for the

2nd (Reserve) Battalion in Toronto. Another Fox served with Lieutenant Ken Kavanagh in Holland where Kavanagh was killed, and the third Fox became Regimental Sergeant Major of the 4th Battalion in 1945–1946. Both Eddie Fox and I had been non-commissioned officers in Charlie Company of The Queen's Own.

Captain Christiansen was fluent in German and started a class to teach German to the Hasty P's who were thinking about volunteering for the Army of Occupation after the war ended. I had decided I would volunteer, so I was one of Christiansen's students.

The Commanding Officer told him that his rank would normally entitle him to be placed as a company Second-in-Command but until we got to know him better, he would be a platoon commander. Captain Christiansen was, therefore, put in Able Company under Captain Max Porritt. Able Company had made the initial approach to the Lamone on 4 December.[84] Captain Porritt decided to go right up to the south dike on the banks of the river to have a look at the situation. He had been given only an hour for his orders and the forced march to the river. Christiansen asked to go along, and Porritt said, "No, it is too dangerous." He protested this decision and commented that he wouldn't learn to be an infantry officer if he didn't practise, or words to that effect. Porritt took him along but told Christiansen quite firmly, "When you put your head up, count to three and that is it, not one second longer." So they went up to do their recce, and Porritt barely got his head down when the Germans responded with small-arms fire. Christiansen took a look but kept his head up just a little too long. A German spotted him and shot him through the head. Porritt recalls seeing his beret fall on the ground and Christiansen rolling back down the south dike. Although we evacuated him to the Casualty Clearing Station, he died a few hours later.

The Lamone crossing was a debacle for The Hasty P's for a number of reasons: certainly, the casualties, but also the poor intelligence about those dikes, the failure of the Royal Canadian Regiment to secure the bridgehead on our left flank, and the inexperience of two of the three company commanders. Perhaps the most basic cause of our failure was the lack of proper recce and preparation for the attack. I think our new Brigade commander was out to make a name for himself, and kept pushing the battalions forward.

There was one interesting situation that arose among the soldiers hit by the artillery fire in Charlie Company. One of the men had his No. 77 phosphorus grenade explode. So the stretcher-bearer had to work fast, getting the man's webbing and battle-dress blouse off, fortunately he was not badly burned. When he arrived at the Regimental Aid Post, he asked about his blouse and was told not to worry about it, as he would be issued a new one when he was released from the hospital. The soldier's response was that he didn't care about the blouse but he did want the six hundred dollars in the pocket. This man was a noted gambler in the regiment and the money represented his recent winnings.

As soon as the word got out, this item of clothing became a hot item! It seemed everyone wanted to get up there to search for the money. I too went up some time later to look for it, and all I could find was the right sleeve, burned off from the blouse at the shoulder. While I was there I decided that the place looked pretty chaotic with all those rifles lying every which way. I started picking them up, ejecting the live rounds in the chambers onto the wet ground, as I knew it would soon sink out of sight. I put the rifles in a line, leaning the muzzles against the side of the dike.

As I was moving the last one into place, I saw two engineer officers walking along the bottom of the dike, probably looking for a bridge site, and they had their eyes on me, watching me fiddle with a rifle in the field. They never came any closer than thirty feet, and I didn't salute or speak to them. When they came to that line of rifles, I saw their heads dip down and then look up at me. I could tell from the look on their faces that they realized this was where the debacle had occurred. Each day that we were at the Lamone, I went up to the dike and brought four rifles back to the Quarterbloke. So the place was tidied up.

The Day I Hugged the Padre

I came up to the front lines the next day after we thought the Germans had withdrawn, and saw one hut in a dike with two bodies out front, the soldiers having been killed as they fled across the south side of the river. I went inside and found a lieutenant, two soldiers and Padre Goforth. The lieutenant refused to let the Padre use his two men to pick up bodies in broad daylight. Padre Goforth asked me to go out with him, and I said, "No, it isn't safe." He responded, "Mr. Fox, I thought you, of all men, would help me." We talked further, and the Padre finally persuaded me, (against my better judgment, mind you) to try while it was still light.

Each of us took a stretcher. I went over to one fellow and bent over to open up the stretcher, and "zing," a bullet flew over my head. That sniper could not have been more than fifty or sixty yards away, and I wonder to this day why he *chose not to kill me.* No trained sniper, and the Germans were excellent, would miss at that range. I dropped the stretcher like a hot potato and started running for the house as fast as I could. The Padre had also heard the shot and was running back. There were mud and cow-pies splashing with every step I took. I then realized we were running on a collision course, and just as I was about run into him, I raised my arms and we ran right into each other, holding on with arms around other. We fell to the ground in a heap. I call it, "the day I hugged the Padre." Later we would laugh about the incident, but not then; we were both too scared!

The Commanding Officer came up to investigate the situation a little while later and I told him that the sniper was shooting in our general direction. I estimated he was no more than sixty yards from us in some bushes across the river, and that he was just warning us that this sort of activity was not kosher. Lieutenant Colonel Cameron did not give me a reprimand, but he spoke rather harshly to the Padre for what Cameron considered Goforth's lack of judgment as well as for risking *two* valuable people in the battalion. I think the Commanding Officer was actually scared about losing Padre Goforth and me, hence his anger. The Padre was almost in tears; no one in the regiment had ever spoken to him like this before, and certainly not Lieutenant Colonel Cameron. To put this whole incident in perspective, the Commanding Officer had issued a standing order many months previous that *no one* was to pick up a corpse during daylight. A wounded man, however, was an entirely different matter.

Now you have to understand that the Padre was not an imprudent sort of man. The men loved Padre Fred. He came alongside them in the line and was able to laugh and share stories with them. The Padre had what it took as far as guts went too. No one in the regiment questioned this at all. He had been with the regiment for a year of combat and had nothing to prove. Padre Goforth had shown his courage during the fighting near Ortona in December 1943, when he stayed with the wounded for several hours in a forward position. Of all the personal qualities that soldiers admire, the greatest is courage. Fred Goforth was quite deservedly awarded the Military Cross for his bravery on that occasion. Perhaps he was suffering from too long in the combat zone, I'm not sure. There were some signs of that, I think, in his demeanour.

The term that is widely used now is "battle exhaustion" or simply, "combat stress." More attention is being given in the Canadian Forces to this subject of Critical Incident Stress and Post-Traumatic Stress Disorder, especially as some of our soldiers who returned from overseas deployments were severely traumatized by what they saw there.

It wasn't just combat soldiers and leaders who "burned out" with the stress of being in the front line, but also non-combatants.[85] The diligent chaplain who ministered faithfully to the men of his unit was also at risk. It was the work of dealing with the aftermath of combat that placed a great emotional strain on the Padre. Padre Goforth was a caring and sensitive man; a year in the combat zone had affected him adversely. One Padre who served in Italy and struggled with combat exhaustion wrote: "As long as I was not tired out, the shelling did not bother me; the brain analyzed the noise quickly enough for the nerves to be controlled. When I was tired, though, the process slowed down and I found myself wincing before [my] rational faculty took control."[86]

Rooms for One Hundred, Please

It was the night after the attempted bridgehead over the Lamone had been repulsed. Lieutenant Colonel Cameron put Tactical Headquarters in a church, and I was standing in front with the sentry, none other than my friend, Corporal Fred Crompton. It was a bad night, cold, with rain and some wind, not a fit night for man or sentry. We heard a vehicle coming, and both of us moved up the road to stop it. Whoever it was, he had no business coming up that road. We waved and shouted at the driver, but he was going probably twenty-five miles an hour. We ran after the truck, yelling and waving, and the men in the back of the truck banged on the truck's tarpaulin to get the driver's attention. The truck finally stopped, and as I ran up to the driver, he did not seem very pleased and asked rather belligerently why I had stopped him? I became equally unpleasant and asked him if he could see that hill ahead. It was the Lamone dike, just visible in the rain. He said, "Yeah, so what?" I replied that that hill was "in Germany," and if he could swim and speak German, he could keep on driving.

It was a narrow road with deep ditches on either side, so the driver had to back the sixty-hundredweight truck up nearly two hundred yards before we got him turned around. I have often wondered about those troops in the back: they did not ask where they were or the name of the nearest town, the tactical situation, or anything. All they did was swear and mutter!

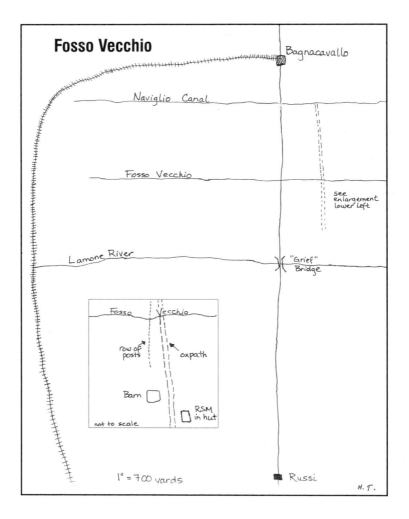

Fosso Vecchio

Bagnacavallo

Naviglio Canal

Fosso Vecchio

see enlargement lower left

Lamone River

"Grief" Bridge

Fosso Vecchio

row of posts

oxpath

Barn

RSM in hut

not to scale

1" = 700 yards

Russi

H. T.

One day following the war, I was back at Eaton's department store in Toronto and I got talking to another fellow, named Wally, who had also served in the Army in Italy. I mentioned this incident, and as soon as I said the driver's name, Wally let out a string of expletives. It seems that on one occasion, Wally, who was a military policeman, was guarding a bridge when this guy drove by him and actually fired shots at Wally from his Tommy gun. The driver was a bad egg, no doubt about it.

As I left Tactical Headquarters I gave strict orders to the sentries that absolutely no vehicle was to be allowed to pass. The regimental policemen seemed tickled to be able to tell very senior ranks to "buzz off." I went back to my bed and had only been there a few minutes when a signaller handed me a message. Just five words: "Roger, Sugar, Mike, Report Sunray." This meant Regimental Sergeant Major report to the Commanding Officer. I headed over to the headquarters and found the Commanding Officer and saluted. He then asked me if we had any available billets for some visiting officers. I did know the status of accommodations, so I took the officer and his eighteen men in two trucks to Franggipangi Street in Traversera, the nearby town, which had about one hundred empty houses. That night, each time I was just getting nicely settled in bed, another call would come from the Commanding Officer. Four more times I hustled off to town to find billets for our guests. Oddly, two nights previous to this I could not find houses for our own men; we could not go into this town because it was out of our designated battalion area.

The next morning during stand-to, the Commanding Officer asked me where I had put everyone, and when I told him that I had put them on the other side of the road in Third Brigade's sector, he grinned and said, "Good. I certainly did not want them cluttering up my regimental area." It was a nice feeling to know that I had pleased the Commanding Officer and also the one hundred men who had a roof over their heads for that wet night.

The next day the engineers came up with a prefabricated Bailey bridge as a replacement for the bridge on the Bagnacavallo road. The bridge was about one hundred feet long and mounted on the top of two tanks. In order to maintain impetus, if the first tank stalled, there was a second tank immediately behind, pushing the first. The first tank driver came up and when he saw the sixty-degree angle of the dike down to the Lamone, he knew he was going to get stuck and so he stopped. That Bailey bridge sat there for about a week until the engineers devised a way to get it across the river. It was eventually called "Grief Bridge" because of all the trouble the engineers had in putting it up.

Fosso Vecchio and The Naviglio

The next obstacle beyond the Lamone River, but before the Senio River, was a ditch called the Fosso Vecchio. In this part of Italy, drainage ditches had been dug to help with rain runoff. The ditches were called *"scuolas."* The Fosso Vecchio was about twelve feet wide at the top, six feet wide at the bottom, and about ten feet deep, built in the form of a flat-bottomed V. The ditches would run across the countryside for about a thousand yards and then suddenly peter out. The Germans had dammed them over on our left and created a huge swamp. The water around here was knee deep, and was it bloody cold! This was December, and "sunny" Italy was as cold a place as you would like to find anywhere. One of our corporals had figured out how to improvise a bridge across the Fosso. However, when I came out of the barn to see how he and his men were doing, I noticed the fifteen-hundredweight truck roaring up the road about three quarters of a mile away. I was furious, thinking they had just abandoned me there all alone. I wanted to catch their attention but how could I do that? They were too far away and anyway they couldn't hear in that big truck. So I grabbed a box of No. 36 grenades in one hand and .303 ammo with the other and started walking up that road, even though I had no map and didn't know where the regiment was located. It turned out that the corporal learned they were being watched from a German artillery observation post in a church spire in the next town. They decided that discretion was the better part of valour, and they left in a hurry.

We were temporarily placed in reserve with the Third Brigade, who were attacking to the east. As if the bloody debacle at Lamone wasn't enough, the higher-ups ordered us to continue on the offensive, across the Vecchio and Naviglio River, from 11 to 13 December 1944. We lost some fine men during these attacks; most notably Sergeant Marcel van Hende, DCM, whom I mentioned earlier, was killed by shrapnel from a mortar shell. Captain Don Weese of Peterborough was killed on 12 December. Weese had been in charge of the Mortar Platoon and had served with the regiment since Ortona. He later moved up to Able Company as Second-in-Command. He went into a building to talk to the Commanding Officer, and a shell hit the roof at the same time; a fragment came down and hit him, killing him instantly.

After the second fight for the Lamone River crossing on 11 December, the Royal Canadian Regiment moved up to our positions and were walking along the top of the dike. I was walking right beside them, when the Germans fired at us and the man walking right beside me was hit and went down, yelling "Stretcher-bearer." I know it sounds terrible, but my first thought was, "Tough on him but good on me. If he had not stopped that slug, I would have."

Later that same day I was carrying two boxes of ammo when I heard a familiar whistling noise, and I hit the dirt. Four mortar bombs exploded all around me; the furthest was ten feet, and the closest, four feet. Fortunately they landed beside the road in the soft mud of the Italian farmland, and most of the impact was cushioned. If the ground had been harder that would have been my "ticket" out of this world. All I got was a headache and a little nick in my left ear lobe. After all these years I can still feel a little gouge there.

A Stroll Down An Italian Lane

About a week after the regiment's abortive attack at "Bloody Lamone," the 48th Highlanders made a successful attack. We were sent through their bridgehead and were to advance down a road parallel to the Lamone. The road had previously been reported as blocked by fallen trees. I decided to do a personal recce and discovered that the road was indeed blocked. It did not seem to have been the result of German demolition but of aerial bombing.

There was a row of trees on either side of the road but beyond the obstacle there were none down. I met with Sergeant Browne of the Anti-tank platoon, and we hiked along the road for several miles. He was concerned about how to support the advance as he could not get his guns across the river. After a few miles we came to the town of Traversera and turned right. The street was about thirty feet wide; on one side was the Lamone dike and on the other were houses. An old woman came out and asked Browne if he was *Tedeschi* to which he responded, *"Canadesi."* The woman started to screech *"Canadesi"* and threw her arms around him and tried to kiss him. I had to laugh at this situation as she was trying to kiss him and he was trying to shove the smelly old woman away from him without hurting her. At the third screech, a group of about two dozen young men, some carrying rifles, came out of the houses, and formed a column of threes and marched off down the street, singing loudly.

The way the newspapers at home reported it, when a town in Europe was "liberated," the troops were given baskets of fruit, bottles of wine, and other gifts. More than sixty years have gone by, and I've yet to get a single bottle for any Italian town that we liberated.

Browne and I then went back to the regiment, and I told the Commanding Officer about the road being blocked. He sent a platoon out with me to clear it up. When we got there, I told the men how I thought they could get the job done. They took their rifles and smashed small branches off the trees. Then they grabbed a hold of each trunk and, with a major effort, flung it into the ditch. The lieutenant asked if I would report back to the Commanding

Officer that the job had been done and I said, "No," his platoon had been tasked so he should report back.

I went to the Regimental Aid Post as all our wounded were still there. It was considered safer to keep them there at the Aid Post until a vehicle could come to evacuate them; otherwise, we would have needed more than one hundred men to carry them across muddy fields to the Casualty Clearing Station. The staff had a roaring fire going when I arrived, and I stretched out to warm up. The warmth and my fatigue got the best of me, and I fell asleep. Some time later, I felt cold and woke up. The fire was just embers winking at me in the dark, and I was completely alone. An ambulance had arrived and the wounded had all been picked up. The Medical Officer told them to leave me alone, as I must be weary indeed, to have flaked out like that.

We were pulled back to the town of Cattolica on 23 December for forty-eight hours rest, just in time for Christmas. For many of the men it was their fifth Christmas away from home, and there was little Christmas cheer or merriment. The only solace was that they would be alive for another two days.

RSM Fox with German prisoners taken during the Gothic Line fighting in northern Italy, September 1944.

German prisoners acting as stretcher-bearers for Canadian wounded, June 1944.

Dykes along the Lamone River in northern Italy. The Hast & PER fought here on December 5, 1944.

Horace Hall, a good friend of Harry's, at Amersfort, Holland, July 1945.

LCol George Rennison, DSO, CD, MiD. He was later made Honorary Colonel. (Hast & PER)

CHAPTER 8

Winter on the Senio River

A Crisis of Manpower and Morale

At the end of December 1944 we moved north from a rear area into a static position on the Senio River, which we occupied until late February 1945. Replacements came in but they were not up to the standard needed for combat. Many had never fired a Bren gun or shot the Projector Infantry, Anti-Tank (PIAT) weapon. Some were volunteers from the reserve battalions in Canada, and some were soldiers dragooned from other trades, like the artillery and the service corps, who had barely fired a rifle.

In any event, with the number of virtually untrained troops in our battalions, it was a good thing that there was no prospect of an attack in the near future. Any weakness in leadership or in the training and fitness of our soldiers showed immediately on the offensive.

There was a story going around that some soldiers had apparently told Mr. Ralston, the Minister of National Defence, who had visited Europe in the fall of 1944, that many infantry replacements had never thrown a grenade. Mr. Ralston didn't believe this story and asked them to look into it. They gave him a report that showed ninety-seven soldiers in a single battalion had never thrown one grenade in training. This story came from the 48th Highlanders during the winter of 1944–1945, and I tend to believe it is true.

We heard eventually about the news of the German attack in the Ardennes in late December and the major fight of the U.S. troops. The American 101st

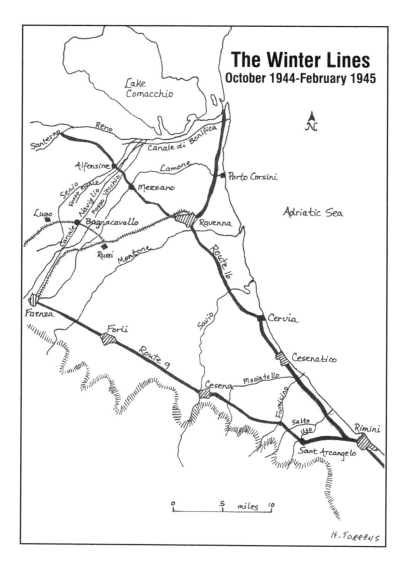

The Winter Lines
October 1944-February 1945

Lake Comacchio

Santerno

Reno

Canale di Bonifica

Alfonsine

Lamone

Porto Corsini

Mezzano

Adriatic Sea

Senio

Canale

Fosso Vetale

Navig lio

Fosso Vecchio

Lugo

Bagnacavallo

Ravenna

Russi

Montone

Route 16

Faenza

Forli

Savio

Cervia

Route 9

Cesenatico

Cesena

Pisciatello

Fiumicino

Salto

Uso

Rimini

Sant Arcangelo

0   5   miles   10

H. TORRENS

Airborne made the headlines because of their stand at Bastogne. They were called "The Battered Bastards of the Bastion of Bastogne." It's too bad that the 10th Armoured and the 82nd Airborne Divisions got so little credit, as they fought well under the same harsh conditions as the 101st.

I think *this* was one of the most trying times for us in the regiment. We were numerically weak, fewer than three hundred, with most of the companies being platoon size, having only thirty or thirty-five men. Morale was at an all-time low as many of us were physically and spiritually spent, having lost any hope of ever getting home. Many of our friends and leaders had been killed in the fall offensives. Losing men is always hard, but when a unit has been in the front-line so long, the loss of fine leaders such as Sergeant van Hende really hurts.

Wire Along the Senio

I was called into the Commanding Officer's office one morning, and he asked me how much barbed wire we had in stores. I replied, "None." When the regiment first landed in Sicily, every truck had a roll of Dennaert wire fastened to its front. Over the last year it had gone rusty and made the newly painted trucks look sloppy. It was potentially hazardous, too, so the practice was stopped.

It seemed that Baker Company wanted to strengthen its defensive position and they had requested wire. The Commanding Officer and I discussed the situation and came to the conclusion that Dennaert wire would be better than ordinary wire. One advantage was that Dennaert took fewer posts and pickets to string it up, and this would mean less noise and confusion. I went back to the engineers' supply dump and picked up fifty coils of wire and had the ammunition truck take it as far forward as was safe in daylight. I left the driver and Freddie Compton, the Provost Corporal, there with the wire. The truck was behind a house, out of sight. There was also an artillery observation post at that location with a sergeant and two gunners.

Shortly after dark, Crompton came running up to me and blurted out that the driver had got into the vino and was threatening to shoot *me*, the Regimental Sergeant Major. We dashed back to the house, and Freddie quickly opened the door as I rushed inside. There was the driver with a rifle in his hands. Before he could raise it to shoot me, I grabbed it out of his hands, knocked him down and told him to get the hell out of my sight, as I didn't want to ever see him again. The driver scuttled out as I unloaded the Lee-Enfield and then tossed it in the corner. I was fighting mad by that point and gave both the driver and Crompton a good dressing-down. Then I told Crompton to get in the truck and drive it up to Baker Company. He protested that he had never driven a thirty-hundredweight truck; I told him that after tonight he would never be in a position to say that again.

So we got in the truck, crossed a field, and drove along a dike and then down a lane onto the main road, which paralleled the Senio River. We passed a burned-out Canadian truck, belonging to the Princess Patricia's Canadian Light Infantry. We unloaded the fifty coils of wire onto the shoulder of the road, each one about six inches apart. Freddie had heavy leather gauntlets as he was a bike rider, but all I had were thin woollen gloves from a Red Cross package. The coils of wire had spikes sticking out every which way and, though not heavy, they were awkward to handle. By the time the job was done, my hands were a bloody mess.

I reported to Major Cliff Broad, the Officer Commanding Baker Company, that the job was completed, and then went back to Tactical Headquarters. Basil Smith, the Quarterbloke, God bless him, had been waiting up for us. He took one look at us and grabbed a jug of rum and poured two healthy tots. I apologized to Freddie for the way I had spoken to him earlier. He just grinned and said, "Well, under the circumstances, I don't blame you." So I went off to sleep and slept the sleep of an honest man.

The Brigadier's Car

The First Brigade's commander drove a small armoured car, and when he got a new one, he gave his old car to Lieutenant Colonel Cameron, our Commanding Officer. He would use it a few times and then give it to the Company Quartermaster Sergeant of the Headquarters Company. I used the wretched little thing only once. It was tiny, having room for less than two persons; the "commander" of the vehicle had to stand up, half in the vehicle and half out. There was a space behind him of about four feet long and perhaps fifteen inches high and wide. It was extremely impractical, far too small to take any kind of a load. If you put a metal box in it, the scraping sound of metal on metal could be heard for a long distance.

One night I delivered two boxes of two-inch mortar bombs to one of the rifle companies. They thanked me for the delivery and then told me in no uncertain terms to "get the hell out of Dodge, *schnell.*" It was a mean and miserable Italian winter's night; upon reflection, I think that the winter of 1944–1945 was worse than that of 1943–1944, but perhaps this is a subjective observation as I was thoroughly weary of the war. The driver seemed to have trouble keeping the little car on the road, complaining that he couldn't see. I was a bit short-tempered with him and told him that his job was to drive and mine was to observe, so, "Carry on."

As you can perhaps guess, very soon we were stuck, with two wheels in the ditch. The only thing that kept the car from turning over was a telephone pole it had come to rest against. I left the driver there with the vehicle because it was amazing how soon tires and other things disappeared from abandoned vehicles. I walked back about eight hundred yards to Advance Echelon, got a driver out of bed and went back for the car and driver with a fifteen-hundred-weight truck.

Unfortunately, that's when our real trouble began. All vehicles were supposed to have a towing cable permanently attached to the front end. The armoured car had none, and we were forced to use the cable from the truck. It had not been used since Sicily, and we had a deuce of a time getting the kinks out of it. The night was pitch black. The wind and rain came swooshing down on us as we stood hip deep in water in the ditch. It was difficult to get any solid hold for the cable on that little scout car. What a job! I never wanted to tackle a job like that ever again. We knew we only had one chance; if the first attempt failed, the car would turn over and the driver would get some very nasty bruises, perhaps even broken bones. He was naturally reluctant to get in. After some very unpleasant remarks from the truck driver and my solemn promise to bend my Tommy gun over his head, the driver finally got inside. Fortunately both drivers hit the gas at the same time and the car started moving out of the ditch, although the fifteen-hundredweight nearly went into the ditch on the other side in the process. We then unhooked the cable and wound it up again. The truck had to back down the road to Tactical Headquarters, and fortunately the road was straight. The driver had to lean out of the truck window to see how he was doing. We finally made it back to headquarters totally exhausted and exasperated.

If anyone had asked me right at that moment how I felt about this little car of the Brigadier's, I would have said, "Set it on fire preferably with the driver inside." But being a non-smoker I carried no matches and couldn't realize this desire. Besides, it would have been the wrong thing to do and would set a very bad example as the Regimental Sergeant Major. I wrung as much water as I could out of my uniform, wiped myself off with a towel and got into bed to shiver myself to sleep. In reflecting on this little incident in later years, I think that on that one dirty night in Italy, I used more bad language than I did during the rest of my Army days put together.

Who's Winning This War, Anyway?

Two orders had come from on high, meaning General Headquarters. In one, the Army Commander said he did not want his men fighting both the Germans and Mother Nature, so the Army would go into winter quarters. There would be no more offensive or forward movement, but intense patrolling would be carried out. What this meant in effect was that the Hasty P's and all the other infantry battalions would still be working.

The second order was more detailed and specified how much ammunition could be expended. The regimental mortar crews could not fire more than five bombs each, and even then they were not to fire unless under direct counterattack and on the express order of the Brigadier. The field regiments (25-pounders) had the same orders, five rounds per gun per day but only on orders from the General Officer Commanding. The medium regiments had the same orders except that their direction came from the General Officer Commanding, Royal Artillery. So the war in Italy had come to a complete halt except for the "intensive patrolling," which meant no rest at all for us in the infantry who grumbled bravely on.

The Plough Jockeys were getting pretty weary of this war and we wondered how life could be made a little easier on the patrolling side. If the guns were not allowed to fire in support, perhaps the tanks could be used as fire support. The question then arose, is the tank an artillery weapon, to which the Tank Corps said, "Absolutely not." In their view, they had basically won the war in the desert of North Africa and so were vital for reconnaissance. We proposed sending a tank up to one of the forward companies and use it to shell a known German position, about a mile and a half away.

This novel concept was sent up the chain of command and it was approved with the caveat that if it failed, we would be to blame!

A tank was loaned to us one January night with the purpose of shelling a group of buildings we knew the Jerries were using. The tankers were happy because they did not like to see their tanks simply rusting away in the fields. Don Company Headquarters was chosen as the firing position because the yard in front of their house was nicely gravelled, unlike most of the others, which were puddles. A January puddle in Italy means a black, gooey, smelly mess that is seventy percent mud and thirty percent cow dung. After all, what else can you expect from a barnyard?

Our Commanding Officer, Lieutenant Colonel Cameron personally supervised the operation, as it was his idea in the first place. I went with him as his escort, bodyguard and message boy. We passed the tank on the road and were surprised at how quiet it was; only a faint sound of gravel crunching could be heard on the ox-cart path. The tank was barely moving, probably one mile per hour. We got to Don Company's Headquarters and the tank pulled in after us. The commander leaned out and politely asked us to move to the other side of the tank as he knew we would not want a red-hot shell casing down the back of our necks. So we moved to the left of the tank, and stood in line with the turret, about ten feet away.

The Don Company commander, Major McDonald stood in the door of the house about seventy-five feet away, directly in front of the tank but far enough away to avoid the muzzle blast. By this time it was first light and we could see the German position with our field glasses. In a few minutes the tank commander indicated they were ready, the Commanding Officer nodded and they commenced firing. It seemed almost immediately that the Germans returned our fire, and a shell landed slightly in front of the tank on the right-hand side. Apparently they had our position zeroed for one of their guns. We heard the splinter of gravel as shrapnel rattled against the side of the tank. The tank commander's warning had saved our lives, as we had been right where that round landed.

There was a yell from the house, and a voice cried out that the major had been hit. The Commanding Officer instantly ordered the tank to cease fire, and the two of us went into the house to see how Major McDonald was doing. Two men were standing over him with candles lit, and we could see that his wound was fatal. Military protocol dictated that the senior rank on the ground call the Regimental Aid Post, so Lieutenant Colonel Cameron got on the radio and told them to come and pick up Major McDonald.

We went back to the tank and told its commander that the operation was over, and to go home. No words were exchanged as the Commanding Officer and I walked back to Tactical Headquarters, but I knew that the Colonel was already worrying about his next decision, whom to appoint as the new Don Company commander. During the last six weeks, including this night's fiasco, we had three company commanders taken prisoner, two killed and one badly wounded. Who was winning this war, anyway? At that point, I wasn't too sure that we were!

Who Fired on Whom?

We in Italy were desperately short of ammunition by this time. In the larger picture, various offensive operations across the Rhine (Op Blockbuster for the Canadians) were using larger quantities of ammunition than had been forecasted.

The only weapon the higher-ups did not bother to restrict was the two-inch mortar. It's not clear whether this was simply an oversight or if they thought we used them on patrol. In any case, we decided to let sleeping dogs lie. Occasionally we would throw a mortar shell or two over the Senio, just to let the Germans know we were still on the job.

It was February 1945 and the mud would freeze in the middle of the night and occasionally crust over, so that it could be walked on. During the day it would become milder and we would have mud again. One day two men in Able Company were wounded by mortar fire. The platoon commander came on the radio and insisted that a bomb launched from our own Don Company had done the damage. This lieutenant was rather eccentric, to say the least, so the story was taken with a grain of salt.

Nevertheless it could not simply be ignored, so I was sent off to Don Company to find out their version of events. I did not go to the Company Headquarters or even the platoons, but went directly to the soldiers in the mortar section. My line of reasoning was that the men would tell me what really happened, even if they were responsible. I soon found the mortar section and explained my mission. The sergeant in charge exploded in anger and began to swear, threatening to punch those out who claimed that they fired that bomb. Finally he looked at me and exclaimed, "I'll show you," and took me over to the mortar emplacement. There I found the mortar jammed into a position with tree branches and hard-packed earth. It was obvious that this set-up had been there for some time and not recently built.

The sergeant grabbed two bombs and proceeded to fire them off in quick succession. I watched the rounds sail high over the Senio and land among the German lines. Having satisfied myself that Don Company was not responsible for the Able Company casualties, I reported back to the Commanding Officer, who thanked me for the report.

A few days later that same lieutenant who had made the unjustified accusation quietly disappeared; he was transferred out of the regiment. We never heard from him again, much to the relief of his Platoon Sergeant, Neil Hoxie.

Harry as Padre

As I mentioned earlier, since I joined the Hasty P's I took on the job of burials to help out the Padre. On one occasion I was assisting Padre Goforth because there were some Plough Jockeys to bury. The graves were dug and the bodies placed in. The Padre was on one knee, conducting the service. Just then, artillery came in, and all those men in the burial party dove into the graves for cover. Padre Fred Goforth remained in his position, trying to finish the words of committal, and was hit in the back with a piece of shrapnel. I think I too may have been hit slightly in that shelling. About 1992 I pulled a small piece of metal out of my head that I never knew was there. The Padre refused to be evacuated until a few days later. His wound wasn't serious but it created a unique situation.

Padre Goforth's evacuation meant that I became the acting but unofficial Padre of the Hasty P's for about ten days. During this time there were a few more casualties. One day I had four soldiers to be buried, and one of them had been a Roman Catholic. However, the only Catholic Padre was at First Brigade Headquarters. One of the Sergeant Majors, who happened to be Catholic, came around a few days later and, seeing the body still half buried, said to me, "A man can't go to heaven without the last rites." So he sent off for the Catholic Padre who came up and performed the burial ceremony.

One other task that I had to perform while acting Padre was to write letters to all the families of the dead soldiers. This was one aspect of a chaplain's work that was very difficult and often unappreciated by the men. Padre Goforth was quite diligent about this task. He tried to find out something about each soldier to make the letter more personal. This was a very commendable thing on his part. Normally the letters followed the same format, saying that the man died a hero and that he didn't suffer. Even if he had been the worst soldier in the battalion, we would never put anything in writing that reflected poorly on him. We didn't want to cause any more pain and anguish to those who received the letters. Sometimes wives or mothers would write back asking how the soldier died. Even if we knew, and in many cases we didn't, we would only speak in general terms. In some situations, the men had suffered greatly, and we wouldn't share that with their loved ones.

Burgers on the Senio

It was early February, and the regiment had moved into an area north of Ravenna not far from the town of Mezzano, which had been the scene of an abortive German attack just days before our arrival, I was doing my usual routine, wandering about being nosey, when I heard a mooing sound coming from a barn. I went in and found five large bullocks, beautiful beasts, about as tall at the shoulder as I am (six feet). They had pink eyes and otherwise were all white except for their hooves, horns and tips of their tails, which were black. The horns were about three feet across, curved, with a sharp tip. If you met one of these fearsome beasts on a narrow trail, you would step to one side, take off your hat and say, "After you, Tommassio."

These oxen were standing about a trough, mooing, so I surmised that they were hungry and thirsty. There was a wheel contraption and by playing around with it, I finally got water to come up from the well. So I started wheeling and watering. It was amazing how much those animals slopped up. I was thoroughly weary by the time they were satisfied. I threw them a few forkfuls of hay and went on my way, having done my Boy Scout deed for the day. I certainly had no intention of making this a part of my daily routine in the town, but we had to find a way to prevent these fine beasts from starving to death.

There is a myth in the Army that Regimental Sergeant Majors know everything. The men were always asking me questions, and I guess this was their way of trying to disprove the myth. For example, there were some hens near the location of the kitchen, and I was asked what type of chickens they were. I told them "Guinea hens," not that I knew but I had to keep the myth alive. So I made up a name. Not many of the men had ever heard of such a breed but they seemed satisfied. One unusual characteristic of these hens was that they could fly six or eight feet off the ground for about a hundred yards. They would fly off and land on top of a building and scowl down on us. They were definitely not your Canadian type of barnyard fowl! In terms of appearance, they seemed to me to be a cross between a sick turkey and a dying vulture. They were very ugly! When we left that area about two weeks later, they were still flapping and squawking; no respectable Canadian soldier would stoop so low as to grab one and put it in a pot.

This next story concerns the hens and my provost squad. The regimental police detachment was made up of a sergeant, a corporal and two lance corporals. They did not have webbing and ammunition pouches like the other riflemen, just a waist belt, a cross-strap and a pistol holster. These items along with the anklets were bleached white. One of the lance corporals had scrubbed his belt and whitened it and then hung it on a post behind the kitchen to dry. Basil Smith, the Quarterbloke and I, were inside the building sitting at a table. I'm not sure what I was doing, but Basil was writing away, perhaps a letter to his wife, more likely some entry in his journal. The kitchen staff had just brewed up mugs of tea for us and all seemed calm and peaceful.

Suddenly breaking the calm came the roar of a Tommy gun outside. What a flap that caused! Tea mugs went flying as the men dove for their bedrolls and their weapons. Basil and I jumped up, knocking over the chairs. My Tommy gun and webbing were on the back of my chair and as I picked them up, I stumbled over the chair nearly losing my balance. I managed to be the first one out of the house, not because I was the bravest but simply because I was closest to the door!

The first thing I saw was the sentry at Tactical Headquarters, which was diagonally across the street about seventy-five yards away. He was standing with his rifle in the firing position, and it was pointed right at me. I didn't stop, however, as I figured that even if he did fire, he would miss, and so I kept on running to the back of the house. When I got there I found one of my lance corporals, a big friendly fellow, usually described in Army fashion, as a man who would not say the word s__ even if his mouth was full of it. On this occasion, he was saying plenty and loudly too. He was stamping his feet in a petulant rage and was crying because he was so angry. He was trying to shove another magazine into his Tommy gun, but he had the magazine backwards, or upside down, because it would not go in. This only made him curse the harder.

I ripped the gun from him and asked him, "What the bloody blue hell do you think you are doing?" He muttered and spluttered and finally explained that he had come out to see if his belts were dry and this Guinea hen had jumped on them, found them inedible and had pooped all over them. The evidence was right in front of me as I could see nasty black streaks still dribbling down his white equipment.

The kitchen gang had arrived by this time, and it looked like an old time necktie party. Handing the gun over to Basil Smith, I said, "You look after things here, while I go to Tactical Headquarters and straighten things out." The sentry had come to the "On Guard" position, and when I got to him, he snapped to attention. I congratulated him on the speed with which he was ready to defend the headquarters. He then thanked me for the compliment and asked what the entire ruckus was about. I replied that one of my regimental policemen had temporarily gone bonkers. The sentry replied that in his opinion, regimental policemen were always bonkers. I didn't stop to debate that point but went inside to face the music.

Gathered in the room were the Commanding Officer, the Second-in-Command, a major from one of the rifle companies, who had probably come back for a mug of tea, as well as the Signals Officer and the Intelligence Officer. All of them were scowling at me, and so I launched into a song and dance about this episode. Before the Commanding Officer had a chance to reply, I asked if he wanted me to place the man on charge in the usual manner, or whether I could handle it in my own way. He looked at me, rather surprised, and then said, "Very well, RSM, do it your way, and if I'm not satisfied, I will put you both on a charge." "Yes, sir," I said and went out. As I walked back to the kitchen I was mentally kicking myself for opening my mouth and putting my big boot in it. Why didn't I just ride with the tide and not make waves? I was thoroughly vexed. I should have just let the Commanding Officer make his decision.

Everyone who was not on duty had crowded into the kitchen, each telling each other or inquiring about what had happened. When I stamped in, they all stood up. Then I sat down, and the lance corporal was brought to stand in front of me. I said, "Corporal, you have a choice. You can go up in front of the Commanding Officer and you know what will happen then: he will bust you to private, probably send you to a rifle company, and you will probably get killed next week. Or you can take my punishment." He replied, "I'll take yours, sir."

"Here is your punishment. You will go over to that cow byre and take care of those bullocks. Clean the place up, too. You will only be allowed to come outside to get your meals, but you must eat them inside the byre. Is that clear?" "Yes, sir." I turned to the Provost Sergeant and said, "See to it."

Very quickly the news of the Regimental Sergeant Major's *cruel and unusual punishment* reached all the corners of the regiment. It was new and different and broke the monotony, so everyone had something to gossip about. Even the Postal Sergeant, who had been with the Newfoundland Regiment in the First World War, and who lived in the furthest rear echelon, was asking questions. In the next few days men who had no business in the headquarters area would come along, open the door to the byre, and yell, "Hi, cowboy. What's the price of beef today in Calgary?" Then they would slam the door and run before something could be thrown at them. It was great stuff for the morale of the regiment.

Now, that lance corporal worked hard, but it was a stable after all, and he couldn't get it clean enough to eat off the floor but he nearly did. I went in one day and saw him down on his hands and knees and yelled at him. He turned with a funny grin on his face and said that the animals smelled so he was giving them a bath. If you can believe it, that animal had a smile on its face with its eyes half shut, chewing the cud and enjoying life. All four of the beasts seemed to be enjoying things with lots of water and food, a pleasant man to talk to them, and a little fire to keep them warm. What more could they ask for? They were on Easy Street and they knew it.

Did I say that there were *five* bullocks when we first arrived in town? Yes, there were, but we shot one and ate it. A pleasant change from the awful British rations, though the beef was a bit tough. The bullock saga was not over yet, though. One day our Provost Sergeant, Art Miller, came to me and said that there was an Italian down the street making noises about the bullocks. I said: "Holy Joe, the last thing I need is an argument with some civilian over an animal. I haven't got the time or patience to get into it. You go back and deal with him."

In a few days the lance corporal was back on duty, all neat and shiny, and the oxen were gone. Now it was very strange; those oxen simply disappeared one night, and no one seemed to know what happened. If large animals like these could be taken from a tightly controlled area such as Tactical Headquarters, perhaps other things would go missing too? Our British comrades on the left were the King's Own Yorkshire Light Infantry, and they had an expression for situations like this: "Eee, it's a rum go, lad."

The Italian civilian who had been complaining got his bullocks, and my cut of the deal was five thousand lire. This sounds like a lot of money but it was about fifty dollars. That was about twelve days' pay for me, so I was happy.

A Big Wheel Rolls Around

My routine was to visit the Regimental Aid Post every day. One day as I came into the room, I noticed that the staff all looked like they were going to be hung on the nearest tree in ten minutes' time. So, naturally I asked what was wrong and was informed that there was a bit of a kerfuffle at higher medical headquarters. It seemed that a casualty from our Regimental Aid Post with undressed wounds had arrived at the Casualty Clearing Station. In the medical world, this was about as serious a situation as you could imagine. It shouted incompetence and carelessness and could not be ignored. The staff was afraid that the Medical Officer was going to get the sack, as the Assistant Director of Medical Services was slated for a visit. He was a full colonel and carried a lot of clout.

I piped up that I had been expecting this all along. What an outcry resulted from that remark! The sergeant yelled, "What do you think we are, a bunch of murderers?" If there had not been a table between us, I'm sure he would have punched me. The other men's faces were distorted with anger, and they were literally snarling at me. I had quite a job to cool them down as I tried to explain what I meant by that statement.

The Aid Post staff was unaware of the situation that I was referring to, as they had deployed at night. The path back to the Casualty Clearing Station passed over a dike, about five feet above the ground. The Germans had a mortar covering that exposed section and regularly shelled our vehicles moving along it. There was absolutely no cover for a hundred yards, and twice in the last week the mortar bombs had chased me off as I had walked along the dike. Only the day before, a burst had killed a cow and her calf. I continued with my explanation: the ambulance driver would know he was under fire and would likely conclude that some were near misses. However, he could not know where the shrapnel went, and it was very possible that some had hit the man on the stretcher in the jeep. As this bit of intelligence sunk in, they visibly calmed down, and they agreed that this was certainly a possible explanation for why the man had had untreated wounds upon arrival at the Station. Sergeant Knight went to talk to the Medical Officer as he thought this information would be important for the pending investigation.

I was leaving the Aid Post as the medical big wig arrived. I gave him a smart salute and kept on moving. I thought it was just as well that I not speak to the colonel, as the expression on his face would have turned milk into vinegar. He was in the Aid Post a long time, finally emerged and drove his vehicle over the dike. As he neared the two dead cattle, he stopped the vehicle, stood up and looked around. I think he was counting the number of bomb craters near the road. There were quite a few, and all were filled with water. Apparently satisfied with what he saw, he drove off.

Several days later a letter came to the regiment with regard to the wounded soldier. It said that the matter had been thoroughly investigated by the

Assistant Director of Medical Services, and there was no sign of negligence. On the contrary, the regiment was fortunate to have such a fine and competent group of medical personnel.

Some time later, a message came through from General Headquarters stating that Dr. Max Lerner, the Medical Officer, had been awarded the Military Cross for his actions at the Naviglio, where he established the Regimental Aid Post just two hundred yards from the front line in order to better care for the wounded. Captain Lerner had consistently maintained the closest Aid Post to the front line in the whole First Division. Everyone in the regiment was happy that the Medical Officer was at last recognized for his fine service.[87]

We stayed in that location for a few more weeks and I bumped into the Assistant Director several times. As we exchanged salutes, he would give me a nice smile and some cheery words. I was impressed that he remembered me from that one brief encounter outside the Aid Post when he was clearly preoccupied with weighty medical matters. I guess that's always the way it's been with me: too easily recognized and remembered. It just goes to show you that in order to get on in this world, you have to know which side of the dike your cows are on.

Civilians

I've spoken about the Italian civilian population several times and normally we got on fairly well with them. On one occasion, however, we had trouble with the some of the locals. Word came down from the top that civilians were to be evacuated from our area immediately, and two Italian policemen were sent to help us out. Each policeman was armed with a short rifle that had a fixed bayonet; the sword could be folded down out of the way.

We went to one big house, with orders for everyone to get out. An old grandmother started to scream when she heard the news, saying she had been born there and she would die there. In her panic she tried to climb into a small dog kennel. Our Provost Corporal and the two *carabinieri* picked her up and carried her to the truck.

On another occasion, in Bagnacavallo I decided to take a look at the local church. I came to the crypt, and when I opened the door, I couldn't believe my eyes! There must have been a thousand civilians in that place. I didn't know whether the Germans had herded them in there or if they had simply fled there for shelter. What hit me hardest was the smell. Ashbridge's Bay (into which Toronto's sewer water runs) on a warm summer day was pleasant compared to that stench! I didn't envy the regiment that was assigned the task of clearing those civilians out of the church.

Our Commanding Officer, Lieutenant Colonel Donald Cameron, DSO, was promoted to full Colonel just before we were taken out of the line in mid-February, and he left the regiment. He eventually made brigadier after the war. Major Ross, who had been the Second-in-Command, took over as Acting Commanding Officer. The Senio River was as far north as we got in northern Italy. We never got to Bologna before the decision was made to consolidate all five Canadian divisions in Holland. So they pulled the First Division and the whole Corps out of the line in late February 1945. Farewell to "sunny Italy." What a crock! The last three months I was there, I had five blankets on my bed, and I was still cold.

Rest and Recreation

Something was in the wind. The Signals Officer had a large number of Italians working to bury the phone lines from Tactical Headquarters a foot underground. This had never been done before and we were all very curious. One night they loaded us into Troop Carrying Vehicles and we were brought to a little town named Ripratransone up in the mountains. The war had never touched this town, and it was good to see buildings that still had glass in their windows! It was wintry up there, though, and one of the regimental policemen slipped and broke his leg. Thankfully he was picked up before he could be seriously frostbitten.

The local police had arrested two women for being suspected enemy agents. One of our provosts decided it was his job to see that they were properly locked up every night. We didn't know exactly what went on, but the rumours were rife.

A group of twelve Plough Jockeys was to go home on the Tri-Wound scheme (thirty days' leave in Canada and then back to the front), so I went over to say goodbye to them before they headed down the mountain. One of these fellows had been my batman for over a year, and I asked him if he was okay and had everything he needed. He said, "Yes, I have a bottle of Dago Red (the local red wine) to keep me company." I casually mentioned that there was a bottle of Scotch in the top of my kit bag, and then went to talk to some of the others. A few days later I had occasion to open up my bag and noticed that the Scotch was no longer there. In its place was a bottle of the local red vino. So I knew then that Bill "Scotty" Brown had gone home happy.

We left on 2 March and headed over the Apennines, which run like a spine down the centre of Italy. We travelled down to the plain and up through Florence, eventually arriving at a place called Harrod's Camp, just outside Pisa. After our ten-day rest in Ripratransone, this was a stark reintroduction to the harshness of military life. Harrod's was an army transit camp such as has existed from the time of the Roman legions. It was a place where regulations and spit polish were the norm, and intelligence and common sense, forgotten commodities.

Harry Fox leads a Hastings and Prince Edward Regiment reunion parade in Belleville, Ontario, 1990.

Harry Fox is made Honorary RSM of the QOR at CFB Petawawa, 1993. In the background is the late Colonel H.C.F. Elliot, Honorary Colonel of the QOR.

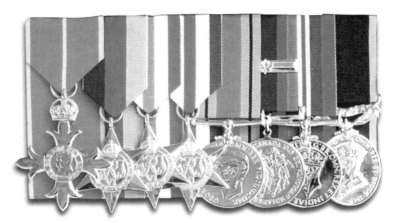

Harry Fox's medals. The MBE (Order of the British Empire, Member) is at left.

D-Day Anniversary at City Hall, 1995. Left to right: Harry Fox, John Missons, Art Gay, Rolph Jackson, Charlie Martin and R. Grieve.

Fred Skyvington, left, Harry Fox and Colonel Willcocks in October 1998 visiting what was the C Coy headquarters at San Tomaso, Italy in January 1998.

Harry Fox, right, and Fred Skyvington at the Cassino Cemetery in Italy, October 1998.

Harry Fox selling poppies at the Manulife Centre, Toronto, ca 2000. He performed this duty voluntarily for many years.

Harry Fox, age 87, at the QOR Association annual shoot at CFB Borden, September 2001.

The Minister of National Defence, Art Eggleton, and Harry Fox at The Queen's Own Rifles 140th Birthday celebrations, April 2000.

Harry Fox on his 90th birthday, 2004.

CHAPTER 9

Northwest Europe and the End of the Second World War

"D-Day Dodgers" Join the Action

We boarded American ships at the port of Leghorn on 13 March 1945 for the trip to Northwest Europe. I think the prevailing sentiment was immense relief, like feeling you had just escaped from a torture chamber or a prison. Surely whatever awaited us could not be worse than what we had been through in Italy, some of us thought. After an almost surrealistic sea voyage, compared to what we had been experiencing, we landed at the port of Marseilles. Army trucks took us through the Rhone Valley, and after war-desolated Italy, the greenness of southern France (under the Vichy regime) seemed almost a kind of paradise.

We arrived in the town of Westmalle, north of Antwerp, and most of the regiment was bivouacked in a Trappist monastery that was famous for its fine beer. It seemed a strange irony for soldiers who had fought through the hills of Italy, to be billeted in a beer-making monastery! The regiment spent almost a month in Belgium where we gained a well-needed "breather" from combat. For once, the leave policy was generous, and many of the soldiers got passes to Brussels. For many, this was unbelievable as Brussels was a major city, unlike most of the towns available to front-line soldiers in Italy (with the exception of Rome).

A group even returned to England to wander down memory lane and reminisce about happier times. To their consternation, England was vastly changed, with the overriding American presence and the war weariness of the English populace.

Training went on, but the men had a hard time taking it seriously, because many thought the war was virtually over. To the more astute, a sure sign of coming combat was the replacement of much of our old, worn-out equipment and uniforms. Mowat mentions several items that irked our men. First, was the order for battle-dress to be replaced by a shirt and black tie. This was the dress of the "Zombies" at home. First Canadian Army wanted all soldiers to be dressed alike, and not to single out the few thousand conscripts who had volunteered for overseas service. Second, we had come to wear the Eighth Army Crusader Cross badge with great pride, and now we had to relinquish it for the meaningless (to us, at least) First Canadian Army flash.

But I think it was the replacement of our weapons that spoke the loudest of what was to come. They took away our Thompson submachine guns and gave us Sten guns. I know a lot of our men hated this weapon. They railed about its poor quality and cheap construction. Someone even composed a poem about its faults, I believe. Perhaps the most serious criticism was its tendency to jam after firing a round or two. This cost some men their lives in combat, hence the soldiers' anger at the Sten and its builders.

It was an all right weapon *if* you knew how to handle it. The secret was that it had to remain cocked. This detail was not in the weapon's manual but was something you learned from experience. The thing with the Sten gun was, if you had to bang it around, it could cock, and you wouldn't know that it was cocked and ready to fire. Then it was truly dangerous. Incidentally, a Third Battalion QOR rifleman was killed accidentally in Debert, Nova Scotia, in 1943 by a Sten gun that was not handled properly by another soldier. You had to cock it and put it on safe; only then could you bang it around and be safe. The Tommy gun was different: you were never sure it was cocked unless you looked at it.

With regard to shooting, the Sten was a better weapon as it had a higher rate of fire. The Thompson was slow and fired a clumsy bullet that travelled six hundred feet a second. You could actually hear the bullet coming but not with the Sten. With the Thompson, if your target wasn't hit with the first round then none of the rest would connect. The funny thing with the Tommy gun is that the bursts always go up; the first round goes on target and then all the rest go up, missing the target. So we turned it on its side. The Tommy gun with a box magazine had twenty rounds initially, and then thirty rounds. The British wouldn't use the Tommy because of its awkwardness. I think another reason was cultural. There was a certain association of the Tommy gun with American gangsters of the thirties. The British didn't want to be connected with what they saw as a "dirty gangster's weapon." In Britain, Tommy guns had originally been issued to section commanders, but they soon were take away from the infantry and given to truck drivers. However, the truck drivers really didn't need them so they were taken away altogether.

We were sent to the Reichswald Forest, just across the Rhine River inside Germany, on 2 April. Although there was the confidence that we were hardened combat veterans, things were very different in Northwest Europe. It was greener, wetter, with more trees, and virtually flat. While we waited for the order to move, I was able to get away for a day and visit the QOR, at least at headquarters, and inquire about the various men that I had known.

Holland: Final Days of Combat

The Hasty P's were taken across the Ijssel River on amphibious vehicles called Buffaloes, which were a marvel to us as we had only heard of these machines but never had the use of them going into action. They were old friends, however, to the troops of the Second and Third Divisions who had used them in the Scheldt fighting during the fall of 1944. This river crossing was mentioned in my Order of the British Empire citation, but I really did nothing that spectacular. Perhaps the only thing that we did differently was that I went up with the reserve company of the 48th Highlanders, who were ahead of us, and established a new Battalion Headquarters right behind their advance.

Our first action in Holland took place on 13 April. We moved through the villages of Hoven and Teuge, where Charlie Company met furious initial resistance. Our troops encountered the dreaded 88-millimetre gun, and several vehicles were knocked out in quick succession. Then, just as quickly, many of the enemy surrendered. The fighting was short and furious as these largely Dutch SS troops knew there was no future for them but death. It was the very young ones, sixteen or seventeen years old, that were most fanatical, however, and they would die before giving up. The late Lieutenant Colonel H. Elliot Dalton, DSO, a QOR veteran of the Second World War once commented: "The SS people were sold on the do or die idea, like the Hitler Division which came into battle on tanks screaming, 'We're Hitler's SS Division,' and expecting you to surrender."[88] Able and Don companies advanced right up to the major canal that runs outside Apeldoorn. Many prisoners were taken in our rapid advance, and although this was a logistical challenge for me as Regimental Sergeant Major, there wasn't the same danger presented as in Italy. The German prisoners we took were older fellows and more mature, often family men and more pragmatic. They wanted to get home to see their wives and children, and everyone knew the war was virtually over.

We suffered a number of casualties during this week of fighting. For example, Sergeant Brott, age twenty-six, from Trout Creek, Ontario was killed on 15 April. A sniper killed Corporal Finton, one of the 1939 originals of the Mortar Platoon, on 17 April. Lieutenant Charles Tompkins from Port Credit (Mississauga) died on 18 April. After the fighting on 14 April, we were put into Brigade reserve and the other two regiments, the Royal Canadian Regiment and the 48th Highlanders, crossed the canal and entered Apeldoorn. While my friends in The Queen's Own Rifles and the rest of the Third Infantry Division were fighting in Friesland in the north, our Division's job was to cut across the heart of Holland, separating the German forces in the south from those in the north. This was the same kind of encirclement the Allies employed for isolating the Ruhr industrial area of Germany across the Rhine.

Earlier I talked about combat stress. I felt I was in that state by this point in the war. I had little ambition or drive while we were in Holland. For example, as the battalion would move forward, I had to set up Battalion Headquarters in the next town. I'd call Brigade and get a report, and then, after hanging up the line, I would forget what I'd been told.

The higher-ups never really accepted this "combat stress" problem because they were never exposed to the same conditions, or at least, their exposure was very short. I recall several posh types in Italy who looked at you as if you were a pig, with mud up to your knees, battle dress not pressed, and looking very unsoldierly. They literally looked down their noses at "we poor beggars in the mud." They had a revolver with six extra rounds in their belt, and their boots shone. Most of the information they wanted could have been given over the phone; it was not really necessary for these staff types to come up to the front. I think it was partly psychological: that is, to assuage their guilt over the comparatively soft life they led while so many of our men lived in the adverse conditions of the front line.

On 17 April we entered Apeldoorn and secured the Palace of Queen Wilhelmina for our Battalion Headquarters. There was mass confusion in the streets as people were ecstatic at being freed from German occupation after five years. Liberation also brought with it some very ugly developments, however. They were first seen, I think, in Eindhoven and other communities on 17 September 1944 during Operation Market Garden when elements of the American 101st Airborne (506th Parachute Infantry) entered that city. In every city and town where the Allies drove the Germans out, the Dutch loyalists rounded up "collaborators," those who had been sympathetic or supportive of the German occupation. The same thing happened in France. We Canadians found it hard to swallow at first, seeing the Dutch people so bent on revenge. Most of the men were shot or hung; it depended on the whim of the group. The women were publically humiliated and had their hair cut off. I know our soldiers intervened in a few cases to stop executions but many of them had the same attitude as the Dutch loyalists; that is, the presumed collaborators deserved their fate for having worked with the Nazis. This was especially true as news of the death camps like Dachau and Auschwitz became widely known.

We moved west from Apeldoorn and encountered the enemy in strength at a wood near the town of Nieuw Milligen. We had to bring in the flamethrowing vehicles (Crocodiles) to clear them out. We had moved forward and, for some reason were restricted to three vehicles: two ambulance jeeps and one fifteen-hundredweight truck, loaded mostly with signal equipment, spare batteries, phone wire and so on. I had loaded three boxes of .303 ammo and there was some material for the Intelligence section. All in all, a pretty skinny Tactical Headquarters!

More Close Calls

One day in Holland I was walking along the road and approached a group of men gathered around a truck. They were priming grenades, and then suddenly there was a mighty bang. A piece of shrapnel, bright and shiny, flew past me, waist height no more than three feet from me. I'm still not sure how shrapnel from a 36 grenade could be shiny unless it was white hot.

Another time I was walking along a road to visit one of the rifle companies. Some of the men yelled to me to watch out for a sniper. No sooner were the words out of their mouths when, WHACK, a bullet went by me. I dropped what I was carrying and jumped into the ditch. I drew my pistol (I refused to carry a Sten gun) and headed for a house a few hundred yards away, surmising that this must be where the sniper was located. There was no cover, and I was a sitting duck if he decided to shoot again! Fortunately nothing happened, and I made it to the house intact. Once inside I found a rifle but no shooter.

We've Lost the CO!

We were in a pine forest, with the trees planted in rows at right angles to the road, which was good for cover as we advanced. Sergeant Major George Ponsford came by and picked up six bandoliers of .303 ammo. He said he had something for me to see and asked me to come with him. I was agreeable, and so we walked along the road passing a Saskatoon Light Infantry truck that had been knocked out.[89] Ponsford and I kept going and soon came to a spot where two lance corporals had an observation post. The Sergeant Major said the two soldiers would be picked up after dark. I thanked him for showing me, as it would have been tricky trying to locate them in the dark. The rest of Charlie Company was about four hundred yards away on the top of small incline. I decided it was best to turn back at that point and return to Tactical Headquarters.

While I was gone, the Commanding Officer, Lieutenant Colonel Rennison, became quite upset over the lack of communication from the rifle companies. The officers had been issued new radios and they had been chatting away all day on them. Now there was nothing but silence. He took a rifleman with him and went out to see for himself what was going on.

A short time later, a soldier came running up to me, huffing and puffing, saying that he had "lost" the Commanding Officer. A flight of mortar bombs had come in to their location and the soldier had hit the ground. When he stood up, the Commanding Officer was nowhere to be seen and so he thought it best to get back to headquarters and tell the Regimental Sergeant Major. I said something to the effect, "Take me back to where you lost him, *schnell, schnell.*" We ran down the right side of the road, and about half a mile down, the rifleman looked over at the road, suddenly grabbed something and then rejoined me.

It seems that a tank officer had been wounded, and the stretcher-bearers had left his web equipment by the side of the road when they had picked him up. The webbing had a pistol and field glasses. The rifleman gave the pistol to me, and kept the binoculars. We kept on going for another half mile or so and then ran across the road to a small clearing where there were fresh bomb craters. The smell of high explosive was quite evident, too.[90]

I knew that Charlie Company was the closest, so I led the way there. In a few minutes we came to another clearing, and there was a Jerry standing in the middle, hands up in the air and shaking like a pot of jelly at a St. Vitus's dance.

The Commanding Officer was standing with his back to a tree, holding his pistol in both hands, and pointing it at the Jerry. Lieutenant Colonel Rennison was shaking just as badly as the German, so I yelled out, "I've got him, sir," and drew my pistol. He looked at me and said, "Thank God, you're here, Sergeant Major. I did not want to shoot an unarmed man, but I could not take him with me, nor could I let him loose in our area."

So I took the prisoner back to Tactical Headquarters and the Commanding Officer went over to Charlie's lines. The major commanding the company had been hit, and Ponsford was alone at Company Headquarters with a signaller and a stretcher-bearer. A platoon commander just happened to call in at that moment, saying that they had reached their objective with little opposition and asked what were his orders? The Commanding Officer told him to keep going, and then he got the other companies moving forward as well. As a result the battalion was able to capture the objective that Brigade had assigned for the reserve units to take the next day. This enabled the whole First Division to move forward ahead of schedule, and everyone was happy. Lieutenant Colonel Rennison was eventually awarded the Distinguished Service Order for his leadership, and Ponsford, the Order of the British Empire.

On 23 April we were pulled out of the line. It turned out that the engagement with the Dutch SS troops were the last shots the regiment would fire in the Second World War. We were resting in a place called Elspeet on VE Day. Then we were ordered to Amersfoort to accept the surrender of the German garrison there. On 8 May we were told to go to Ijmuiden (south of Amsterdam), as there were 20,000 Germans there who had to be disarmed and taken prisoner. Along with the Royal Canadian Regiment, we moved across the country through Amsterdam, and the Dutch celebrated wildly their Canadian "liberators." For many of our young soldiers, this was heady stuff. Some of us had an intuition that the Dutch would soon tire of our presence as they tried to return to the "normalcy" of peace.

There were some happy reunions with people in The Queen's Own Rifles as the whole Canadian Army was in Holland together in the spring of 1945. The first time I was back to see the old regiment since my departure from them in England in October 1943, was on 9 April when the QOR was on its way to Deventer. The Medical Officer, Captain R. Douglas Oatway, mentions my visit in his diary: "RSM Harry Fox, who used to be with the QOR and of whom everyone speaks so fondly, was at BHQ."[91] Because of the relative proximity, there were comings and goings of a social nature between units. Other former QOR riflemen who had been sent to serve with other units came by the Hasty P's lines. Sergeant Horace Hall, for example, had been sent on a Pooch draft to the 48th and he came over to visit me one day.

Return to Canada

The Hasty P's remained in Holland on occupation duties while men were constantly sent home and others posted in, often simply because they had come from eastern Ontario, Military District No. 3. We finally left Holland on 1 September and travelling via Britain, took a ship for Canada. The Hasty P's got off the train on 4 October 1945 to a jubilant crowd in Belleville, made up of well-wishing civilians and reservists who had longed to join the regiment. Perhaps the saddest ones there were the women with children, who hoped to see someone get off the train and didn't. This is the ultimate cost of defending freedom, the lives of men.

After returning to Toronto I was able to get my old job back at Eaton's and counted myself fortunate. Many returning veterans found there was no job waiting for them, and so many returned to school or had to change their trades. For me, there was an adjustment issue as I had been a Regimental Sergeant Major for two years and I was used to having men jump when I spoke. A First World War veteran shared with me that I needed to be less crisp and mellower in my demeanour with the customers. He said that he too had had to adjust his manner when dealing with civilians after the Great War. I decided to rejoin The Queen's Own Rifles of Canada again as Regimental Sergeant Major in 1947. I served for about a year (a second tour of duty, so to speak), and then for a variety of reasons, I decided that I had had enough of Army life.

For many years I tried to forget all that had happened in the Second World War. It's a funny thing though, you can never really forget. In the late 1980s Regimental Sergeant Major Brian Budden invited me to come to a Queen's

Own function. I came, and since then I've been back in my regimental family. Every second Thursday I meet with my friends at the Royal Canadian Legion Branch 344 on Lakeshore Boulevard, in Toronto, for lunch and cribbage, often retelling the old war stories. Padre Craig Cameron started coming to the lunches soon after joining The Queen's Own Rifles in 1992. I've told him a lot of the stories that you've just been reading and eventually he decided to write them all down.

I felt privileged to be able to go with the QOR Association to support the regiment in Normandy for the Fiftieth Anniversary of D-Day in June 1994.[92] The regiment had an impressive number in attendance, over one hundred serving soldiers, including the regimental band. I believe this is the largest number of riflemen from a *reserve unit* to travel abroad to France since the Second World War. The QOR had the largest number of members in attendance (just under two hundred including veterans), though other units like the Royal Winnipeg Rifles had approximately forty veterans on their tour.

Perhaps the hardest aspect of the trip was commuting from Rouen to Bernières for the ceremony on 6 June. We had to get up very early to make it to the beach for 0730 hours. Somehow the regiment's guard didn't show and so we held a small ceremony in the evening on a clear and windswept beach setting. Padre Cameron read the names of the sixty-one men killed on D-Day; it was a special moment.

The year 2000 was a significant one for The Queen's Own Rifles as the regiment celebrated its one hundred and fortieth birthday. A parade was held at Moss Park Armoury, Toronto, and the Minister of National Defence, the Honorable Art Eggleton, acted as the Reviewing Officer. He presented four other veterans and me with a commemorative coin that the regiment had struck for the occasion.

I was also privileged to attend the Fifty-fifth Anniversary of the Liberation of Holland, shortly after the parade at Moss Park Armoury. I was "double hatted" during that visit, wearing the scarlet beret of The Plough Jockeys for several events including the parade in Apeldoorn where the regiment liberated the Queen's palace of Het Loo. On the other occasions, I wore a green beret with the QOR cap badge.

There were parades to the two major Canadian cemeteries at Holten and Groesbeek. One was memorable when at exactly 1100 hrs three Air Force planes flew over and dropped thousands of poppies on the cemetery. It brought back memories of the trip to Normandy when pigeons had unleashed something on us slightly less pleasant than poppies! The trip was mostly well planned, as we had every other day to relax, drink beer and tell tall tales. I guess the low point for me was when I got off the bus one day and lost my balance, making a perfect two-point landing on the pavement, left elbow and knee contacting the hard stuff. A local policeman checked me over, and I think I said something like, "No, officer, I'm not tipsy." There was no injury, thankfully, except for some skin loss. However, this wasn't the only physical discomfort on the trip. Several days we were on the bus for seven hours, and my feet and ankles swelled up like puddings. But, all in all, it was a first-class trip, and I was glad that I went!

POSTSCRIPT

Harry's Luck Finally Runs Out

Harry was scheduled to meet Queen Elizabeth during the recent Jubilee Tour in 2003 when Her Majesty was visiting Toronto. He received an engraved invitation to come to the Canadian National Exhibition to which he replied that he would attend. He checked in and was given some information and a white tag with a number 1600 to wear around his neck. Suddenly he felt that he needed to sit down. This is not normal for Harry, though he is now ninety-one years of age. He has selling been poppies every November at the Manulife Centre in downtown Toronto, standing on his feet for up to six hours at a time, since the age of eighty!

Harry walked over to a window ledge and propped himself against it. "The next three hours passed very quickly," he says. He asked various women who were passing by if they were called Janet, his contact. They all said that they were not. To kill the time, he tried to calculate how many yards of red carpet had been used for the floor, but couldn't do it. He had worked for Eaton's in the Floor Covering department for forty years until retirement.

A man walked by Harry and asked him if he knew that he bore a striking resemblance to Field Marshall Montgomery. Harry's response was to the effect that he had been accused of that several times, including once in the United States. The fellow laughed at this witty comeback. Another fellow came by and said he was a riding representative, and did Harry know the name of his Member of Parliament or his Ontario representative? He came up with one name but couldn't think of his Member of the Provincial Parliament. This fellow soon left Harry alone.

Then around the corner came a woman who made a beeline for Harry once she saw his face. It turned out to be Flora MacDonald, former Liberal MP and Cabinet minister. They chatted for a while, and she told Harry of her recent trip to Afghanistan. When she turned to leave, Harry saluted her. He doesn't know why; it was just an impulse, he says.

Finally, a young woman with a clipboard came to him and said there was a seat for him on the platform. So she led him through the sea of people along the red carpet to the top of the stand where she showed him a chair. Harry looked around at the crowd of people and tried to count them but gave up at about nine hundred. While sitting there he had a good view of the royal couple, particularly when they signed the guest book. Harry says he enjoyed the experience and was happy to see Her Majesty and Prince Philip.

Then it dawned on him that the whole event was over and yet he was supposed to have been personally presented to the Queen herself, shake hands and exchange a few words. This would have been a thrill of a lifetime and a wonderful way to top off his military career. "But my luck had run out," Harry says.

ORDER OF THE BRITISH EMPIRE (MBE) CITATION

B 63612 Warrant Officer Class 1
(Regimental Sergeant-Major Harry Fox)

Regimental Sergeant-Major Harry Fox has served with the Hastings and Prince Edward Regiment since 1 January 1944. It has been his particular duty during operations to ensure that the forward companies were always adequately supplied with ammunition. In addition to this he had displayed outstanding ability in organizing and directing stretcher-bearer parties.

On one occasion in Italy, one company had secured a narrow bridgehead and had withstood thirteen counter-attacks over a period of twelve hours. Throughout the whole of this engagement Regimental Sergeant-Major Fox worked ceaselessly, maintaining the company concerned with ammunition and supplies, evacuating casualties and rendering every possible assistance to the company commander.

Similarly in Holland during the operation of crossing the Ijssel River and subsequent engagements, Regimental Sergeant-Major Fox continued to be an inspiration to all those working with him. His fine personal example and his outstanding courage during the heaviest of fighting and shelling have contributed largely to the many successes of the battalion. He has always maintained a high standard of morale and good discipline and he has earned the respect and the esteem of all personnel in the battalion.

First Canadian Infantry Division Formations in Italy

First Infantry Brigade

The Royal Canadian Regiment (RCR)

The Hastings and Prince Edward Regiment (Hast & PER)

The 48th Highlanders of Canada – (48th)

Second Infantry Brigade

Princess Patricia's Canadian Light Infantry (PPCLI)

Seaforth Highlanders of Canada (Seaforths)

Loyal Edmonton Regiment (Loyal Eddies)

Third Infantry Brigade

Royal 22nd Regiment (Van Doos)

Carleton & York Regiment (CYR)

The West Nova Scotia Regiment (WNSR)

First Canadian Armoured Brigade

The Ontario Regiment (Ont R)

The Calgary Regiment

The Three Rivers Regiment

4th Princess Louise Dragoon Guards (PLDG) Reconnaissance

Artillery

1st Field Regiment (Royal Canadian Artillery)

2nd Field Regiment

3rd Field Regiment

1st Anti-Tank Regiment

2nd Anti-Tank Regiment

Support troops

The Saskatoon Light Infantry (SLI) -MGs and Heavy Mortars

1st Armoured Car Regiment – (Royal Canadian Dragoons)

7th Anti-Tank Regiment

1st Survey Regiment

1st Light Anti-Aircraft Regiment (Lanark and Renfrew Scottish Regiment)

Royal Canadian Engineers (RCE)

Royal Canadian Army Service Corps (RCASC)

BRIEF HISTORY OF THE QUEEN'S OWN RIFLES OF CANADA

The Queen's Own Rifles of Canada began on 26 April 1860 as the 2nd Battalion, Volunteer Militia Rifles, drawing together six existing Toronto and area militia companies. *The Militia Act* of 1859 formally organized the Canadian militia for the country's defence following the withdrawal of British troops. The regiment was the second to be registered following this act and hence the number "2" on its cap badge.

The regiment became The Queen's Own Rifles of Toronto in 1863 in honour of Queen Victoria. Canada's oldest continuing and non-amalgamated infantry unit, The Queen's Own Rifles has served in virtually all of Canada's military engagements. The first combat seen by soldiers of the regiment was against the Irish-American Fenians at Ridgeway on 2 June 1866, where they sustained thirty casualties, nine of them fatal. Members of the regiment served in The Red River Expedition (1870), the Northwest Rebellion (1885), and the Boer War (1899–1902).

In 1914, the QOR sent a battalion of 1,000 men to Valcartier, Quebec, upon the outbreak of war against Germany. Forming the majority of the 3rd Battalion Canadian Expeditionary Force, the 3rd Toronto Regiment fought at St. Julien, Festubert, St. Eloi, Mount Sorrel, the Somme, Vimy Ridge, Passchendaele, Amiens, and Drocourt-Queant with distinction. During the First World War, the QOR raised five other overseas battalions, the 83rd, 95th, 166th 198th and the 255th led by QOR officers. Substantial contributions were made to seven other battalions as well, including an initial draft of 422 men to the 35th Battalion. In addition, 938 men volunteered for other arms of the military. Nearly 8,000 men from the regiment served in the Great War and over 1,200 never returned.

During the Second World War, the QOR fielded three battalions: two reserve battalions in Canada and the 1st which was mobilised for active service in June 1940. After training in England, the 1st Battalion landed on D-Day (6 June 1944) as one of four Canadian first-wave assault units, suffering the highest casualties of any Canadian unit (one hundred forty-three). The QOR fought with the Third Infantry Division in Normandy, the Channel ports, the Scheldt (Belgium-Holland), Rhineland campaign and northern Holland.

In 1953, two existing Rifle battalions were designated the 1st and 2nd Battalions, The Queen's Own Rifles, with the reserve Toronto battalion becoming the 3rd. The two regular battalions served overseas in peacekeeping in Korea, Germany and Cyprus, and were stationed in Calgary and Victoria. Both battalions were reduced to nil strength in 1968 and 1970 respectively.

The regiment continues to be a vital part of Canada's reserve Army and has spearheaded innovative training involving various branches of the Canadian Forces, such as Exercise Neptune Strike, a joint arms exercise held each spring. Since 1982, the QOR has maintained an airborne tasking; first, in support of the Canadian Airborne Regiment until 1995; and subsequently to provide a jump company of sixty-six paratroopers in support of The Canadian Parachute Center (Trenton). It regularly provides riflemen to Regular Force units. Several former riflemen serve with the Joint Task Force 2 and fought with 3rd Battalion Princess Patricia's Canadian Light Infantry in Afghanistan in 2002.

Soldiers of the regiment have also served on missions as augmentees to the Regular Force in such places as: Namibia, Egypt, the Golan Heights, Western Sahara, Cambodia, Somalia, Croatia, Bosnia, Sierra Leone and Dubai.

More than 1,750 riflemen have died serving with the regiment since its inception.

As one of only five Rifle regiments currently on the Canadian Order of Battle, The Queen's Own Rifles of Canada proudly maintains its distinctive traditions of Rifle drill and dress.

In Pace Paratus

BRIEF HISTORY OF THE HASTINGS
AND PRINCE EDWARD REGIMENT

The origins of the Hastings and Prince Edward Regiment, though stretching back to the beginning of the nineteenth century, officially dates to the formation of the 16th Battalion of Volunteer Militia in 1863, and the 49th Hastings Battalion in 1866. Soldiers of both battalions served in the Northwest Rebellion (1885) and the Boer War (1899–1902). The regiment also perpetuates the 9th Anti-Tank Regiment (Argyll Light Infantry), formerly the 15th Battalion Volunteer Rifles which was formed in January 1863, as well as the Midland Regiment.

During the First World War the parent militia units formed the 2nd, 21st and 59th Infantry Battalions and also raised the reinforcement 39th, 80th, 136th, 155th and 254th Battalions as well as the 1st Forestry Battalion. The 21st Battalion fought in all the major engagements of the Canadian Corps from Mount Sorrel in 1916 to Amiens in 1918.

The 16th Prince Edward Regiment and the 49th Hastings Rifles amalgamated in 1920 to form the Hastings and Prince Edward Regiment. In 1934 an official affiliation was established with the Royal Sussex Regiment of the British Army, now perpetuated in the Princess of Wales's Royal Regiment.

The regiment was mobilised and placed on active service at the outbreak of the Second World War in 1939 as part of the First Brigade and First Infantry Division. After six months in England, the First Brigade landed in western France in June 1940, but was withdrawn prior to engaging the German Army. The regiment's baptism of fire came on 10 July 1943 at Pachino, Sicily. The Plough Jockeys served with the Eighth Army throughout the Italian campaign, fighting at such famous battles as Ortona and the Hitler Line and at such lesser-known ones as Bulgaria and the Lamone River. In March 1945 the First Division joined its sister Canadian divisions in Holland and fought for a month there before the end of the war. Despite earning thirty-one Battle Honours, 343 Plough Jockeys would never return to Canada.

A 2nd (Reserve) Battalion functioned throughout the war, providing replacements for the 1st Battalion. A third battalion was formed as the 2nd Canadian Infantry Battalion for service against Japan, but its services were not required as the Pacific war ended in August 1945.

In 1951 the regiment was called to provide two companies for the new 27th Canadian Brigade formed to serve NATO in Germany, one of which deployed overseas. Some individual Hasty P's volunteered for service with the 25th Brigade in Korea. In 1954, the 9th Anti-Tank Regiment and the Midland Regiment amalgamated into the Hastings and Prince Edward Regiment. The result was that the regiment had a presence in seven locations: Belleville, Trenton, Picton, Port Hope, Madoc, Millbrook and Norwood until 1965 when all the armouries were closed with the exception of Belleville. This trend was somewhat reversed when "B" Company was formed in Peterborough and "C" Company in Cobourg in 1992.

Since that time, the Regiment has provided a Mortar Platoon to the 3rd Battalion, Royal Canadian Regiment from 1992 until 1995. Individual members have served as augmentees with the Regular Force in a variety of overseas locations including Bosnia.

The Plough Jockeys were part of Op Recuperation, military assistance rendered to the civilian population in eastern Ontario during the devastating ice storm of January 1999. The regiment continues to live up to its motto *Paratus*, "Ready."

BIBLIOGRAPHY

The following books were consulted in the production of these memoirs.

Ambrose, Stephen E. *Band of Brothers: Easy Company, 506th Regiment, 101st Airborne: From Normandy to Hitler's Eagle's Nest*. New York: Simon & Schuster, 1992.

Barnard, W.T. *The Queen's Own Rifles of Canada 1860–1960: One Hundred Years of Canada*. Don Mills, Ont.: The Ontario Publishing Company, 1960.

Beattie, Kim. *Dileas*. Toronto: 48th Highlanders of Canada, 1957.

Blackburn, George G. *The Guns of Normandy: A Soldier's Eye View, France 1944*. Toronto: McClelland & Stewart Inc., 1995.

————.*The Guns of Victory: A Soldier's Eye View, Belgium, Holland and Germany, 1944-45*. Toronto: McClelland & Stewart Inc., 1996.

Brokaw, Tom. The *Greatest Generation*. New York: Dell Publishing, 1998.

Burns, E.L.M. *Manpower Crisis in the Canadian Army*. Toronto: Clarke, Irwin, 1966.

Comfort, Charles. *Artist at War*. Revised. Pender Island, B.C.: Remembrance Books, 1995.

Copp, Terry and Bill McAndrew. *Battle Exhaustion: Soldiers and Psychiatrists in The Canadian Army, 1939–1945*. Montreal and Kingston: McGill-Queen's University Press, 1990.

Cottingham, Peter Layton. *Once Upon a Wartime: A Canadian Who Survived the Devil's Brigade*. Brandon, Man.: Leech Printing, 1996.

Coughlin, Bing. *"Herbie!"*. Toronto: Thomas Nelson, 1946.

Crawford, Steve. *Battleships and Carriers*. Etobicoke, Ont.: Prospero Books, 1999.

Dancocks, Daniel G. *The D-Day Dodgers: The Canadians in Italy, 1943–1945*. Toronto: McClelland & Stewart, 1991.

Feasby, W.R. ed. *Official History of the Canadian Medical Services,1939–1945*, Vol. 1. Ottawa: The Queen's Printer, 1956.

Fussell, Paul. *Wartime: Understanding and Behavior in the Second World War*. New York: Oxford University Press, 1989.

Granatstein, J. L. *Conscription in the Second World War, 1939–1945*. Toronto: McGraw-Ryerson, 1969.

Granatstein, J.L. and Desmond Morton. *A Nation Forged in Fire: Canadians and The Second World War 1939–1945,* Toronto: Lester & Orpen Dennys, 1990.

Gray, J. Glenn. The *Warriors: Reflections on Men in Battle*. New York: Harper & Row, 1959.

Keegan, John. *The Face of Battle*. New York: Penguin Books, 1976.

Kuhn, Volkmar. *German Paratroops in World War II*. London: Ian Allen, 1978.

Majdalany, Fred. *Patrol*. New York: Ballantine Books, 1947.

Margolian, Howard. *Conduct Unbecoming: The Story of the Murder of Canadian Prisoners of War in Normandy*. Toronto: University of Toronto Press, 1998.

Marteinson, John. *We Stand on Guard: An Illustrated History of the Canadian Army*. Montreal: Orvale Publications, 1992.

Martin, Charles Cromwell. *Battle Diary: From D-Day and Normandy to the Zuider Zee and VE*. Toronto: Dundurn Press, 1994.

Morton, Desmond. *A Military History of Canada*. Edmonton: Hurtig, 1985.

Mowat, Farley. *And No Birds Sang*. Toronto: McClelland and Stewart-Bantam, 1979.

——————. *The Regiment*. Toronto: McClelland and Stewart, 1955. reprint., 1974.

Nicholson, G.W. *The Canadians in Italy*. Ottawa: The Queen's Printer, 1957.

Portugal, Jean E., ed. and comp. *We Were There: The Army A Record for Canada*. Volume 2. Toronto: Royal Canadian Military Institute Heritage Society, 1998.

Regan, Geoffrey. *Fight or Flight*. New York: Avon Books, 1996.

Smith, Basil. *Memories of a QuarterBloke*. Privately printed: Belleville, 2002.

Smith, Kenneth. *Duffy's Regiment*. Don Mills, Ont.: T.H. Best, 1983.

Smith, W. *What Time the Tempest*. Toronto: Ryerson Press, 1953.

Stacey, C.P. *The Canadian Army: 1939 1945*. Ottawa: The Queen's Printer, 1948.

Stevens, G.R. *The Royal Canadian Regiment, 1933–1966*. London: London Printing, 1967.

Taber's Cyclopedic Medical Dictionary. Toronto: Ryerson Press, 1969.

Whitsed, Roy J. ed. *Canadians: A Battalion at War: Canadians in The Queen's Own Rifles of Canada, 1940 to 1945*. Burlington, Ont.: Mississauga Books, 1996.

Zuehkle, Mark. *Ortona: Canada's Epic World War II Battle*. Vancouver: Douglas and McIntyre, 2003.

ENDNOTES

1 Harry Fox has no middle name.

2 Canadian infantry battalions used the names Able, Baker, Charlie and Dog for their companies. An infantry company in World War Two normally consisted of about one hundred and thirty soldiers: one hundred and fifteen were infantrymen, and fifteen others included engineers, gunners and stretcher-bearers.

3 In Italy, "D" Company of the Hastings and Prince Edward Regiment had two officers named Don who commanded them: Major (later Brigadier General) Donald Cameron and Major (later Lieutenant Colonel) Donald Ross. Neither officer liked the term "Dog" so we called it "Don's" Company, or most often, simply "Don" Company.

4 Gordon Weiss, the Regimental Quartermaster Sergeant was given number B 63502; the Provost Sergeant was B 63504. Bill Ives, who was in 13 Platoon, and later became Company Quartermaster Sergeant of Charlie Company, was B 63511. Clay Bell, who had joined the regiment in 1937, became B 63520. David Hazzard received the last allotted number, B 64448, even though he originally joined the QOR in 1936. He worked at Dunlop Tire and had to get a man to cover for him so he could enlist.

5 Sergeant David Hazzard was later commissioned and killed in action with Baker Company of the QOR on 5 July 1944 in Normandy while moving up to Carpiquet.

6 Roy J. Whitsed, ed. *Canadians: A Battalion at War: Canadians in The Queen's Own Rifles of Canada 1940–1945* (Mississauga, Ont.: Burlington Books, 1996), p. 252.

7 For example, Rome was declared an "open city" in June 1944 to prevent destruction of many historical treasures and sites.

8 Whitsed, *Canadians*, pp. 251-252.

9 Ibid.

10 Ibid., p. 303.

11 "Quarterbloke" was the Canadian Army term for the Company Quartermaster Sergeant, in charge of all supplies for the company. Today he is simply called CQ.

12 *The Rifleman*, 1999, p. 33.

13 Ken MacLeod was later commissioned from the ranks, and rejoined the regiment in Normandy. He was serving as a platoon commander in Able Company of the QOR at Giberville, near Caen, when he was killed in action on 18 July 1944.

14 Coxey's Army was a group of five hundred unemployed men who walked from Ohio to Washington, D.C. in 1894 during "The Great Panic" (economic depression of 1893-96). Their leader was Jacob Coxey (1854–1951), a quarry owner who believed the federal government should deal with the unemployment problems through various public works projects.

15   There aren't many of these in Canada; one that was constructed on the Queen Elizabeth Way from Hamilton to St. Catharines caused too many accidents and deaths. I believe Tim Horton was killed at that location on 21 February 1974.

16   "Singed Boots," *The Rifleman*, 2002 – 2003, p.44.

17   Charles Cromwell Martin, *Battle Diary: From D-Day and Normandy to the Zuider Zee and VE.* (Toronto: Dundurn Press, 1994), pp. 28-29. This passage describes Charlie Martin's run-in with a British brigadier in Normandy.

18   Just a note of clarification: the officers had soldiers assigned to assist them with meals, kit and other matters. Officers in the rank of captain and above had their own personal batman to look after them. In subsequent years, when the batman position was eliminated, the officers always ate *after* the men while in the field, which is a fine tradition, I think. It is still the custom in the Army today.

19   A Canadian infantry battalion in the Second World War at full strength had approximately seven hundred and fifty men. The battalion was divided into seven major sub-units: Battalion Headquarters (Commanding Officer and his staff); about sixty personnel; Headquarters Company, about seventy people; Support Company encompassing seven numbered platoons including, mortars (No. 3), carriers (No. 4), anti-tank (No. 5), and pioneer (No. 6); and four rifle companies. Each rifle company had about one hundred and fifteen riflemen; Able Company, 7 to 9 Platoons; Baker Company, 10 to 12 Platoon; Charlie Company, 13 to 15 Platoon; and Dog Company, 16 to 18 Platoon.

20   George G. Blackburn, *The Guns of Normandy: A Soldier's Eye View, France 1944* (Toronto: McClelland and Stewart, 1995), pp. 350-351.

21   Ibid., pp. 346-47.

22   A trained private's pay during the Second World War was one dollar and forty cents a day. After six months of experience, it was raised ten cents to a dollar fifty.

23   A warrant officer class one was paid four dollars per day and got an extra twenty cents for a Regimental Sergeant Major appointment. When you compare the pay of the different ranks, the ratio is not a great deal different than the ratio these days. In 2005, a chief warrant officer (reserve) receives about $180 a day and a rifleman (reserve) is paid about $ 70 a day.

24   Dr. Homer Eshoo was the Hastings and Prince Edward Regiment's Medical Officer from December 1943, and after the death of Dr. Charles Krakauer, until June 1944. Captain Eshoo was a graduate of the Manitoba Medical College, class of 1941.

25   Howard Margolian, *Conduct Unbecoming: The Story of the Murder of Canadian Prisoners of War in Normandy* (Toronto: University of Toronto Press, 1998), pp. 115,126.

26   Whitsed, *Canadians*, p. 203.

27   *The Rifleman*, 1999, pp. 33-34.

28 The lance sergeant was a kind of "floater" in the company, not being assigned to a specific platoon.

29 Farley Mowat, *The Regiment* (Toronto: McClelland and Stewart, 1955, reprint 1974), p. 129. Padre Fred Goforth replaced Padre Essex in November 1944. Goforth became the unit's third combat Padre since the regiment landed in Sicily.

30 Daniel G. Dancocks, *D-Day Dodgers: The Canadians in Italy, 1943 –1945* (Toronto: McClelland and Stewart, 1991), p. 187.

31 Farley Mowat, *And No Birds Sang* (Toronto: McClelland and Stewart, Bantam Limited, 1979), pp. 193 – 194.

32 Soldiers in the Hastings & Prince Edward Regiment are called "plough jockeys" because of the predominantly rural nature of the two counties in Ontario from which the regiment hails.

33 "Hasty P's" or alternately, "Hasty Pees," are other colloquial terms used in the Army for the Hastings and Prince Edward Regiment and its soldiers.

34 Mowat, *The Regiment*, pp.161–162.

35 Regimental Sergeant Majors are often called "Mr." by the officers to reflect their special position.

36 A "stonk" is a sudden artillery bombardment on a specific location.

37 Mowat, *The Regiment*, p. 177.

38 Charles Comfort, *Artist at War* revised ed. (Pender Island, B.C.: Remembrance Books, 1995), p. 103.

39 Kim Beattie, *Dileas* (Toronto: 48th Highlanders of Canada, 1957), p. 493.

40 Allied Military Government Occupied Territory.

41 Dancocks, *D-Day Dodgers*, p. 189.

42 Terry Copp and Fred McAndrew, *Battle Exhaustion: Soldiers and Psychiatrists in The Canadian Army, 1939–1945* (Montreal and Kingston: McGill-Queen's University Press, 1990), p. 57.

43 Fred Majdalany, *Patrol* (New York: Ballantine Books, 1947).

44 Dancocks, *D-Day Dodgers*, p. 215.

45 Mowat, *The Regiment*, pp. 169–170.

46 Kenneth Smith, *Duffy's Regiment* (Don Mills, Ont.: T.H. Best, 1983), p. 143.

47 Steven E. Ambrose, *Band of Brothers: E Company, 506th Regiment, 101st Airborne From Normandy to Hitler's Eagle's Nest,* (New York: Simon and Schuster, 1992), p. 142.

48 Dancocks, *D-Day Dodgers*, p. 213.

49 Mowat, *The Regiment*, p. 167.

50 Dancocks, *D-Day Dodgers*, p. 213.

51 A "dixie" was a steel pot eighteen inches high and twelve inches wide with a lid.

52 "Pot-walloper" was the colloquial Army term for cook's assistant. These men performed menial tasks such as peeling potatoes, serving food to the troops and creative scrounging for fresh rations.

53 Saluting is normally forbidden in the front lines; soldiers call it a "sniper check." Some officers however, insisted on being saluted regardless of the danger.

54 "Padre" is Spanish for "Father," the normal term for a Roman Catholic priest.

55 Ambrose, *Band of Brothers*, pp. 134,155.

56 Mowat, *The Regiment*, p. 165.

57 Mowat, *And No Birds Sang*, pp.160–161.

58 Peter L. Cottingham, *Once Upon a Wartime: A Canadian Who Survived the Devil's Brigade* (Brandon, Man.: Leech Printing, 1996), p. 107.

59 Margolian, *Conduct Unbecoming*, p. 112.

60 W.R. Feasby, ed. *Official History of the Canadian Medical Services, 1939–1945*, Volume 1 (Ottawa: The Queen's Printer, 1956), p.165.

61 Basil Smith, Memories of a Quarterbloke, (np, nd) entry for Thursday, 4 May 1944. Smith states that he and RSM Fox set out at exactly 1730 hours and touched the wooden cross on top at 1928 hours, one hour and fifty-eight minutes.

62 Dr. Homer Eshoo was the Hastings and Prince Edward Regiment's Medical Officer from December 1943, after the death of Dr. Charles Krakauer, until June, 1944. Captain Eshoo was a graduate of the Manitoba Medical College, class of 1941.

63 The Schmeisser machine pistol was a German semi-automatic weapon, equivalent to our Tommy gun.

64 Lieutenant Colonel Steven D. Brand, CD, was Commanding Officer of The Queen's Own Rifles of Canada from 1992 to 1995.

65 A "William" is a five-round salvo from all the guns supporting the attack on one position.

66 Mowat, *The Regiment*, p. 189

67 Ibid., p.190.

68 The Regimental Sergeant Major had some of the same privileges as an officer: the men called him "Sir," and he was entitled to the services of an aide (batman).

69 Cottingham, *Once Upon a Wartime*, p.147.

70 St. Vitus's dance is a medical condition known as "chorea," a functional nervous disorder with muscular spasms (*Taber's Cyclopedic Medical Dictionary*, Toronto: Ryerson, 1969, C 49). In the late Middle Ages, largely in Germany, people danced before the statue of St. Vitus (a fourth century Christian martyr), in order to ensure good health for the year ahead. The religious emotional neurosis that developed manifested itself in frenetic dancing. In time, this activity became confused with the shaking associated with chorea, and the term "St. Vitus's dance."

71 *The Plough Jockey*, Volume 3, Issue 2, Spring-Summer 2001, pp. 34-35.

72 Bill Graydon was Honorary Colonel of the Hasty P's from 1976 until 1982 and he died in 2001.

73 Mowat, *The Regiment*, pp. 219-221.

74 Corporal Raymond D. Playfair, "San Maria di Scacciano," *The Plough Jockey*, Volume 3, Issue 2, Spring-Summer 2001, pp. 30-32.

75 The Lance Sergeant was a kind of floater really, because technically he was still a corporal and not assigned to one of the platoons. The section commanders were corporals (sergeants today) and the sergeant was the platoon second-in-command (warrant officer today).

76 These small collapsible foot-bridges were called "Olayson" bridges after its inventor. They were made of steel pipe about ten feet in length and about one half inch thick.

77 Mowat, *The Regiment*, p. 242

78 John Keegan, *The Face of Battle*, (New York: Penguin Books, 1976), pp., 335-336.

79 "A Lesson in First Aid," *The Plough Jockey, Spring* 2002, p. 36.

80 As other writers point out, this shortage was an *infantry* shortage primarily. There were more than 465,000 men and women in the Army in the fall of 1944. Burns, *Manpower Crisis in the Canadian Army* (Toronto, 1956), showed that this Army had only 38,000 infantry soldiers, less than ten percent of the whole, largely because of the way the Canadian Army was structured.

81 Mowat, *The Regiment*, pp. 259-260.

82 Porritt had previously been awarded the Military Cross for his actions in attacking and knocking out several tanks in a little village called Bulgaria on 14 October.

83 *The Plough Jockey*, Volume 3, Issue 5. Spring 2003, pp. 14–15. Captain (later Lieutenant Colonel) Max Porritt was a German prisoner of war until the end of the Second World War. He served in the Hastings and Prince Edward Regiment after the war, eventually commanding the militia battalion from 15 September 1949 to 14 September 1952. Max Porritt died in 2002 at the age of ninety.

84 Mowat, *The Regiment*, p. 258.

85 Copp and McAndrews, *Battle Exhaustion*, p. 75.

86 W. Smith, *What Time The Tempest* (Toronto: Ryerson Press, 1953), p. 278.

87 Dr. Max Lerner served as the Hastings and Prince Edward Regiment's Medical Officer, replacing Dr. Homer Eshoo, from June 1944 until the end of the war. Like Dr. Eshoo he was a graduate of the Manitoba Medical College, Class of 1934.

88 Jean Portugal, ed. and comp. *We Were There: The Army A Record for Canada, Vol.* 2 (Toronto: Royal Canadian Military Institute Heritage Society, 1998), p. 646.

89 An armour-piercing shell decapitated the driver of the truck, a sergeant from the Saskatoon Light Infantry.

90 Some Second World War writers talk about the "stink of cordite." Cordite itself does not have an odour, as Vaseline is one of its main ingredients. The distinctive smell from high explosive shells comes from a mixture of sulphur and picric acid. In a confined place, like a cellar, the odour alone can be fatal. Fortunately, the gas is hot and rises up quickly where the wind can blow it away.

91 Whitsed, *Canadians*, p. 175.

92 About twenty-five QOR veterans visited Normandy for the Fiftieth Anniversary of D-Day.

ABOUT THE AUTHORS

RSM Harry Fox, MBE

Harry Fox was born in England, and moved to Canada with his family in 1920. Harry went to work for the T. Eaton Company in Toronto at the age of fifteen. Apart from his wartime service, he worked for the company for his entire career, retiring in 1976. He joined The Queen's Own Rifles (militia) in 1932, volunteered for overseas service when the regiment was mobilized in 1940, and was then promoted from Sergeant to Warrant Officer 2, Company Sergeant Major of Charlie Company. In 1942 Harry Fox was again promoted, to Warrant Officer 1st class, becoming the Regimental Sergeant-Major of 1st Battalion, QOR. Wanting to gain combat experience, Harry transferred to 1st Division in Italy in 1943, later serving as RSM of the Hastings and Prince Edward Regiment until the end of the war. He was awarded the Order of the British Empire (Member) for his outstanding service with the regiment in Italy. He rejoined the QOR in 1947 as RSM, and retired permanently from military service in 1948.

Harry Fox has participated in several commemorative tours to Normandy (1994), Italy (1998), Holland (2000) and Normandy (2004). He is an active member of the Royal Canadian Legion, Branch 344 in Toronto.

Captain the Reverend, Craig B. Cameron, CD

Born and educated in Winnipeg, Manitoba, Craig Cameron received his Master of Divinity degree from Acadia University, (Wolfville, Nova Scotia) in 1980. He subsequently pursued further studies at the Toronto School of Theology, and for a time, also taught history at a college in Toronto. He joined the Canadian Forces as a chaplain in 1992, serving with The Queen's Own Rifles of Canada, where he met Harry Fox. He attended the fiftieth anniversary of D-Day celebrations in Normandy with the regiment in 1994, and later compiled a Book of Remembrance, a Second World War Honour Roll for the QOR. He had a significant role in helping to create a memorial kiosk for the QOR at the Juno Beach Centre (Courseulles-sur-mer, France) and attended the Centre's opening in 2003. Since September 2004, Captain Craig Cameron has served with 25 (Toronto) Field Ambulance, a Reserve medical unit. He and his wife live in Toronto.